POPULAR MUSIC AND FILM

edited by

Ian Inglis

WALLFLOWER PRESS

LONDON & NEW YORK

First published in Great Britain in 2003 by
Wallflower Press
4th Floor, 26 Shacklewell Lane, London, E8 2EZ
www.wallflowerpress.co.uk

A catalogue for this book is available from the British Library

ISBN 1-903364-71-X (paperback)
ISBN 1-903364-72-8 (hardback)

Printed in Great Britain by Antony Rowe, Chippenham, Wiltshire

POPULAR MUSIC AND FILM

CONTENTS

NOTES ON CONTRIBUTORS

Lauren Anderson graduated from and subsequently completed her MA at Massey University, New Zealand. She worked in the film industry in that country, before travelling in Europe.

Lee Barron is Lecturer in Sociology at the University of Northumbria. He completed an MA in Cultural and Textual Studies at the University of Sunderland and his doctoral research considers postmodernist themes within contemporary film and television. He has published in a variety of areas, including popular music, sport, and the effectiveness of teaching and learning strategies.

Melissa Carey studied contemporary music at Southern Cross University, Australia, completing an interactive multimedia exploration of chaos theory and chance in music and audiovisual composition. Her current research interests include film score analysis and film music's capacity to create mood and meaning.

K. J. Donnelly is Lecturer in the Department of Theatre, Film and Television Studies at the University of Wales, Aberystwyth. He is the author of *Pop Music in British Cinema* (BFI, 2001) and editor of *Film Music* (Edinburgh University Press, 2001). He has published in journals such as *Popular Music*, the *Historical Journal of Film, Radio and Television* and *Irish Studies Review*. He is currently preparing books about film music and *Moulin Rouge*.

Michael Hannan is Associate Professor and Head of Contemporary Music at Southern Cross University. He is a composer, performer, musicologist and music journalist who, in addition to concert and electronic works, has written music for film, radio and theatre. His research interests include the work practices of professional musicians and music lexicography.

Ian Inglis is Senior Lecturer in Sociology at the University of Northumbria. He is the editor of *The Beatles, Popular Music and Society: A Thousand Voices* (Macmillan, 2000) and his doctoral research considered the significance of sociological and cultural theory in explanations of the career of the Beatles. He is a member of the editorial board of *Popular Music and Society*, and his articles have been published in numerous journals including *Popular Music*, the *Journal of Popular Music Studies*, *Visual Culture in Britain*, *American Music*, *Popular Music and Society* and the *International Review of the Aesthetics and Sociology of Music*.

Antti-Ville Karja is a doctoral student in the Department of Musicology at the University of Helsinki. His current research presents an analysis of the historical conjunctures of Finnish popular music and audiovisual media. He has additional research interests in the areas of national identity and historiography.

Anahid Kassabian teaches in the Department of Communication and Media Studies at Fordham University, New York, where she also serves on the faculties of Women's Studies and Literary Studies. Her book, *Hearing Film* (Routledge, 2001), examined identification processes in the scores of contemporary Hollywood films. She has published widely in areas such as music and disciplinarity, and Armenian diasporan film. Her current research focuses on the intersections of music, technology and subjectivity in the wake of new media. She is Chair of the International Association for the Study of Popular Music.

Jaap Kooijman is Assistant Professor of Film and Television Studies at the University of Amsterdam. He completed a doctorate in American Studies in 1999, and has taught courses on 'Motown and the Civil Rights Movement' and 'The Politics of Soul and Disco'. He is currently working on a study of Diana Ross and the Supremes.

Anno Mungen is a musicologist in the Department of Music at the University of Mainz, Germany. His doctoral research examined the works of Gaspare Santini and early nineteenth-century German and French opera. Publication of his current research into the prehistory or 'archaeology' of film music and the simultaneous fusion of sound and image is forthcoming. His other research interests include Wagner, opera history, and music in Nazi Germany.

Phil Powrie is Professor of French Cultural Studies and Director of the Centre for Research into Film and Media at the University of Newcastle-upon-Tyne. His publications include *Nostalgia and the Crisis of Masculinity* (Clarendon Press, 1997), *Contemporary French Cinema: Continuity and Difference* (Oxford University Press, 1999), *Jean Jacques Beineix* (Manchester University Press, 2001), and he is the co-author of a forthcoming student introduction to French cinema. He is the general co-editor of the journal *Studies in French Cinema*. His current projects include a study of film adaptations of *Carmen*, a co-edited collection (with Bruce Babington and Ann Davies) entitled *The Trouble With Men: Masculinities in European and Hollywood Cinema* and the edited volume *The Cinema of France* (both forthcoming from Wallflower Press).

Lesley Vize teaches the Pedagogy of History at Trinity College, Dublin, focusing on the social and cultural history of the nineteenth and twentieth centuries. Her research interests include the use of music, film and primary documents to aid understandings of the past, and the semiotics of music and the body in dance and film.

Robb Wright is a film composer, sound editor and recording engineer who has worked on more than seventy feature films, television movies, documentaries and independent dramas, and numerous music projects for theatre, dance and CD recording. He teaches in the Department of Music at York University, Toronto, and in the School of Media Studies at Humber College, Toronto, where he is Co-ordinator of the Graduate Program in Post-Production.

This book is dedicated to Annette, Eleanor, Christopher and Susannah.

p.s. I Love You

Introduction

POPULAR MUSIC AND FILM

Ian Inglis

The separate historical trajectories of popular music and film display substantial and significant similarities. Both were stimulated by technological innovations in the late nineteenth century and a series of constant refinements throughout the twentieth century; both were and are dependent on the existence of a new kind of mass audience which shares a common interest but whose members are largely unknown to each other; both grew from novelty beginnings to become major international industries with huge annual turnovers; both have been variously accused of contributing to anti-social, criminal and irresponsible activities (particularly among the young); and both have been increasingly approached and consumed from perspectives which have redefined their intellectual status from products of popular/mass culture to examples of high/elite culture.

In addition, the two mediums share a long history of artistic affinities. The Lumière brothers' first film show, in Paris in 1895, was to the accompaniment of a pianist and, three decades later, the introduction of sound to the cinema was first demonstrated in a musical – *The Jazz Singer* (Alan Crosland, 1927) – whose impact was so great that more than two hundred musical films were produced over the next three years. And although themes and traditions overlapped, subsequent decades were able to broadly reinterpret and continue that relationship in a variety of ways. The 1930s were characterised by the production of films (such as the lavish song and dance spectaculars of Busby Berkeley and the glamorous screen romances of Fred Astaire and Ginger Rogers) in which music provided occasional, if important, interludes. In the 1940s, Hollywood began to produce a new kind of musical film in which the elements of song and dance were *integral* rather than *incidental*, and which seemed to arise naturally from their narrative context; they included *Meet Me in St Louis* (Vincente Minnelli, 1944), *Anchors Aweigh* (George Sidney, 1945) and *On the Town* (Gene Kelly & Stanley Donen, 1949). In the 1950s, the cinema's adaptation of successful stage musicals proved a hugely lucrative strategy via movies like *Oklahoma* (Fred Zinneman, 1955), *The King and I* (Walter Lang, 1956), *Carousel* (Henry King, 1956), *South Pacific* (Joshua Logan, 1958) and *Gigi* (Vincente Minnelli, 1958). The 1960s were a decade in which pop stars sought to become movie stars as they realised that the cinema offered an alternative or additional strategy to touring. Individually, the films of Elvis Presley (the world's top box-office attraction at the start of the decade) and the Beatles competed with the role of the solo concert as the principal mechanism through which these performers were able to satisfy the demands of fans. Collectively, films like *It's Trad, Dad* (Dick Lester, 1962), which featured performances by Helen Shapiro, Craig Douglas, John Leyton, Chubby Checker, the Temperance Seven, Gene Vincent, Sounds Incorporated, the Brook Brothers, Gary U.S. Bonds, Del Shannon, Gene McDaniels and the Paris Sisters replaced the functions and contents of the multi-artist package tour.

It was not until the 1970s that popular music, which had by then reconstructed itself in significant part as 'rock' rather than 'showbiz' (following the emergence of rock'n'roll in the United States in the 1950s and the impetus of the British Invasion of the 1960s) was able to participate in film in ways which departed from the traditional conventions of the musical interlude and the 'escapist' functions commonly associated with the screen musical. Facilitated by the growing industrial, commercial and aesthetic links between popular music and film, a number of sub-genres or 'treatments' have been established. Documentaries including *Woodstock* (Michael Wadleigh, 1970), *The Last Waltz* (Martin Scorsese, 1978) and *Stop Making Sense* (Jonathan Demme, 1984) have reported and preserved particular segments of popular music's history. Fictional narratives have used the popular music industry as a setting in which to tell dramatic or comic stories – *This is Spinal Tap* (Rob Reiner, 1983), *The Commitments* (Alan Parker, 1991), *Grace of My Heart* (Allison Anders, 1996), *Velvet Goldmine* (Todd Haynes, 1998) and *Still Crazy* (Brian Gibson, 1998). A growing number of popular musicians – Mick Jagger, Cher, Phil Collins, Sting, David Bowie, Madonna, Adam Ant – have attempted to become serious actors in non-musical films. There has been a spectacular if sporadic resurgence of the dance movie. Numerous biopics have purported to tell the stories of some of the more celebrated or idiosyncratic of popular music's leading figures, from Elvis Presley to Sid Vicious. And, perhaps most significantly, the use of popular music as a soundtrack device, or as the provider of a theme song, is now commonplace.

Given the persistence of these correspondences, it is surprising that relatively little academic attention has been directed towards popular music and film, and the dynamics of the relationship that exists between them. This is despite the proliferation of film studies departments and degree programmes in universities around the world, and more recent similar developments in the study of popular music.

Much of this neglect might stem from a desire among those who create film or music to preserve some sort of disciplinary autonomy. In the case of cinema, this may reflect a tradition which maintains that film is essentially a visual and spoken medium, to which music may be a useful but ultimately peripheral addition. In the case of popular music, it may reflect a belief that the emotions, excitement and unpredictability of rock'n'roll can only be fully appreciated in the context of live performance. While neither of these beliefs are wholly incorrect, they are mistaken. All popular music contains visual elements; all film relies, in varying degrees, on musical elements.

In addition, it has to be said that within the academic world, there remains a degree of uncertainty about the appropriate perspective from which popular music and film ought to be approached and analysed. While the status of cinema-as-art is well established, there is less agreement over the status of popular music. Inquiries into such areas as the cultural history of film, the separation and definition of genres, political and ideological characteristics, and auteur theory do not sit comfortably with details of chart placings, gold/platinum records and sales of merchandise – even though such apparently distinct concerns have become inextricably intertwined in recent years. The complications introduced by music video (is it to be analysed as film or as something else?) only add to the difficulties.

There is thus a pressing need to expand the range of strategies and emphases that can be usefully employed in the examination of popular music and film. Some important contributions have already been made (Romney & Wootton 1995; Buhler *et al.* 2000; Kassabian 2001; Donnelly 2001). The following essays seek to aid in that expansion by a varied and systematic exploration of contemporary topics, theoretical and substantive, which builds on work already done and suggests new directions for research in the future. The international composition of the contributors – from Ireland, Australia, the United States, Finland, Germany, New Zealand, Canada, the Netherlands and the United Kingdom – and the variety of academic backgrounds from which they come – sociology, history, film studies, musicology, media/communication studies, film production – reflect the complexities of inquiry into the popular music/film dynamic, and the position both mediums occupy as transnational sites of production and consumption.

In Chapter One, Robb Wright provides an insightful and comprehensive analysis of the contexts and motivations which surround the increasingly common decision to employ pre-recorded popular music, rather than a specially commissioned original score, as film soundtrack. Reflecting his experience as a film composer, and his academic interest in audio/video post-production and music technology, his essay suggests that in addition to economic, aesthetic and technological factors, the move towards the use of popular music in film demonstrates the desire of producers to give their movies a particular, but very elusive, commercial and artistic signature. As he explains, it can be a risky strategy.

The association between music, film and dance is explored in Chapter Two. Lesley Vize chooses to concentrate her analysis on the innovative and hugely successful dance-based movies of the 1980s, which were triggered by the impact of *Saturday Night Fever* (John Badham, 1977). While dance has long been an important component of screen musicals, she argues that the specific form it took in those movies requires a new form of analysis if it is to be properly understood. In place of the often inadequate methodologies of musicology and film theory, she suggests an analytical approach in which the three elements of vision, sound and dance are given equal prominence, and in which the inter-connections between them are made explicit.

As noted above, a notable feature in recent decades of the relationship between popular music and film has been the career diversification of a number of established pop/rock stars into the world of film. In Chapter Three, Phil Powrie presents a detailed and critical account of one of the more celebrated performers who have attempted such a transition. His analysis of Sting's career is especially appropriate – not simply because of the relative success of many of the films in which he has appeared, or the musical contributions he brings to them, or the complexity of the screen persona he presents, but because it evinces a key binary of 'good' and 'evil' which recurs throughout the production and consumption of Sting-as-popular musician and Sting-as-film actor, and which structures our understanding of the nature of (his) stardom.

One of the first musical documentaries to be produced by the cinema was *Monterey Pop* (D. A. Pennebaker, 1967); and one of the central components of the movie, and the festival it recorded, was the performance of Jimi Hendrix, who concluded his set by burning his guitar on stage. It remains today a startling and evocative image of the provocative, flamboyant and political role that rock music was steering towards in the late 1960s. In Chapter Four, Anno Mungen uses his investigation of Hendrix's actions to argue that an awareness of the close relationship between music, performance and audio-visual media is necessary to fully illuminate the musical events of that (or any) day. The real significance of his behaviour emerges from the visual or theatrical nature of music and the socio-cultural status of music-as-art. To that end, the participation of cinema at Monterey serves to emphasise the manner in which Hendrix's sound and music may only become meaningful through their visual images.

The critical neglect of the film biography – the biopic – may perhaps be seen at its most acute in the context of popular music, where in recent decades it has become a familiar category. In Chapter Five, Ian Inglis considers the reasons for the popularity of such movies, and the implications they may have for our understanding of historical explanation, through a comparison of two movies which have purported to tell the (early) story of the Beatles. Three components coincide within the design of pop music biopics – narrative, music and nostalgia; the manner in which they are manipulated (individually and together) determine the readiness with which we are likely to accept the truth (or untruth) of the particular tales they tell.

What has underpinned popular music's displacement of the traditional composed film score has been an assumption that it performs its required tasks with equal (or greater) effectiveness. Indeed, the contention that while the form of music has changed, its functions have not, may be one of the principal arguments in favour of its use. However, in Chapter Six, Anahid Kassabian suggests that the gradual disappearance of effective distinctions between noise, sound and music offers new possibilities for the roles that music might play within film. As the boundaries between sounds recede, film soundtracks may be constructed from a variety of aural materials, in which traditional concepts of melody, progression and narrative are replaced by technicity, repetition and iteration. The consequences of these tendencies – not least in their proposal of new understandings of gender – might, it is argued, herald the arrival of a new film form.

While theory and conjecture surround many debates in studies of film and music, there is a real need for substantive pieces of research which examine the specific mechanisms through which the two mediums interact. In Chapter Seven, such a case study is provided by Lauren Anderson's detailed analysis of the ways in which meaning in two films is assigned by popular music. Her investigation of the music in *Sliding Doors* (Peter Howitt, 1997) and *Topless Women Talk About Their Lives* (Harry Sinclair, 1997) considers the nature of popular music's general incursion into film soundtracks, and suggests that although the devices employed may differ slightly from those of the composed score, the same functions are performed and fulfilled.

There is an understandable tendency to concentrate on British and North American sources in the historical evolution of popular music, overlooking the fact that in the mid-1950s the new musical form of rock'n'roll spread to many other countries around the world – one of which was Finland. In Chapter Eight, Antti-Ville Karja contextualises the traditions of Finnish music and film within the broader societal response to rock'n'roll, to consider the specific and unique form that such music was to find within that country's domestic cinema. A combination of political anxiety and creative caution resulted in a marginalisation of popular music through cinematic approaches which rendered it largely powerless. It is a fascinating historical account of the Finnish film industry's 'solution' to the 'problem' posed by the arrival of popular music.

The historical significance of genre music in the cinema is well established; the ease with which we adapt to previously unheard musical cues to immediately locate ourselves within the world of the western, the thriller, the epic or the science fiction fantasy testifies to the strength of associations that exist between music and genre. In Chapter Nine, K. J. Donnelly argues that some recent cinema of science fiction has challenged these perennial associations by relying on music that is neither consciously 'futuristic' nor explicitly contemporary, and which is indifferent to the concept of 'the future' that the film (re)presents. The apparent irony of employing popular music of the past to construct ideas of the future may be resolved by acknowledging that in such cases, music is an independent discourse.

The clearest evidence of the commercial connections between popular music and cinema may be seen in the near-obligatory release of soundtrack albums which accompany new films. In addition to expanding a movie's commercial presence (along with other products) soundtrack albums have provided a vehicle through which the audience may 'revisit' it by another route. In Chapter Ten, Lee Barron considers the policies which have defined this kind of practice. However, his discussion also charts the development of a recent tendency whereby the increasingly aggressive promotion of such albums utilises music which does not appear in the original film. The success of those strategies by which audiences are persuaded to purchase non-related items provides a telling example of the centrality of popular music to the consumption of contemporary film.

One of the first films to rely solely on a soundtrack of pre-recorded popular music was *The Big Chill* (Lawrence Kasdan, 1983). The case study by Melissa Carey and Michael Hannan in Chapter Eleven assesses the efficiency with which its soundtrack is able to meet the traditional functions of film music. While it has been suggested that the presence of lyrics may threaten to disturb the balance between music and narrative, their analysis concludes that, in fact, song lyrics, musical genre, and their interplay with film narrative can bring additional and significant advantages. Furthermore, the enhanced level of intertextuality supplied by the film's soundtrack is a key element within the body of changed listening habits and responses which typify the contemporary audience.

In Chapter Twelve, Jaap Kooijman returns to the study of the popular music biopic. His analysis, however, is less on the presentation of 'history' (which characterised the study in Chapter Five) and more on the competition for our attention that is created between subject and star. His consideration of two films, which present apparently similar images of black female triumph over adversity, suggests that one film sets out to reaffirm the star image of its subject rather than its actress, while the other consciously strengthens the image of its star rather than its subject. Such a distinction raises important questions about the commercial motivations that lie behind biopic construction and the popular expectations that explain audience consumption of the genre.

Academic interests often reflect personal experiences. In my case, a childhood spent in a small North Staffordshire town, in which the principal out-of-home entertainments were the juke-box and the cinema, provided opportunities for discovery, excitement and enjoyment, whose emotional and intellectual benefits have stayed with me; anyone who has grown up with similar access to a Majestic, Palace or Grand Cinema will have shared in those pleasures. That sense of pleasure has been continued and consolidated through the exchange of opinions, insights and knowledge with the contributors to this book, and I want to express my real gratitude to them for their patience, support and effort. Finally, this book could not have been realised without the help and encouragement of my fellow traveller, rock critic and movie-goer, Annette Hames, in whose company every scrap of music becomes a love song, and every midweek matinee a Hollywood premiere.

Chapter One

SCORE VS. SONG: ART, COMMERCE, AND THE H FACTOR IN FILM AND TELEVISION MUSIC

Robb Wright

Since the late 1970s, the formal overlap among the various forms of popular culture, especially those distributed through mass media, has been expanding steadily. This trend is most evident in the increasing presence of popular music in the visual media – song-driven movie trailers, music videos, television commercials crafted to resemble music videos, trendy themes to topical television shows, and the gradual encroachment of popular songs in the soundtracks of dramatic film and television production.

There are numerous factors – demographic, technological and economic – driving this development, although they are difficult to isolate. And, as is the tendency with any cultural expression, as one formal avenue for pop songs grows in prominence, others mimic, quote and mutate from it. Music videos, for example, are the cultural offspring of variety show performance and story-form television spots; the visual and structural language they have spawned has, in turn, been co-opted by computer games, theme park rides and by later television spots.

This cross-pollination is, of course, natural and inevitable. But there is a functional difference among the various forms through which popular music has made its way into the visual media. While most are more or less overt tools for marketing, only in dramatic film and television are popular songs used in order to help tell a sustained narrative story – a role that has traditionally been played by commissioned musical score. Today, the musical landscape of a feature film may contain a full score, a soundtrack of radio hits, or different combinations of source music and score, including commissioned music composed to resemble successful pop songs. The displacement, partially or entirely, of score by popular music in dramatic film and television constitutes a significant departure from the traditional narrative language of film. It merits a thorough examination of the mechanics of its execution, its qualitative effects, the economic, cultural and technological factors that contribute to the decision to use popular music, and the motivation of its proponents and its detractors.

An informed discussion of music for film and television must encompass an understanding of the larger production process into which its purveyors must fit themselves. However we may regard the fact, making a film is not fundamentally different from any other collaborative construction, such as building a house. The process does afford great variation in order, timeframe and priorities, according to the production's budget, genre, and delivery medium, but at heart it is a complex assembly of co-ordinated elements, most of them provided by outside suppliers. This remains true, irrespective of any artistic merit we ascribe to the script or its execution – it is a characteristic dictated by the time, money and labour involved in film-making. In this sense, those that provide music for film and television are among a production's sub-contractors.

It is important here to make the first distinction between films whose music is composed and those for which some component of the music is pre-recorded. Pre-recorded music is in principle a 'prefabricated' element. It enters the process already formed, and the options for manipulating it are limited. For whatever reasons producers may elect to use pre-recorded music, it is a decision that is typically made (at least tentatively) early on in the process, often well before any film has been shot. It is quite common for picture editors to place the music first and edit the picture to it, allowing the rhythm and pacing of the music to drive that of the picture edit, thus giving the whole piece a certain unity that would be harder to achieve by merely adding music to a finished edit. Whether or not the picture is edited to the music, it is often necessary to edit the music for length; but in most cases, pre-recorded music comes with its own contours to which a picture edit must generally conform.

On the other hand, music composed for a film is designed in place, its form and content determined exclusively by the needs of the production. The later in the production process a musical element is provided, the more enshrined is the film's structure, and the more the music must be tailored or altered to accommodate it. Composers are often engaged for a film much later than they would prefer; consequently their contribution must adapt to a structure that is already essentially complete. By the time a composer is brought on to a project, the picture edit is generally locked, and the director and picture editor – and others – have discussed and often confirmed the character and placement of all the musical cues. While a good composer will review these decisions and make the case for desired changes, it can be an uphill battle.

So it would appear that score and pre-recorded music offer different approaches to the post-production process: one is tailored to the picture, the other has the picture tailored to it. The question of whether either of these approaches better serves the dramatic interests of the film is more complex than it may appear.

The most fundamental observation that can be made about music in any audio/visual medium is that it enjoys a rather direct route to our subconscious. Humans are by nature visually oriented. Our evolutionary development is such that we are primarily aware of the visual world, and of subtle changes in what we see. While we are also aware of what we hear, we digest visual information more consciously – and more critically – than we do aural information. This tendency has long been understood and exploited by sound editors and mixers for film and television. Many dramatic film soundtracks contain a remarkable amount of sound that cannot be justified, in any rational way, by the films' visual or dramatic content. Scenes with substantial emotional weight are often rife with extraneous elements, usually mixed at a low volume relative to the other tracks – animal sounds, thunder, heartbeats, babies crying. Such sounds are not chosen arbitrarily, but for their evocative power – their ability to trigger an emotional response. As long as a sound is quiet enough not to broach the threshold of direct, conscious perception, it escapes our analytical radar, and we accept its associations unfiltered. Used judiciously, this process can have a considerable effect on a film's impact on a viewer.

The access that sound has to our subconscious is not something that applies uniformly. Among the three general areas of sound in film, dialogue is, for the most part, interpreted rationally and is usually delivered in straightforward manner. Ambiences and sound effects are less the focus of a viewer's attention and thus have more potential for emotional provocation. But it is music more than anything that carries emotional freight, precisely because in most cases it is completely removed from the specific logic of the film's story line.

Music is the primary instrument of emotional direction in film – it tells us what to feel about a character, a place, a situation. It also reinforces the identity of a place or time; specific rhythms, dynamic patterns, ranges, timbres, instrumental textures and other musical devices are used to evoke a mood, a season, a historical period, a location, an ethnic flavour. Crucial to the emotive power of music in general, but especially in film, is this ability to evoke – to subtly call to the viewer's mind a related or comparable situation, to act as a shorthand to steer the viewer emotionally. As with any such shorthand, its successful execution depends on a shared context, a body of ideas, experiences, associations and cultural touchstones to which the composer can refer, even obliquely, to strike a desired emotional tone.

Some emotional triggers are universal. Certain natural elements – breath, birdcalls, thunder – can be evoked musically and will elicit a (broadly) similar emotional response in virtually any listener, as an experience of these things is common among humans. Other references are effective only among a targeted audience whose background includes the suggested material. To a typical contemporary Canadian viewer, for example, trumpets and snare drums will reliably telegraph a military setting. Fanfares and marches are so established in our collective musical ear that even a viewer who had never heard one directly would have heard its quotation in countless orchestral pieces, advertisements, and other film scores. By contrast, a viewer from a traditional village in Borneo might have no such associations, and her reaction to the cue in question would be very different.

This represents a major qualification to the discussion of the evocative capacity of music: it is culturally and historically relative – a shared experiential vocabulary is essential, and the greater that shared experience, the more effective its associative power. Music and film are, after all, forms of communication, and their message is necessarily mediated by their context. Thus, the role of music in film and television is very much a function of the musical and cinematic tradition in which a production is rooted. Much of the popular cinema in India, for example, is unfamiliar and bizarre to a Western viewer, and has less in common with Western cinema than it does with nineteenth-century Italian opera.

Cultural context assumes even more importance in analyses of the use of popular music in film, since – the McCulture juggernaut notwithstanding – meaning and significance in popular music vary considerably with geography and, especially, with time. Popular music by definition is of the moment. What has huge significance today can have little ten years hence; even worse, it can be painfully dated, potentially distracting from, or working against, the desired emotional effect. Even in a contemporary context, regional distinctions are critically important. A song that serves as an unofficial anthem for a group or generation in Spain might, although intelligible, have no similar resonance for an equivalent group in Venezuela. By associating itself with the passing success of a song, a film may severely limit its distribution and its shelf life.

Of course, it may be argued that film itself, with rare exceptions, is a popular medium whose expressions lose their currency over time. A thirty-year-old feature film will almost inevitably present at least a few glaring artefacts of its era in those areas where fashions change most rapidly – clothing, hairstyles, automobiles. We notice these things when we watch old films, and we occasionally find them quaint or even funny. But these are components of the picture – they are more consciously observed than is music. Even dated language, because of its logical, verbal content, is not as damning to an audience's receptiveness as dated pop music. It is precisely because the message in music is so implicit, because it influences us somewhat subliminally – through the back door, as it were – that we find its failings so noteworthy. The stakes are high: when it works, it moves us mysteriously, but when it fails, we cringe at the attempt.

For dramatic films therefore, it appears that there are significant risks in using popular music rather than score. Why, then, do producers do it? If score can be specifically tailored to fit the length and mood of a scene, and if pre-recorded popular music limits its relevance to a few years, why take the risk? Pragmatists might suggest that the opportunity to garner quick commercial returns via a successful soundtrack justifies any long-term compromise, and there is some logic to this. The commercial film industry has learned through experience that while only one in ten of the productions it finances may return a profit, the success of that one will more than pay for the losses of the others within the first two weeks. There is no doubt that similar reasoning will be heard when decisions are made about how to approach the music for a film … although it would clearly be unfair to ascribe mercenary motives alone to every pop music soundtrack.

Many producers are inclined to regard popular songs as 'road tested', a term to which composers justifiably take offence. The logic and function of radio airplay is very different to the logic and function of film accompaniment, and an assumption that the two are in any way interchangeable would be naïve. But the familiarity that radio and television exposure gives to a popular song can still be useful in a cinematic context. Film scores are usually brand new to each viewer and it falls upon the composer to create every nuance of feeling and association that the music seeks to produce. By contrast, previously heard pop songs carry their own sets of feelings and associations, often developed over months or years of repeated hearings. The potential emotional punch of those established associations is considerable, and arguably greater than a virgin score could hope to elicit. The right song in the right place can be an extremely powerful device, which enables a film to effectively build on the work that the song has already done.

Furthermore, there are occasions when the right pop song, regardless of its familiarity, might simply function more effectively to set the desired scene, period or emotional mood than a score. A common criticism of pop music in film is that it is too uniform to be useful: the degree of variation in tempo, volume and instrumental texture which film composers commonly use to steer viewers through a scene, is normally not present in popular songs, and cannot be injected into pre-recorded music in any practical way. But for scenes where the setting and action are not changing, or are changing in a regular progression, such variation is generally undesirable, and in fact the regular groove of a pop tune often works very well as featured score. The most typical example is the road trip sequence. The prototype of this is the motorcycling scene from *Easy Rider* (Dennis Hopper, 1969), accompanied by Steppenwolf's 'Born To Be Wild', a gritty, hard rock song that quickly became an anthem for defiant individualism. The association of this kind of music with this kind of situation has become so common in American films that it is now a universally familiar part of cinematic language. In the archetypal scenario, two or more characters embark on a trip, usually in a car. The departure, and the exhilaration of movement that highway travel brings, are often successfully supported by a driving rock song. There is resonance on several levels: a steady, repetitive groove reflects the state of motionless confinement in (or on) a moving vehicle; the power of amplified instruments evokes the power of the engine; and the process of leaving – and its suggestion of illicit escape from the regulated grid of the city – is aptly captured by rock music and its associations with protest and rebellion. All of these connotations are usually implicit, and largely unnoticed by the viewer, and therefore function that much more powerfully. The fact that road trip scenes in many films are accompanied by scored cues that were deliberately designed to emulate a driving rock groove is evidence of the genre's success.

When the subject matter of a film involves a specific era in recent history, popular music from that period is often evocative in ways that a score could only imitate. For those who lived through that era, familiar examples of its music can have a powerful effect on their reaction to accompanying images, carrying with them not only the musical memories of the day, but the attitudes and mores that were current at the time. The decade of the 1960s is a period that, for demographic as much as historical reasons, maintains a powerful presence in the popular consciousness. Its successful recreation in *Apocalypse Now* (Francis Ford Coppola 1979) was achieved, to some extent, by the judicious use of 'vintage' songs th recalled not only the era but also the spirit of iconoclasm that pervaded the popular movements of the day, and ultimately pervades the darkening sensibility of Captain Willard, the film's central character. The musical landscape is largely a counterpoint between source music that punctuates the various, often bizarre, contexts through which the story moves and a sombre, muted score that starkly illustrates the deepening unease within Willard as he travels deeper into the bush.

For example, the Rolling Stones' 'Satisfaction' accompanies a scene in which the crew of doomed young sailors, charged with transporting Willard up-river, cope with their confinement by engaging in what comforting rituals they can – dancing, singing and water-skiing. The ironic contrast between the song's infectious groove and its lyrical message of discontent runs parallel to the contrast between the characters' lighthearted activities and the unpleasant reality of their circumstances. In addition, the song's oblique drug references find resonance with the characters' periodic use of drugs as a further coping mechanism. It is unlikely that any composed score could have provided so much for the scene and so effectively recalled the historical period. Later, when the focus turns from the group's partying to Willard's private reflection on the serious details of his mission, the song simply backs off in the mix and the score takes over. Part of what raises this device above a mere contrivance is the fact that the song begins as a diegetic element, playing on a crewman's radio. When it crossfades against the score, we accept it as a transition from outward action to inward reflection; the effect is one of withdrawing into Willard's thought.

This leads on to another important distinction in the use of pre-recorded music in dramatic films. When a song appears to originate from within the drama – live musicians, a recording, a PA system, a radio or TV broadcast – it helps to justify its existence. The current state of cinematic language is such that we are somewhat conditioned to regard songs as more than accompaniment to the visual element. Their lyrical content demands our attention, and their musical structure usually precludes their adoption of any supporting function in the manner of a traditional underscore. When we hear a non-diegetic song, we may be distracted by it, expecting at some level to see a singer, or at least some dramatic rationale for what we are hearing. The distraction may be only momentary and not inevitably problematic. But it can be quite harmful if the viewer's distraction undermines the dramatic thrust of the scene. Such distraction is often avoided by introducing as an ostensible part of the action – from a car radio, for example – a song which then proceeds to function like a score, punctuating dialogue, continuing at full volume during shots where its source would realistically be muted, even bridging to another scene. We do not object to this detachment, and may not even notice it, because our introduction to the song provided a logical justification, allowing us to hear it in a realistic context, even though the scene then effectively departs from this logic.

This effect can also apply on a wider scale when a film provides a dramatic context that sets up a musical or quasi-musical environment, or an ongoing rationale for recurring musical interludes. In *The Talented Mr Ripley* (Anthony Minghella, 1999) Tom Ripley has been hired by a wealthy man to travel to Italy in order to persuade the man's hedonistic son to return to the United States. Knowing of the son's passion for jazz, but being unfamiliar with the genre himself, Ripley undertakes an intense listening study before his departure. During this sequence, as we listen to a number of records with the character, a particular brand of 1950s small-combo jazz is established as a sort of musical aesthetic, which then becomes the thematic tissue that unifies the rest of the film musically. Whenever jazz is heard in subsequent scenes, its presence is accepted – even when no source is evident – as emanating from the ubiquitous record player that is a natural element of the bohemian milieu the characters inhabit, or as a lyrical suggestion of this world. The latter grounds are notable: the diegetic introduction and acclimatisation of the music early in the film has, in effect, served to condition the viewer to inhabit the characters' musical landscape, rendering later non-diegetic music quite natural.

A similar process is at work in *High Fidelity* (Stephen Frears, 2000). The story revolves around Rob Gordon, who runs an ultra-trendy alternative record store, and his employees, all of whom pride themselves on their knowledge of what they consider worthy popular music. The explicit musical setting and a plotline concerning aesthetic elitism provide many occasions for pop music to figure diegetically in the soundtrack. But even when the setting is remote from any source of music, songs appear throughout the film, functioning essentially as score. Again the viewer's ears accept these more readily since the musical pattern has already been introduced in what we accept as a logically admissible way.

In both these cases, the films' setting and structure function to reinforce the legitimacy of non-diegetic songs by quickly establishing a justifiable model of music recordings playing in the characters' environment. Without this conditioning, the songs would be likely to call undue attention to themselves, and their presence may be perceived by the viewer as indulgent, contrived or manipulative.

Another more subtle effect in the use of non-diegetic songs is their tendency to put distance between the viewer and the action. Sometimes this is deliberately used by directors. In the opening scene of *Apocalypse Now* we observe from distance a hazy confusion of slow-motion military activity that we eventu-

recognise as the napalm torching of a jungle village. We do not hear the planes, the bombs, the flames or the victims' cries, nor any ambience or sound effects at all, save the faint impressionistic thumping of helicopter rotors which fade in and out of the mix. Accompanying the entire scene is The Doors' 'The End', a meditative and seemingly nihilistic ballad that eventually evolves into a sort of hypnotic vamp. The song clearly does not originate from anything in the action, and its consequent detachment reinforces the distance established by the long lens, the slow movement and the lack of sound effects. The music imparts to the scene a calmness that is disturbing, all the more so as we gradually realise what is happening, with all its horrific implications. Here again, Coppola uses ironic juxtaposition to make his point with music. The use of popular songs in *Apocalypse Now* is particularly successful because the director and his editor were sensitive to the music's effectiveness as a signifier of the period and its values, but were also aware of the risks inherent in the substitution of finished musical material for the more flexible instrument of traditional score. It is noteworthy that where a dramatic situation was better served by score, Coppola made that choice. Throughout the film, he was consistent in selecting musical content – score, pop songs, a Wagnerian aria, a disembodied wailing guitar – that most effectively conveyed the story and its sub-text.

Occasionally, directors choose to dispense with score altogether, opting instead for a soundtrack which consists entirely of pre-recorded songs. One of the earliest and most celebrated examples of this is *The Big Chill* (Lawrence Kasdan, 1983); it also provides a telling illustration of why this approach to film soundtracks rarely succeeds completely. The story involves the reunion of a tight group of college friends, a decade after graduation, to mourn the suicide of one of their own. Nostalgia plays a big part in the film, especially for the years the characters spent in college together, the late 1960s and early 1970s. Popular hits of that period feed the sentiment throughout the film. Kasdan chose some 'classics' of the era and, for the most part, they are thoughtfully integrated with the plot. In several places the songs are introduced diegetically and evolve into score-like musical accompaniment. This works best during the funeral scene where a solo organist plays the Rolling Stones' 'You Can't Always Get What You Want' while the mourners are filing out of the chapel. As we move outside, the organ gives way to the group's own, original version of the song, which continues under a sequence of intercut conversations among the characters in the different cars; now, the music plays mostly low in the mix, as plausible radio accompaniment. At the cemetery, the song becomes foreground again and plays out over a wide rising crane shot of the ceremony. The vaguely gospel groove captures the sense of a gathering of irreverent souls in a reverent situation, and the choir adds a solemnity that reminds us of the underlying gravity of the scene.

However, not all of the songs work this well. The film is an ensemble piece, and there are several emotional subplots among the characters. Each of these has its climactic points, and at some of these points there is no musical support when it is clearly needed. On other occasions, songs are rather clumsily introduced, at points where the subtlety and flexibility of a composed score would have been more appropriate to frame the emotional truth of the scene. At times it appears that songs have been used that may not have been the director's or the editor's first choice for a scene – the Exciters' 'Tell Him' and the Beach Boys' 'Wouldn't It Be Nice?' seem signally inappropriate and anachronistic. The acquisition of the rights to use popular songs in films requires considerable effort and money, and in the case of *The Big Chill* it is hard to resist the conclusion that Kasdan was forced to settle for a few songs he might not have selected, had other choices been available. It is likely that the scenes in question were originally edited to music that worked better, but which subsequently proved unavailable. This is the price paid by directors who choose to dispense with score altogether.

One of the most powerful associations that popular music can bring to a film is a political message. In *Do The Right Thing* (Spike Lee, 1989) the character of Radio Raheem carries a portable tape deck whenever and wherever he appears, which always plays (at high volume) 'Fight The Power' by Public Enemy. Ostensibly, the song's repetition is a comical sideshow, the signature of an ill-tempered homeboy who refuses to depart from the familiar; while other characters and relationships in the film are moving and evolving, he seems to be stuck. But, in fact, the song was chosen for its overtly political content. In 1989 Public Enemy had only recently emerged as the first truly successful rap group to embrace black militancy. Their public image borrowed liberally from the language and imagery of 1960s black power activism, and their song lyrics consistently advocated political consciousness-raising and subversive action. As its title suggests, 'Fight The Power' was typical of these sentiments. In the film it functions as a sort of reprise, subtly reminding the audience that the larger context in which this story is played out is not a neutral one. Public Enemy's presence also serves to implicitly, but powerfully, evoke the voice of Malcolm X, the story's moral compass and invisible character. The music has the effect of giving Radio Raheem's character a political point-of-view status, designating him as a silent narrator in the political meta-drama that underlies the surface of the story.

The reasons film-makers choose a particular approach to music are near important as the kind of music they use. In the mid-1980s, commercial tele saw a new generation of dramatic programming that was attempting to position itself to appeal to a younger fashion-conscious audience. At the head of the pack was the police drama *Miami Vice*. The show set a new standard for leading-edge chic in its look – clothing, set design, cars – and in its sound – dialogue and, above all, music. Each episode featured a soundtrack that was a blend of current pop songs and a catchy, synthesizer-dominated score by Jan Hammer. The use of pop music gave the show 'street credibility' with its target audience and it became a huge commercial success, running for five seasons.

Predictably, *Miami Vice* looks and sounds rather antique to modern audiences. The trendy features show their age plainly, including the hit parade soundtrack. With a few exceptions, the songs are conspicuously out-of-date, and their prominence even impedes the flow of the plot. In many cases they appear to have been chosen for their (then) currency, rather than for any specific resonance with the narrative thrust of the scene, its emotional content, the characters' thoughts, or any of the other traditional functions of music in film. Thus, what may have succeeded in its day on the strength of its musical relevance fails a decade or two later, when its relevance is exhausted. Yet the show's composed score seems to have aged rather better, despite the fact that it shared an idiomatic musical language with much of the pre-recorded music that surrounded it. The likely explanations for the relative freshness of the score include many of the factors discussed above but, more than anything else, it may stem from the composer's motivation. Hammer has consistently cited storyline as his primary guide in scoring. The need for this may seem self-evident, but on many occasions, composers are instructed to ignore the emotional or sub-textual content of a scene and simply blanket it with a piece of music meeting specific stylistic requirements. That Hammer had both the artistic freedom and the competence to create music that was driven by plot and sub-text, yet still blended stylistically with the songs around it, is striking in itself, and this is what accounts for its success as musical score and for its apparent longevity.

Here, we would do well to distinguish between theatrical film and dramatic television. Television in North America is itself so obsessively current that, except as archival material, its content rarely survives beyond a brief window of currency of around five years. Dramatic shows in syndication beyond that range quickly assume a kind of 'legacy' status, where they become valued for the oddity that their age confers on them. With limited exceptions, the prevailing ethic seems be that television needs no shelf life. Indeed, if a television programme does show its age within a few years, it might even be seen as evidence that its cers had too conservative an approach for TV. In the light of this, we might find the dated music in *Miami Vice* less problematic. *Miami Vice* is only a rather conspicuous example of what has emerged as a primary objective in the design of musical soundtracks in recent years: the pursuit of 'hipness'. While we may use other words, we are all familiar with some version of it. By definition, 'hip' is a difficult concept to isolate, as it is enormously variable over time, place and demographic group. Any meaningful definition must therefore consider the larger context.

Films are made for the most part in modern societies that see the world in terms of progression and growth, as opposed to pre-literate cultures that see the world in terms of natural, unchanging cycles. Not surprisingly, progressive societies tend to value manifestations of progress and change, a doctrine that, in modern Western countries, has developed into a kind of mythology of hipness. The further our lifestyles take us from nature and the unchanging features of the world, and the closer we are to the central institutions of modernity – consumerism, mass communication, automobiles – the greater is our veneration of hipness. Hipness, so designated, denotes that which is worldly, up-to-date, informed and appealing in a modern sense.

There is, therefore, a great incentive for film producers to seek out ways to identify their films as hip. Considerable energies are devoted to researching trends and determining appropriate symbols in order to achieve that designation in the public's eye. It is not easy: people readily distinguish between hip and trendy, the latter tending to denote a more transitory popularity, a passing fancy, a flash in the pan. But the selection of those qualities which make something substantial enough to be elevated to hipness is extremely subjective. It is generally understood that hipness is an inherent attribute, rather than an acquired state, so that people and things that are hip achieve that status without any special effort; in the context of film, the viewing public are thus quite sensitive to contrivance, to something that 'tries too hard' to be hip. This awareness is particularly acute among younger audiences, a group that increasingly represents the majority of the film-going public. Moreover, while most of us may like to think of ourselves as at least somewhat hip, each of us may define it in different terms, making agreement across a broad audience very difficult. Hipness itself is in many ways a moving target, anchored as it is in 'the modern', a notion that is itself constantly evolving. This is one reason that an enduring statement is so elusive in popular culture.

Given all these difficulties, music, with its 'back door' access to our consciousness, is a powerful tool in the quest for hipness. It stealthily pilots the audience's mood and emotional response to a film's content. More than that, allows film-makers, in some measure anyway, to bypass our cynical sensibil and to speak directly to the part of us that prefers red wine, brown hair or black jeans, and cherishes or loathes the barest fragment of a distant memory. A piece of music that manages to reach and touch the source of our blind, illogical attachment to apparently insignificant distinctions – that unknowable aesthetic core of each of us where our taste lies – has made a friend for the long term. Its grip on us is beyond analysis, and beyond our control. By appealing fundamentally to our taste, not just to our notion of what is appropriate or current, it ensures a deep and lasting effect on us. Precisely what it is in a piece of music that does that for each of us is a product of many factors, and much of the process is specific to the individual. But the most successful music will engage us with its freshness and originality while simultaneously resonating with a timeless sense of authenticity.

For each of us then, our idea of hipness in music arises in part from the success of a given piece in moving us on that impenetrable level. Well-crafted popular music can do this if it is married to images that reinforce the universal dimension of its message. At face value, pop music is the domain of the hip; we are predisposed to regard it as an expression of the contemporary and the aware. To the extent that a song is able to sustain this engagement and furnish a broader truth, it may have better success harnessing the appeal of hipness than would be possible with a score.

The need for a universal dimension cannot be overstated. Consider the mechanics of the post-production process. Picture editors regularly edit to the timing of substitute or 'temp' music before the final music – prerecorded or composed score – is available. Often this means that the editor and the director of a film are working with that version of the film, and that music, for weeks or months at a time. It is all too easy for directors to fall prey to 'temp love', a phenomenon wherein the victim has seen the images and music together for so long that s/he can not imagine any other music in its place. Other music can be tried, but simply does not seem to possess the magic, the resonance, the appropriate feel – the hipness – that the temp music has. Sometimes this is indeed the case, and the great efforts that are often made at the last minute to secure the rights to the temp music may prove worthwhile. But in most cases the magic that the director feels is due to a private relationship that s/he has developed with the music over time. It may have great depth and substance but it does not reflect what a viewer, who has never seen or heard the film before, will experience at a single screening, and it is this which must be the primary consideration when assessing film music. Even when others share the director's enthusiasm, the question that has to be ~ked is whether the larger public will echo their perception. A song may bring ♦ scene just the right touch of groove and attitude to underline the characters' unspoken thoughts, but that will not guarantee its success or that of the scene. If the musical or lyrical content that creates those associations is dependent on a very local or current sensibility and lacks a sense of universal truth, it may be perceived as trite or irrelevant by those outside its circle.

Notwithstanding all of the above, film music is not something that can be codified in a manual of absolute laws. What succeeds as musical accompaniment to a film is subject to a range of factors, many of them quite subtle, and all of them evolving over time. Popular music as a form of cultural expression is itself evolving rapidly, and the gradual popular acculturation to songs with images, through music videos, advertising and related media, continues to re-define the cultural role of popular music around the world. The popular cinematic palate also changes gradually, including our taste for different musical conventions. Just as it was once unthinkable to score a feature film without a full orchestral score in the style of Brahms or Berlioz, the use of songs in anything but a designated musical has been, until fairly recently, widely denigrated. The language of film will continue to grow and change, but the principles that determine what does and does not succeed as film music will remain consistent.

Chapter Two

MUSIC AND THE BODY IN DANCE FILM

Lesley Vize

The impetus for this chapter came originally out of previous investigations into the place of *Saturday Night Fever* (John Badham, 1977) in contemporary cinema. While researching the topic, it struck me that surprisingly little had been written on a film which my own memory told me had an enormous influence on the popular culture of the late 1970s. I was 21 at the time of its release, and could imagine that its impact on myself and my peers was comparable with that of *The Blackboard Jungle* (Richard Brooks, 1955) on the youth of the 1950s (see Marwick 1996: 131–2). As someone who spent much of her leisure time at discotheques, I can remember that they were crowded and popular places where we would dance until the early hours. Saturday nights were especially important: much time and effort were spent dressing (often a new item of clothing would have been purchased for the occasion), applying make-up and anticipating the evening out. We went to the disco primarily to dance and to listen to music, usually in the company of ne or more girlfriends, or occasionally a boyfriend. I doubt if any of us believed would meet someone 'special' there, although obviously the presence of men art of the attraction. The combination of heat, coloured lights flashing from the floor and ceiling, strobe lighting (which frequently endowed the scene with a slow-motion filmic quality), music pulsing loudly and rhythmically, and of course the relaxing effects of alcohol, made the disco an avenue of escape from reality into fantasy.

Although at the time discotheques, music and dance were very much part of the mainstream popular culture, my research revealed that 'disco music' was not considered seriously, if at all, by many commentators. For example, while Frith & McRobbie admitted that 'from a sociological point-of-view, the most interesting film released in Britain last year was *Saturday Night Fever*' (1978: 3), their overall assessment of the film and its music appeared rather patronising in its focus on the passive consumption, 'teenybopper' appeal, and promotion of John Travolta as star/pin-up.

In fact, *Saturday Night Fever* was enormously popular with a broad cross-section of the population and, indeed, has retained its popularity (both the video and the soundtrack album were re-released in October 1998). In addition,

> *Saturday Night Fever* … set the stage: it was not only the first film of the decade to focus on the life of contemporary youth, it also demonstrated the mutual benefits of the close relationship between film and soundtracks. (Grossberg 1993: 191)

While it is not one of my favourite films (the mysogynistic attitude towards the female characters still makes me wince), I did enjoy it. Its music and dance gave it a novel dimension, to which I could relate; without these twin elements it would be a rather trite social drama. *Saturday Night Fever* created a vivid iconographic image of disco music and dance, and its somewhat unexpected success encouraged Hollywood to exploit the music/dance movie genre throughout the 1980s, in films such as *Fame* (Alan Parker, 1980), *Flashdance* (Adrian Lyne, 1983), *Staying Alive* (Sylvester Stallone, 1983) and *Footloose* (Herbert Ross, 1984). The cycle culminated with the hugely successful *Dirty Dancing* (Emile Ardolino, 1987). It was released a decade after *Saturday Night Fever*, and was set in the early 1960s – differences which had important dialogic and semiotic repercussions. However, although ten years older and well out of the 'youth audience', I still derived considerable pleasure from that movie too, largely – again – through its presentation of music and the body.

Subsequent viewings of the two films have led me to begin to explore how the relationship between music, the body and dance film creates a particular synergy. One significant factor lies in the staying power of such popular musi forms as disco (in *Saturday Night Fever*) and soul (in *Dirty Dancing*). One of the primary qualities they possess is a capacity to encourage people to dance and/or to take pleasure in watching others do so – whether on the dance-floor or in the dance movie. A useful starting point for an exploration of these and other related characteristics is Nicholas Cook's analysis of 'musical multimedia':

> There are multimedia genres which really *are* 'musical': that is to say, in which music plays a constitutive role that has been conspicuously neglected in the critical literature. The most obvious example ... is the music video. Another is a genre which does not even have a name: what I call 'music film'. (1998: vi)

Following Cook, I wish to call films such as *Saturday Night Fever* and *Dirty Dancing* 'dance film', and will argue that they constitute a separate genre. Although there is a considerable literature about film music, Hollywood musicals, music video and MTV, little work has been produced on 'dance film'. First, the music itself has often been denigrated:

> Dismissals of dance music can be found throughout the critical history of Western 'serious' music. To the extent that the appeal is to physicality rather than abstracted listening, dance music is often trivialized at the same time that its power to distract and arouse is regarded with anxiety. (McClary 1991: 153)

Secondly, dance music – and consequently dance itself – has been widely regarded as 'feminine' and therefore not deserving of serious study. And finally, it has been marginalised through its conventional associations with youth.

I hope to demonstrate how the relationship between popular music/rock and the body is an important aspect of 'dance film' and that dance, as the body's authentic response to music, is both cerebral and somatic. Certainly, the commercial strength of dance film became ever more evident in the aftermath of *Saturday Night Fever*:

> In the 1980s ... film [became] an important source of origination, distribution and profit. In 1984, all five of the best-selling pop singles came from movies. There were eight platinum soundtrack albums (including 'Flashdance', 'Footloose' and 'Saturday Night Fever'). This relationship, perfected in such films as *Flashdance* and *Footloose*, has become the norm and

it has radically changed not only the system by which films are exploited and promoted, but also the shape of the pop charts. (Grossberg 1993: 191)

The relationship between image and music is a complex and powerful one. Andrew Goodwin has referred to the 'phenomenon of *synaesthesia,* the intrapersonal process whereby sensory impressions are carried over from one sense to another, for instance, when one pictures sounds in one's "mind's eye"' (1993: 50). What we see and hear goes beyond the somatic experience of the aural and the visual to tap into deep personal resonances within each individual. Sometimes these resonances are related to iconography: who can listen to the Bee Gees singing 'Night Fever' without seeing the white-suited John Travolta dancing on the floor of the discotheque? At other times, the synaesthesia is more subjective and idiosyncratic. The suggestion that in our consumption of music video, 'the essential element of pleasure in viewing the clips must involve more than purely visual pleasure (scopophilia, voyeurism), since this in itself provides no incentive to buy the aural commodities that are being promoted' (Goodwin 1993: 70), can be related to films too. Thus, in order for the soundtrack albums from *Saturday Night Fever* and *Dirty Dancing* to have sold in such great numbers, there had to be more of an interest than merely the images in the films.

Dance film communicates to us on many different levels creating a synergy of the aural, the visual and the cerebral to which the audience can relate and through which it can escape. Dance film reinforces its effect (and affect) doubly – through the music and the spectacle of the dance. Parts of the soundtrack can be listened to many times, in both casual and specific contexts. The dance itself provides an initial excitement and engagement, which can be repeated via memory or a rewatching of the film (or video). Film can also remind one of a particular moment in one's personal history. And it can act as a cultural 'map' for reading change and diversity in an increasingly globalised popular culture. Just as Goodwin suggests we should analyse music video *as* music video (1993: xv–xviii) rather than as film, so I believe we should analyse dance film *as* dance film, rather than as film which happens to feature music and dance. And in that analysis, we must acknowledge equally three elements of multimedia; music, film and dance. They interact with each other to create a new, different, 'novelised' form in which music and dance propel the plot.

Such an analysis possesses real advantages over the traditional approaches of film theory and musicology. Film theory largely ignores music and dance while musicology's emphasis on musical notation continues to perpetuate the assumption that popular music is an inferior form. Multimedia analysis recogn the significance of the various contributors to dance film – the director, the choreographer, the dancer, the musician – and dispenses with the notion of the supremacy of the work itself.

Dirty Dancing

Dance is assumed to be a non-representational art form, yet in dance film it becomes momentarily representational by virtue of the reality of its image. The posture of the dancers, the way in which they respond to the music and the movements they enact within the dance tell us much about representations of, for example, gender and power. Popular music, dance and dance film are *heteroglossic*: they are forms of communication or language which speak to us in different ways – via the camera lens, the specific dance steps, the characters' clothing, the soundtrack, the dialogue. Larry Billman's assessment of *Dirty Dancing* correctly recognises this:

> The producers use dance as a language, trusting its basic value. Director Ardolino says that 'dance is used to advance plot and to reveal character … dance is a metaphor for what was about to happen across the country, both politically and sexually'. The simplicity of showing an 'old fashioned' social dance blossom into a wilder, freer, physical expression makes the film highly accessible. (1997: 160)

By reading dance as language in *Dirty Dancing*, we begin to understand how the effects of music on the body can be beneficial in bringing about a personal propinquity between the main protagonists through communication. Music and dance create an alternative space where the protagonists can meet. This may be demonstrated through a detailed analysis of six minutes of *Dirty Dancing*, in which I will expand the twofold categorisation of 'sound' and 'vision' employed by Goodwin in his analysis of music video (1993: 121–7) to incorporate a third category of 'dance'.

Dirty Dancing tells the story of shy seventeen-year-old Frances Houseman (known as Baby) on holiday in the Catskills with her mother and father, and sister Lisa. At the resort camp, she meets dance instructor Johnny Castle, whose job is to teach dancing to the guests. When his regular dance partner, Penny, is unable to perform with him (she has an abortion) Frances seeks to take her place. This particular sequence maps Frances's growing confidence and expertise as a dancer, and cuts between two locations: the bridge separating the guests' accommodation from the staff quarters, and the dance studio itself.

	Vision	Dance	Sound
1	Establishing shot: Baby right, Johnny left. Johnny in black trousers and shirt, Baby in jeans and long, loose shirt. Close-up of calves and feet; metonymy of dance.	Johnny is teaching Baby to dance traditional Latin American ballroom style.	Mambo (Latin American) music.
2	Mirror shot. He is dressed the same but this time she is wearing jeans with a top tied at the midriff. Rhythmic edit with 'and'.	He stands by as she dances, instructing her, arranging her body into the correct posture.	Guitar solo, 1950s sound.
3	Baby is on the bridge between the staff quarters and the rest of the holiday camp. Wearing jeans and loose shirt again. Mid-shot of her practicing her new dance steps. Camera shots are jerky and montage-like reflecting her lack of confidence in the dance. We see her from the front. Five times there is a rhythmic edit where she starts the steps again on the cymbal clash. She jumps up and down and kicks the bridge in her frustration.	On her way back from the staff quarters she is practicing the dance on her own, counting time whilst doing the steps. Her movements are unsure and wooden. She is frustrated at her incompetence in the dance.	On the bridge. Drum solo, continuation of 2. Non-diegetic. She is imagining the music in her head.
4	Long-shot of her dancing up the steps at the other side of the bridge; this time she is wearing tight shorts and spaghetti strapped teeshirt. We only see her back.	She wiggles her hips as she dances up the steps and now seems to be enjoying herself.	Continues with non-diegetic drum solo.

5	Indoor mid-shot of Johnny, establishing shot again with close-up of calves and feet. This time she is on the left (significant of binary opposition typical of non-dialogic readings of cultural texts). She moves back skilfully to the right. She now wears footless flesh-coloured tights and plimsolls.	At first he is instructing her, then they dance together. She appears more proficient.	Drum solo continues but we assume that it is now diegetic as they are practicing: He is issuing instructions: 'Don't put your heel down. Don't put your heel down! Stay on the toe. Just listen to me... the steps aren't enough, feel the music!' He urges her to give her body to the rhythm. Guitar comes in.
6	On the bridge again. The same outfit as when she first danced up the steps.	On the bridge dancing by herself. Again she is more relaxed, her dance movements are flowing and she appears to be enjoying herself. She uses her body in a stylised erotic way: leaning back against the side of the bridge which she previously kicked in annoyance; pouting using her arms in a less rigid manner, overtly sexual movements.	Non-diegetic guitar and drum duet.
7	Close-up from waist up. She is wearing a loose shirt. He places his hand over his heart and in mirror fashion she places her hand over her heart. Then, in order to accentuate the rhythm he places her hand over his heart. The 180 degree rule is broken in this shot – We see the back of her head, then of his – the viewer's perspective is suddenly reversed, causing a sense of	They are moving in time to the rhythm.	'It's not the mambo, it's not on the 'one'; you feel it: a heartbeat...gu gung...gu gung. Close your eyes.' Music is heard – diegetic or non-diegetic? There is no evidence that any record has been put on. Instrumental of 'Hungry Eyes' – '2,3,4, Breathe.' His instructions are not shouted but spoken tenderly. She is affected by his tone.

	confusion, reflecting the obvious confusion of Baby and Johnny; they are practicing a dance figure but something else is going on as well. Not only are they practicing moving rhythmically as part of the dance, they are connecting somatically and cerebrally.		
8	Mid-shot of Baby running towards a building in pedal-pushers and cardigan.	No dance.	Instrumental opening continues non-diegetically.
9	Mid-shot inside the building towards the same window, of what appears to be a dance studio. Baby and Johnny dancing together. This time the establishing shot is reversed as she is on the left and he is on the right. She wears a pink bra-top and shorts.	Johnny is teaching her the arm positions; they are not relaxed.	Vocals begin: Male voice singing: Johnny is shouting instructions at her: 'Head up! Lock your frame, Spaghetti Arms! This is my dance space…this is yours!' He is domineering again.
10	Camera gives a revelation pan to mid-shot of window under which is a record player being adjusted by his partner. We haven't been aware of her presence in the room until now. She is wearing black leotards and tights. She adjusts the volume then moves purposefully over to Baby and Johnny to adjust Baby's posture and placing one hand on Baby's hip the other on her back, dances	They dance: he is in effect dancing with two women, both facing him.	No more instructions. 'Hungry Eyes' continues.

	behind her guiding her movements. Baby is now in the centre.		
11	Close-up as they dance, of their upper bodies; both pairs of female eyes gaze at Johnny as they dance. The metonymy is of sex rather than just dance.	They dance in a concentrated and sensuous way around the floor.	'Now I've got you in my sights, with these hungry eyes.' With this line the music literally sings about the visual.
12	Metonymy of dance again: Close-up of calves and feet. Baby is clumsily trying dance steps. She is wearing very little: a midriff baring top, knickers and flesh coloured footless tights. He is wearing a short sleeve teeshirt which reveals his biceps. Close-up of her torso, he is behind with his arms around her waist.	He is instructing her. She is working hard but frustrated. The swings and twirls are proving difficult to synchronize.	'I feel the magic between you and I.' This is ironic as he looks annoyed; he sticks his finger in her eye by mistake whilst trying to get her to maintain eye contact during the dance figure. 'I want to show you what love's all about.' This scene suggests it's all about hard work.
13	Close-up of calves and feet. She is on the left wearing plimsolls and footless tights. Jump shot to high-heeled silver dance sandals.	More proficient dancing.	'Darling tonight.'
14	Close-up of Johnny back in the studio seated cross-legged on the floor, looking up at something and nodding in time to the music, Camera pans out to mid-shot and he is framed by two pairs of female legs dancing opposite each other in black tights and silver high-heels. These are the subject of his gaze. Baby on the right	Partner is teaching Baby to dance in a more erotic manner with gestures metonymic of a sexually aware woman, suggesting that these dance dance lessons form part of a 'rite of passage' for Baby.	'Now I've got you in my sights.' An appropriate line as Johnny gazes at both women dancing together.

	wears black knickers and short grey top; her partner wears red leotards.		
15	On the bridge again: Mid-shot of her in tight shorts and white top applying lipstick. This is the first time she is wearing make-up.	No dancing.	Chorus continues.
16	Close-up of side view of her waist and bottom in black knickers and flesh-coloured tights. His hand on her hip as she dances. Metonymy of sex.	Dancing close, gazing at each other.	Chorus. Saxophone.
17	Pans up to close-up of their head and shoulders, dancing: for the first time he is naked to the waist. He smiles encouragingly and nods his approval.	They dance in a relaxed way together, their bodies in tune. Metonymy of sex.	Rasping saxophone. He is issuing instructions; the geno-song of the saxophone matches the eroticism of the dance.
18	Close-up of feet and calves as she moves from right to left. Close-up of upper bodies, we see his muscles because he is bare-chested. Close-up of Baby leaning with her back on his chest; he strokes her arm downwards as part of the dance practice; she is ticklish and it causes her to laugh; Johnny is annoyed; the move works when he gazes at her and she returns his gaze – they make a connection which seems to go beyond the dance move.	They dance very well together, they are moving as one, smiling.	'Hungry Eyes.' Screaming saxophone. Fade out.

Within these six minutes, we have seen Baby transformed from a virginal girl to a sexually aware young woman ... through her increasingly provocative costume (vision), and through her increasingly eroticised dance gestures and movements (dance). The music adds to the significance of these shifts (sound) by providing a series of signs which direct the audience to particular readings of the text. Thus, at Sound 9, a male voice sings 'I've got this feelin' that won't subside, I look at you and I fantasise, darlin' tonight'; at Sound 12, the erotic promise is repeated by 'I feel the magic between you and I'; at Sound 16, the introduction of the soul-based saxophone presents a contrast with the song up to that point, complements their new physical closeness, and is suggestive of sexual intimacy; at Sound 18, the male voice singing 'hungry eyes' has been replaced by a female voice, indicative of a union of male and female.

These, and other, signs are familiar and powerful inducements to the audience to read the scene in a particular way. Alan Durant has noted that:

> Movement and gesture are figured important pleasures of the body in music, to be felt and to be viewed. But these are always addressed across specific conditions and aesthetic purposes, in rhetorics of deportment, clothing and mannerism through which are represented the mobile, the muscular and the physical. (1984: 97–8)

Furthermore, the location of the scene is significant. In addition to the obvious symbolism of the bridge as a transition or point of departure, McRobbie's comments on 'the mysterious eroticism of the rehearsal room' (1984: 134) indicate how the paraphernalia of the dance studio – the leotards, tights, dance shoes and mirrors – provide a sensual milieu, an escape through fantasy for protagonists and audience alike. It is also self-referential in the sense that it shows the development of dance as human/social process against a polished product.

While this scene is in many ways crucial to the narrative construction of the film, it is by no means alone in its celebration of the (potentially) liberating effect of music and dance for the body. *Dirty Dancing*'s final scene makes this explicit. Johnny has been fired because of his association with Baby. Despite this he enters the dance hall on the last night of the holiday during the final party, in jeans and leather jacket, and walks over to where Baby is sitting with her parents. Announcing that 'Nobody puts Baby in a corner – come on', he takes her up on to the stage:

> 'Sorry for the interruption folks, but I always do the last dance of the season. This year somebody told me not to. So I'm going to do *my* kind

of dancing with a great partner, someone who's taught me that there are people willing to stand up for other people no matter what it costs them, somebody who's taught me about the kind of person I want to be: Miss Frances Houseman.'

Both audience and her parents are shocked as this is the first occasion on which she has been addressed by her proper name rather than the pet-name of Baby. All its connotations – young, virginal, child, dependent – are suddenly challenged. There follows a dance sequence to Bill Medley & Jennifer Warnes' 'The Time Of My Life' which interrupts the sedate chorus line routines from the other guests and demonstrates how, through dance, Johnny can confront and overcome the hypocrisy and repressiveness of the 'official culture'.

Johnny and Baby slowly begin the dance. His body is rigid, hers is leaning slightly in his grasp, gazing up at him, a pose which does not possess any sexual charge (she looks almost maternal in a conventional white dress). They begin to dance, easily and proficiently, smiling and obviously enjoying it. A strong rhythmic beat comes in unexpectedly after the song starts as a slow, romantic ballad, and the musical style suddenly shifts to 'contemporary'. Significantly, the record is a male/female duet or dialogue, whose lyrics mirror what has happened to Johnny and Baby, and which contains repeated phrases suggestive of physical, sensual and emotional communion:

'With passion in our eyes ... we take each other's hand 'cos we seem to understand the urgency ... you're the one thing I can't get enough of ... with my body and soul I want you more than you'll ever know, so we'll just let it go ... don't be afraid to lose control ... yes, I know what's on your mind when you say "stay with me tonight".'

We are left in no doubt that the ability to 'let go' and 'lose control' are important aspects of the beneficial effects of music and dance.

Johnny leaps off the stage exactly as the chorus begins. Baby tilts her head back and laughs joyously as he dances down the aisle through the audience amidst screams of encouragement from the rest of the entertainment staff at the back of the hall (who are, at this point, outsiders, excluded from the official culture's final show). The camera tracks backwards as he approaches them. The rest of the guests are clapping now and moving in time to the music. The entertainment staff start to dance towards Johnny who continues to solo dance; then the camera angle switches to Baby on the stage, and we see Johnny and other dancers approaching her. She smiles in anticipation. She is lifted off the stage by a number of the male dancers, nods at Johnny, then runs and leaps into his arms and is held horizontally aloft executing the dance figure which had given her difficulty in the past, and which had prompted him to say 'you have to trust me'. Her success shows us that now, at last, she obviously does. This is dance as carnival: it provides a cathartic finale to the film, particularly for the two main protagonists. The dance staff invite members of the audience to dance, two elderly ladies discard their fur stoles and join in, much to the amazement of the holiday camp boss Max Kellerman. There are close-ups of the different characters – administrators, guests, entertainment staff – all 'dirty dancing' happily together. The language of dance has brought them momentarily together. Baby is liberated from parental control and Johnny is allowed to give his last dance performance to his kind of music.

Official culture has always in the past sought to denigrate aspects of popular culture, particularly those associated with the feminine, such as dance and the affective appreciation of music: 'To the very large extent that mind is defined as masculine and body as feminine in Western culture, music is always in danger of being perceived as a feminine (or effeminate) enterprise altogether' (McClary 1991: 151). Such binary oppositions as male/female, strong/weak, rational/emotional, good/bad, virgin/whore are imposed on us in all forms of communication. They are at best overly simplistic, at worst pernicious forms of proselytisation for the conservative bias of official culture.

However, I believe that in the early years of the twenty-first century, these oppositions are less readily accepted, and that early clues towards such rejections may be found in texts like *Dirty Dancing*. While it is true, as Anahid Kassabian observes, that 'music and dance, inseparable throughout the film, define two constellations of identity: middle-aged, middle-class, repressed and Jewish versus young, working-class, sexual and not-quite-white' (2001: 78), the behavioural barriers (stereo)typically associated with these divisions are not rigidly upheld. Thus, for example, when Baby loses her virginity to Johnny, she is not castigated for her behaviour; rather, it is seen as a necessary part of her 'rite of passage'.

Changing partners, changing contexts

Unlike some of the other dance music films of the 1980s, *Dirty Dancing* contains an eclectic mix of musical styles and periods, from 1956 to 1987, including rhythm'n'blues, doo wop, soul, girl group ballads, Latin American dance such as the merengue and mambo, and disco/soul hybrids written specially for the film. While not possessing the same degree of 'historical realism' as *Saturday Night*

Fever, the film attempted to portray dialogically the cultural contours of a time fourteen years before its release. The 'structure of feeling' (Williams 1961: 64) it created – via the clothes, the music, the dance, and the setting of the holiday camp – may not have been *exactly* how it was to live at the time and in this sense the film is an interpretive fiction, whose topography can be accepted or rejected by the audience. Nonetheless, the fact that music and dance are so central a part of the film adds to its effectiveness in portraying a general sense of time and place. The *affect* of music and dance accentuates the *effect*.

We see this in the opening sequence of the film, when the Houseman family are driving towards their destination. The music playing (we assume on the car radio) appears to be diegetic but could also be non-diegetic. It is the Four Seasons' 'Big Girls Don't Cry' which is significant in relation to the 'rite of passage' of Baby's evolution from girlhood to womanhood. Baby tells us: 'That was the summer of 1963 ... before President Kennedy was shot, before the Beatles, when I couldn't wait to join the Peace Corps, and I thought I'd never find a guy as great as my dad. That was the Summer we went to Kellerman's.' And at the end of the movie, just before the final dance sequence, Max Kellerman tells the band-leader: 'It's not the changes Tito. It's that it all seems to be ending. You think the kids want to come with their parents and take foxtrot lessons? Trips to Europe, that's what the kids want: twenty-two countries in three days. It feels like it's all slipping away.' His is an interesting insight into the nascent, and largely unrecognised, process of globalisation. Of course, from the vantage point of 1987, when the movie was made, this is clearly evident. Social, cultural, political, demographic and economic change is foreshadowed by Kellerman's example of changes in dance – from the foxtrot to 'dirty dancing'. There is a nostalgia for a lost innocence, for a pre-assassination, pre-Vietnam America which has long disappeared. Baby on the brink of womanhood and America on the brink of massive change are suggested and explored in the film through music and dance.

Hollywood film musicals from the 1930s to the 1950s used dance as a necessary part of the ritual of courtship to bring couples together in a socially approved unit (as in the Fred Astaire/Ginger Rogers series). Dance film from the 1970s onwards has used it in a more oblique way, often for enjoyment and escape. In the 1960s of *Dirty Dancing*, the musical popularity of rock'n'roll, soul and funk were both cause and consequence of less restrictive attitudes towards sexuality and gender. Thus, the dancing couples in the film scene may not necessarily sleep together, but simply dance together. Watching Johnny and his dancing partner, Baby and her cousin speculate: 'They look great together.' 'Yeah, you'd think they were a couple.' 'Aren't they?' 'No, not since we were kids.' Although their dancing is sexual, their relationship is not. They dance for themselves and for each other, and take pleasure in their virtuosity.

However, the possible link between dance and sex is always on the periphery. Baby visits Johnny's room to apologise for her father's hostile behaviour. 'Dance with me,' she says. The music playing on Johnny's record player is Solomon Burke's 'Cry To Me', the lyrics of which are appropriate as both Baby and Johnny are unhappy. 'What, here?' he asks in surprise. They start to dance closely, in time with the sensuous rhythm provided by the insistent horns and 'churchy' piano. Burke's melismatic voice asks: 'When you're all alone in your lonely room, don't you feel like I'm cryin'? Don't you feel like cryin'? Well here I am honey, come on, cry with me/Loneliness, loneliness, is just a waste of time, oh yeah, you don't ever have to walk alone, come on, take my hand, walk with me.' As Johnny holds Baby to his chest, they both seem less unhappy and more aware of each other. She is leaning back slightly, his arms supporting her around her waist. Their knees are bent, their legs intertwined, pelvises touching. She gazes up at him. He is naked from the waist up, displaying his athletic physique; she is wearing tight white jeans and top, accentuating her curves. This is an erotic presentation of both male and female bodies dancing. It is dance as foreplay.

Soul music (through its adoption of secular subjects to the gospel style of call and response, melismatic singing, repetition and syncopation, and its emphasis on heterosexual love and love-making) is particularly appropriate for this type of scene. In the late 1950s and early 1960s, its juxtaposition of what was regarded as the divine and the profane created significant frictions within the musical establishment. Simon Frith explains that 'the sounds made by soul singers around and between their notes ... seem expressive of their deepest feelings because we hear them as if they've escaped from a body that the mind – language – can no longer control' (1996: 192). The moans, groans and shrieks so common in soul music were regarded as revolutionary in both musicological and sociological terms. Later in the film, Otis Redding's 'These Arms Of Mine' performs a similar function, when Johnny dances with other female dancers and then tries to teach Baby. All are enjoying themselves; all have escaped their prescribed roles, albeit briefly, through communion of the mind and body in dance.

Although it is the heterosexual tension between Johnny and Baby that lies at the heart of *Dirty Dancing*, it must be noted that the film provides a context for alternative readings to be satisfied. Richard Dyer (1995) has drawn attention to the important part played by structurally subordinate groups such as women, blacks and gays in the promotion and definition of entertainment. The appeal of Patrick Swayze's (as Johnny) rippling muscles is not just to the female audience;

nor is John Travolta's (as Tony) bedroom routine in *Saturday Night Fever*, which sees him narcissistically dance in front of his mirror, wearing only underpants, lovingly fondling his clothes, carefully grooming his hair, embracing his medallion – surrounded by posters of such male icons as Al Pacino, Bruce Lee, Sylvester Stallone (and Farah Fawcett). The fact that *Saturday Night Fever* may not have set out to attract a gay audience (in fact, there is a scene in which a gay couple are insulted and heckled by Tony and his friends) does not detract from the manner in which an ostensibly heterosexual text has been successfully reappropriated. Referring to the erotic, romantic and materialist characteristics of disco music, Dyer has argued that it is a manifestation of 'camp': 'It is a contrary use of what the dominant culture provides, it is important in forming a gay identity, and it has subversive potential as well as reactionary implications' (1995: 521). In the same way that Carol Vernallis has pointed to the 'homo-erotic perspective' (1998: 179) afforded by the mermen in the video to Madonna's 'Cherish', the images of semi-naked men in *Saturday Night Fever* and *Dirty Dancing* should not be overlooked in their appeal to alternative gender practices.

Whether heterosexual or homosexual, time and place become irrelevant through the escape into fantasy permitted by music and dance in film. Wayne Bowman's suggestion that 'the temporal experience of music occurs not in flat chronological time but in experientially overlapping and simultaneous past, present, and future ... the body is a synergetic system which responds to a musical situation addressed to tactile and visual, as well as auditory, functions' (1998: 272–3) emphasises that it is the synergy between mind/body as represented in the combined agency of music/dance that enables one to escape the realm of the ordinary, to go 'outside' time. As Susan McClary (1991) has discussed, music *does* 'move' people but, unlike advertisers and film-makers, academics are reluctant to accept this, regarding affect as a rather nebulous and subjective concept. However, it remains true that in our 'use' of dance, dance film and dance music, the mind and body are not separate, but are part of the entire experiencing person.

It is significant that *Dirty Dancing*, like *Saturday Night Fever* before it, conferred stardom on the male lead rather than the female. While this is not entirely new (both Fred Astaire and Gene Kelly may be better known than some of their female partners), it does clarify the construction of 'the male gaze' in both films. While dance film presents a highly stylised version of the way we traditionally perceive male/female relationships (through a conservative choreography in which the male always leads), the depiction of the actual male body in these films is a new departure. The lean, muscular, controlled man (white-suited or bare-chested) is foregrounded; the pliant or novice female dancer retreats into the background.

As a result of such depictions, 'men are now beginning to participate in dance in a less sexually frantic way. They too have taken up its narcissistic, auto-erotic dimensions' (McRobbie 1984: 144). On a more routine level, 'mirrors have gone back up on locker-room doors and there's often a dryer and as many as five brushes on the shelf' (Andrews 1998: 89).

The recognition and analysis of dance film thus addresses many concerns regarding contemporary popular culture, acknowledging and articulating issues around sexuality, gender, ethnicity, power and pleasure. Investigations into the nature of the relationship between music and the body in dance film entail an appreciation of philosophy, phenomenology, psychology, sociology, musicology, history, anthropology and cultural studies. While some academics may remain reluctant to approach a subject from an interdisciplinary perspective, my investigation of *Dirty Dancing* presents compelling evidence that this is the only plausible or effective route for the proper study of new and relatively unfamiliar genres such as dance film.

Chapter Three

THE STING IN THE TALE

Phil Powrie

Every breath you take
And every move you make
Every bond you break
Every step you take
I'll be watching you
                – 'Every Breath You Take'

It is not unusual for major British rock stars to appear in feature and television films, either as themselves, or more frequently as characters. Phil Collins has had leading roles in two feature films: *Buster* (David Green, 1988) and *Frauds* (Stephan Elliott, 1993). Mick Jagger acted in two feature films in 1970 – *Performance* (Nicholas Roeg) and *Ned Kelly* (Tony Richardson) – returning to features over twenty years later in *Freejack* (Geoff Murphy, 1992), *Bent* (Sean Mathias, 1997) and *The Man From Elysian Fields* (George Hickenlooper, 2001). Roger Daltrey has acted in some twenty features since the mid-1970s, most famously as the

and he plays Eddie Cochran's 'Three Steps To Heaven', accompanying himself on guitar. Unlike *Quadrophenia*, where the association with music is incidental, Sting plays music, but it is, as it was in *Quadrophenia*, a look back to the past: 'the tenor ... of a certain level of British life in the late 1950s and early 1960s is evoked with startling immediacy by the brief conversation between the two rock'n'roll fans' (Pym 1979: 234). The nostalgia is sentimentally presented, as the hero of the film and Sting's garage attendant share a privileged moment: 'the song offers ... a cultural reference point, a return to an age of innocence from which one can look forward to the future' (Nowell-Smith 1979–80: 35).

In his first two film roles, then, Sting encapsulates two opposing sides of his star persona: apparently dangerous rebellion, and sentimental nostalgia. The two shade off into each other: the rebellion is figured by music from the past which Sting does not sing, while the nostalgia of the Cochran song is also a statement of rebellion against a stultifying environment, which 'contrasts the musical impulse with the damp gloom of the weather and the junk-yard clutter of the station', thereby 'establishing a dialectic between a patently sterile wasteland setting and the transformative possibilities evoked by the sheer presence of the music' (Hogue 1982–83: 50). As discussed below, rebellion and nostalgia were to be key to Sting's first major role, in *Brimstone and Treacle* (Richard Loncraine, 1982).

The Police were arguably at the height of their success in 1979–80. In 1979 they had sold five million singles and two million albums (Sandford 1998: 85). In 1980 they began a year-long world tour and claimed a number of awards, including *Evening Standard* top band, top singer, top album and top single (Ibid.: 118). In 1981 Sting was named *Songwriter of the Year* at the Ivor Novello Awards, and was offered a number of film roles in Hollywood, including the villain in *For Your Eyes Only* (John Glen, 1981) and Mordred in *Excalibur* (John Boorman, 1981), both of which he declined. He accepted the part of Helith, the Angel of Love, in a surreal three-hour-long BBC television film, *Artemis 81* (Alastair Reid, 1981).

Whereas two of Sting's previous roles had been associated with music, his first lead role, as Martin Taylor in *Brimstone and Treacle* (a part turned down by David Bowie) had nothing to do with music at all, although several Police songs, including 'I Burn For You', 'Only You' and 'Spread a Little Happiness', were on the compilation soundtrack issued in September 1982. The last song, a cover of a pre-war classic composed by Vivian Ellis, was, paradoxically given its absolutely straight 1930s musical treatment, Sting's first solo hit, remaining in the charts for eight weeks and rising to sixteenth position (Donnelly 2001: 111), testament to the popularity of the band at this time. If this surprised fans, they were even more surprised by the issue of two cover versions from a film in which Sting did not act, *Party Party* (Terry Winsor, 1983): Fleetwood Mac's 'Need Your Love So Bad' and Little Richard's 'Tutti Frutti', part of a long list of film score contributions.[4]

Brimstone and Treacle was based on a BBC television play by Dennis Potter which was withdrawn three days before broadcasting in 1976 (Sellers 1989: 50). Echoing Joe Orton's 1964 play *Entertaining Mr Sloane* (later made as a film by Douglas Hickox in 1970) and *Teorema* (Pier Paulo Pasolini, 1968), the story is about a young con-man, Martin/Sting, who insinuates himself into a middle-class family whose daughter Pattie lies catatonic after an accident, while her parents bicker about whether or not she is conscious of what goes on around her. Martin drives a wedge between the mother (Norma) and father (Thomas); the mother eventually persuades the father that Martin is not, as he thought, the Devil. Shortly after this they catch him raping the daughter. In a moral twist, however, the rape causes the daughter to speak again, and it was this 'therapy by rape' (Coleman 1982: 28) which had led the BBC to withdraw the play. The debate following what was seen by some as unacceptable censorship had been long forgotten by the early 1980s, although it was to resurface in the tabloid press on the film's release despite the film winning the Grand Prix at the Montreal Film Festival.

In the course of softening up the mother, the only honest emotion Martin seems to show is a need for motherly love. This transpires less from his affectation of the sobriquet 'Mumsy' which she accepts, than from his trying on her jewellery and gloves while she is out, and collapsing onto her shoulder when he discovers a dead sparrow in the garden. Martin, as it turns out, is the Devil after all, but has a soft sentimental side, the paradoxical combination seemingly legitimised by the result: his frantic rape of Pattie awakens the Sleeping Beauty. I shall show below how this reading of the play/film's narrative is made more complex by Sting's performance, however much his casting may have seemed at the time to be 'a fundamental directorial misconception' (Brown 1982: 196). Potter himself thought that Sting combined 'bottled-up warmth' and 'a slightly arrogant air very necessary for this part' (McKay 1981). However, Sting's star status proved to be problematic for many other reviewers: 'Sting's charisma isn't the right sort or of sufficient power to compensate for his dramatic inexperience' (Cassell 1982).

Sting's iconicity, generated both by his status as singer and actor led to several offers of film roles after *Brimstone and Treacle*. He turned down the part eventually played by Christophe Lambert in Luc Besson's *Subway* (1985), and that of Fletcher Christian in Dino de Laurentiis' production of *The Bounty* (Roger Donaldson, 1984), a part eventually played by Mel Gibson; but he did accept a part in Rafaella de Laurentiis' production of *Dune* (David Lynch, 1984).

Consonant with his Police persona of 'Prince of Darkness', upon which he had traded for *Brimstone and Treacle,* he plays the villain Feyd. The film was shot in May 1983, a month before the release of The Police's final album 'Synchronicity', an album which sealed the band's success in the USA, where it stayed at the top of the charts for 17 weeks (Sellers 1989: 62). The part of Feyd was in many ways similar to that of Martin in *Brimstone and Treacle* – 'Martin in a space-suit', as Sting commented (ibid.: 65) – although Sting's role is more memorable for a scene in which he emerges from mist wearing only a V-shaped codpiece. It is perhaps for this reason that, according to one biographer, the film 'remains Sting's most renowned' (ibid.: 69). And as another explains, Sting dressed as Feyd 'made headlines in Britain and America. Stills of him dressed in his black fetishist's garb enjoyed almost iconographic status in the years ahead. Several, if not many, gay men adopted him as their cover-boy' (Sandford 1998: 135). Sting's star status was used to rescue the film, which did not do very well, with many press reports featuring pictures of him at the expense of other actors, as for example in a two-page spread in the *Daily Mirror.* And, as had been the case with *Brimstone and Treacle*, Sting's character and persona melded: 'To some he was Feyd, a villainous feudal lord with a soft side, like the schizophrenic Taylor' (ibid.).

Sting's 1985 album 'The Dream of the Blue Turtles', with a group of US jazz-funk musicians (from the Miles Davis/Weather Report stable), effectively signalled the end of The Police, and the shifting of musical styles away from The Police's reggae beat to jazz inflections. In the same year, Sting married Trudie Styler with whom he had lived for ten years, and had a son by her. Two films released later in that year suggested that his career had shifted with film acting playing a major role. Both films were released in November 1985; the month is all they have in common, however, since Sting's film persona, just like his career more generally, changed across the two films.

The Bride (Franc Roddam, 1985) is very much part of the first Sting film persona. It re-united him with the director of *Quadrophenia* and its star, Phil Daniels, who has a small part as the son of a circus owner. It was a reworking of Mary Shelley's *Frankenstein*, in which Sting plays Frankenstein opposite Jennifer Beals, the young star of *Flashdance* (Adrian Lyne, 1983). It failed, first because it traded horror against fairytale romance, the major theme of the film being Frankenstein's moulding of Eva, the woman he had originally created for the monster Victor, for himself. A second reason for failure was that the film was overly camp, as Sting himself admitted: 'It was camp because it took itself too seriously' (Sellers 1989: 85). As in *Dune*, Sting appeared in a period costume, this time eighteenth-century high collar, ruffs and tails, his hair longer and flowing in typical Romantic style; the film's French producer, Victor Drai, is reported to have commented 'How can you find anyone more beautiful than Sting?' (Edelstein 1985: 54). There are several scenes on horseback, and as a Baron living in a castle, Sting's film character supports the superstar status he had by this time acquired. There are nods to contemporary issues such as women's liberation, as the Baron states that he wants his creation to be a new woman, 'bold, proud and free', and equal to men. Like *Brimstone and Treacle*, however, his persona is contradictory. There are dark undertones from the very beginning with the Gothic *mise-en-scène*: a castle décor, period costume, dark lighting, plunging camera angles. As the film progresses, we see the Baron attempting total control over his creation. He tries to rein in her impulses for freedom, in one self-reflexive sequence arguing with her over the author of *Prometheus Unbound*; he claims it is Byron, she correctly claims it is Shelley, the reference obliquely being to Mary Shelley, whose Frankenstein is subtitled 'the Modern Prometheus'. The Baron develops an obsessive jealousy for Eva, and, in a similar denouement to *Brimstone and Treacle*, attempts to rape her.

The gender tables were turned for *Plenty* (Fred Schepisi, 1985). Like *Brimstone and Treacle* before it, *Plenty* was originally a stageplay, dating back to 1978, by David Hare. The film focuses on the character played by Meryl Streep, a wilful woman disillusioned by post-war Britain, and who gradually becomes mad as a result. She decides she wants a child, but without the burden of a husband and marriage, and chooses Mick/Sting, a Cockney black marketeer, as her partner. The 'experiment' as she later calls it, fails, and she rejects him, shooting at him when he tries to remain close to her. Mick is coded very strongly as part of the new Britain. They meet in a jazz club where the conversation is about the authenticity of the instruments, with Mick saying he doesn't care about the 'traditional' instruments of New Orleans jazz. His working-class status is emphasised in the dialogue of both of his main scenes with her, the one where she proposes the deal in a tryst on the Embankment, and the one where she takes pot shots at him with her revolver. Unlike *The Bride*, where Sting's acting ability, particularly in relation to voice projection, was sorely tested, the small part he plays in this film allows him to play less with the voice and more with the body. We see him, for example, walking convincingly through a 1953 Coronation street-party, greeting friends, his walk all working-class swagger, a point made in an American review: 'He's got a Cockney sexuality that doesn't seem to require a wardrobe to make the point, and an underlying sincerity that makes him believable' (Sellers 1989: 87). The film also signalled a move up for Sting in terms of his co-actors who included, apart from Streep, Sir John Gielgud, Ian McKellen, Charles Dance and Sam Neill.

Indeed, comments made by Sting about his acting career in 1986 confirmed that he saw acting as a major interest: 'I'm growing as a cinema performer all the time. I don't expect to be Hoffman or Olivier overnight' (ibid.).

The rockumentary *Bring on the Night* (Michael Apted, 1986) was commissioned by Sting to show the life of a rock band as it slowly takes shape. Sting chose Apted to direct largely because he had directed the feature *Stardust* (1974) about the rise and fall of a rock singer, played by pop star David Essex. The film was conceived by Sting, according to Apted, as a way of undoing the 'Prince of Darkness' image which was associated with his Police days, and which his first films had traded on. In that sense it underlines the change in persona from *The Bride* to *Plenty*. It attempted to reveal the man behind the mask, even including footage of the birth of his and Trudie Styler's son. 'Conceptually appalling' (Newman 1986: 167) though this may have seemed to many, its 'staging of the backstage', to paraphrase Jonathan Romney (1995: 91), clearly signals the allegory of a new birth which Sting was attempting to promote post-Police, and which also informs his change of screen persona. The film did not do well, but the album tie-in reached sixteen in the album charts. It was seen as 'uncannily like the spoof 'rockumentary', *This is Spinal Tap*' (Newman 1986: 167), apparently Sting's favourite film, even if the concert performances were 'efficiently filmed' (ibid.).[5]

Three years later, *Julia and Julia* (Peter Del Monte, 1988), an Italian/British co-production, reprises the situation in *Plenty*, with Sting as lover to another disturbed woman played by another well-known American actress, Kathleen Turner. There are two time frames. In the first, with which the film opens, and which we assume is the film's 'reality', Julia is widowed on her wedding day when her husband is killed in a car crash; she works in a travel agency, quietly living a hermit-like existence. The other time frame intrudes later in the film when she uncomprehendingly realises that she is married with children to her husband, and also has a lover, played by a globe-trotting photographer, Daniel/Sting. Happy to have rediscovered her married existence, she rejects Daniel and rushes 'home', only to realise that she has fallen back into her first time frame. The next day Daniel arrives in the travel agency. Initially disturbed by this appearance from her 'other' life, she initiates a love affair with him, and returns 'home' only to discover that she is back in the 'happy marriage' time frame, and that her husband knows about the affair. She returns to the hotel room for Daniel and kills him with the scissors he has used to trim his photographs of her when they made love. The time frame is not clear to us in this sequence or in the final sequences when Julia ends up in a mental hospital. The film's two temporalities thus slide into each other, legitimising Julia's madness. Sting's role is pivotal in the film, since he is the link between the two time frames, and, as was the case in *Plenty*, he is connoted as 'the lover'. Once again, we see him making love to the lead actress; indeed, in this film, unlike *Plenty*, he is seen completely naked in one sequence. And, again unlike *Plenty*, but much like his 'evil lover' roles in previous films, he becomes violent with Julia when she rejects him, hitting her in the town square, and (improbably) raping her in a dark corner while people go about their business a few feet away. The film was released in the UK in February 1988, but seemed to confuse audiences and did too badly to go on general release. It went onto video later that year, just after Sting had released his second solo album 'Nothing Like the Sun', and just after the beginning of the Amnesty International World Tour. The album went to Number One in the UK, despite being snubbed by the critics, and stayed in the charts for 47 weeks.

Stormy Monday (Mike Figgis, 1988) was released in the same year in the USA, and a year later in the UK. Sting plays Finney, the owner of a Newcastle jazz club who stubbornly refuses to sell to an American entrepreneur, Cosmo. Figgis had originally thought of Albert Finney for the part, settling on Sting because he needed 'someone from the North with a more ambiguous image, but who could turn on the tough stuff when required' (Floyd 1989: 20). It is paradoxical that it came in Sting's career at a point when he was beginning world tours which would make him a global figure, given that the film returned Sting to his roots in Newcastle and more particularly to the local jazz circuit where he had started his career in the band Last Exit. Its Newcastle-based setting compared unfavourably for many with *Get Carter* (Mike Hodges 1971), not least because of the underlying theme of Anglo-American politics. The *Monthly Film Bulletin* reviewer, Kim Newman, complained about 'an overdose of American-influenced style' with sporadic American images such as 'Clark Gable, an Edward Hopper-style diner, a club whose Geordie bouncers sport New York cop uniforms, a baton-twirling parade' (1989: 58). Newman criticised the film's loose structure, evidenced amongst other things by Sting's 'irrelevant throwaway in which he fools about with a double bass to establish his jazz credentials', and also its 'infuriating vagueness' (Ibid.): is Kate a call-girl or Cosmo's mistress? is Finney a womaniser or happily married? Although many did not like the film, Sting's performance was judged a success: he 'manages to neatly convey self-contained menace' (Heal 1989: 28) as Figgis had hoped; 'Sting acquits himself with a gritty stoicism that is the only believable ingredient in the film' (Romney 1989: 18).

Sting's final film of the 1980s is a cameo as a heroic officer in *The Adventures of Baron Munchausen* (Terry Gilliam, 1988). There was then a long break from acting until his role in the mid-1990s as the butler Fledge in *The Grotesque* (John-Paul

Davidson, 1996), with Trudie Styler as his wife Doris. The film was produced by Styler for their production company Xingu Films, named after the Xingu Indians in the Brazilian rainforest whose plight Sting had brought to the attention of the world during the late 1980s and early 1990s.[6] *The Grotesque* is a black comedy of manners in which an aristocratic British couple, Sir Hugo and Lady Harriet Coal are in a loveless marriage. The new butler, Fledge, much like Martin in *Brimstone and Treacle*, or Steerpike in the Gormenghast trilogy so admired by Sting,[7] worms his way into the family by sleeping with Lady Harriet and with her daughter's boyfriend, Sidney. The film was ridiculed by many critics, and seen as considerably worse than similar films such as the Vivian Stanshall-scripted *Sir Henry at Rawlinson's End* (Steve Roberts, 1980), even if Sting himself came in for qualified praise. *Sight and Sound's* reviewer, for example, wrote of Sting that 'when lit in the right way, he exudes a gimlet-eyed menace, even if he never approaches the seething class hatred and cold Machiavellian stealth that might have made Fledge a butler to rival Dirk Bogarde's in *The Servant* [Joseph Losey, 1963]' (Darke 1996: 50). But as this comment suggests, the self-contained menace which Sting had managed as late as *Stormy Monday* had more or less disappeared: 'Sting lacks even half the menace needed to give the film an edge' (Gowers 1996: 20).

Sting's final film to date, *Lock, Stock and Two Smoking Barrels* (Guy Ritchie, 1998) recalls his role in *Stormy Monday*. He plays a cameo as JD, the bar-owning father of Eddy, who has lost a large amount of money at cards to the porn king Hatchet Harry and who risks losing the bar. Like *Stormy Monday*, the film was said by Sting to represent a kind of return to roots, even though it is set in London's East End: 'My brother owns a bar in Newcastle so I'm actually playing my brother' (DVD liner notes).

Sting's film star persona

This section will focus on the meanings generated by Sting in his films. Before doing so, it is worth emphasising the binary with which this discussion was introduced, that of good and evil, emblematised by the sensitive and the steely, Gordon the good Geordie working-class lad close to his Mum, and Sting, the ruthless band-leader and entrepreneur – Sting the average guy and the star: 'I used to be the same sort of guy on stage that I was in private life, but now it's a kind of monster' he is reported to have said once The Police began to become stars (Sandford 1998: 85), a theme which recurs constantly in interviews: 'I am sort of two people ... and I have a dark side' (Getz 1985: 37; see also Sandford 1998: 109, 127).

Diversification and Closeness

From a relatively simple functional point-of-view, Sting's film roles diversify his persona. In the case of Bowie, film roles complemented changing performance roles in his music (Ziggy Stardust, Aladdin Sane, the Thin White Duke). Sting's on-stage image, however, is more or less consistent, characterised by a 'deadpan, equivocal stare' (Sandford 1998: 72), and relatively simple clothes: 'T-shirts, outsize jackets and military garb' (ibid.: 71). Off-stage, he adopted similar clothes for interviews or television, reverting to Cerruti suits and other designer outfits for the more prominent social life (ibid.: 186). Film roles therefore offered him a way of diversifying and extending a more monolithic image than Bowie's. Diversification occurs at a number of levels: temporal (Britain in the 1950s and the 1960s, eighteenth-century Hungary, a sci-fi future); geographical (Central Europe, Italy, a distant planet, London's East End); life-style (mod, con-man, Prince, Baron, black marketeer, photographer, jazz-club owner).

Diversification becomes all the more obvious when roles are linked in some way to music or other aspects of his stage persona, since the roles contrast with that persona in a more direct manner. This can occur directly, as in the case of the garage attendant who wants to be a guitar star, or the jazz-club owner who nostalgically plucks his bass, both contrasting markedly with the rock star Sting had become. It can also occur more allusively, as in the case of Ace Face, connected with the music of The Who (although it is important to note here that Sting subsequently played on the association with period in a mod revival, for example, wearing parkas during gigs for a while); or even more allusively, in terms of professional lifestyle, as the photographer whose globe-trotting hotel-room-living life is one shared with the rock star.

Costume is connected with diversification. Where Bowie's stage costumes support the fictional personae he adopts, Sting has not worked through such obvious stage personae, and his costumes, as pointed out above, are more stable. Film roles thus allow costume diversification, affording audiences the pleasure of the star body in different 'frames' – the same but always different.

A special case of costume diversification is nakedness or semi-nakedness. Unsurprisingly, given his frequent roles as lover, Sting is frequently seen semi-naked. We see his bare buttocks as he washes in a lake in *Artemis 81*, and again as he tries to rape Pattie in *Brimstone and Treacle*. In the latter film, the father, Mr Bates dreams of a half-naked Martin trashing his daughter's room, eroticism and violence again combined. He wears nothing but a codpiece in *Dune*; in *Plenty* we see him making love with Susan as she tries to conceive a child by him. In *Julia and Julia*, we similarly see him making love with Julia, and it is in this film that there is a fetishising full-length shot of his naked body, laid out for the kind of consumption normally reserved for the female body. Shots of the star body in various states of undress, quite apart from the obvious erotic charge created, allow an impression of unmediated access to the star body. That access is normally denied in the concert situation where the star is usually too far away from the majority of the audience for the immediacy of his body to make an impression. Where there is a large screen at a concert, its very presence, to say nothing of its fuzzy and/or multi-screen-segmented image, constantly reminds audience members of the star's distance from them, whereas a cinema screen with its high-resolution celluloid images combined with frequent close-ups (as in *The Bride* and *Dune*) does precisely the opposite.

The closeness discussed here is not abstract. It functions for a specific youth audience, at least until *The Bride* in the mid-1980s. In the period 1979–85 Sting's characters are youthful rebels, often pitted against father-figures. Ace Face is a mod gang leader. Martin accosts older men for his cons, and is insistently framed against a poster of James Dean in Mr Bates's dream. Feyd is almost androgynously hairless and beautiful in the well-known sequence where he steps out of a steam 'shower' to the admiring gaze of his uncle. It was only at the end of the Police period, around 1983–84, that Sting began to accept roles which were less youthful.

Stereotypes and binaries

As considered above, diversification is inevitably bound up with sameness. Sting's film persona is predicated on readily-available types which give audiences the sense of stability upon which diversification can play. In Sting's case the types are those of the lover and the criminal, which often run together. They appear so frequently, and are so frequently underdeveloped as characters that they are more stereotypes than types.

Underdevelopment is only to be expected in cameo roles such as the intergalactic thug Feyd in *Dune*, or the roving photographer of *Julia and Julia*. These roles however have the same characteristics as more developed roles; in films such as *Brimstone and Treacle* and *The Bride*, Sting's character threatens or rapes women, and in others he threatens or injures men (*Quadrophenia*, *Stormy Monday*, *Lock, Stock and Two Smoking Barrels*).

The lover/criminal binary is often paralleled by another binary: appearance/reality. Many of Sting's characters have something to hide, whether it is Ace Face who is no more than a weekend rebel, or Martin the con-man, or the Baron who does not want the world to know that Eva is his creation, or Fledge the Steerpike-like butler.

Even his roles in *Julia and Julia* and *Stormy Monday* suggest characters who are in some sense fractured. Daniel the photographer is caught in Julia's two worlds and acts as the gateway between them. Finney the jazz-club owner shows evidence of a similar fractured topography, this time not so much temporal as cultural. He resists the American invasion on one (business) level, while accepting it on another through his advocacy of jazz, a quintessentially American art form. This explains in part the need to have a European avant-garde jazz group as part of *Stormy Monday*'s narrative, since their European-ness papers over Finney's fractured cultural position. That fracture is neatly encapsulated in two key moments of the film, both of which have to do with bridges. The first is when Finney breaks the thug's arm by placing it like a bridge on two supports, suggesting metaphorically his break with London (from where the thugs have come) and with Cosmo (for whom they are working, and who is himself trying to build bridges metaphorically between the USA and Tyneside in his entrepreneurial activities). The second sequence has real bridges, when Finney meets Cosmo on Newcastle's High Level Bridge, with the Tyne Bridge in the background. The two meet in the precise centre of the bridges' spans, and the scene concludes when Cosmo follows Finney onto his side of the bridge as Finney intimates that he will accept Cosmo's offer after all.

Sting's first major role, in *Brimstone and Treacle*, is perhaps the most useful through which to capture the overlapping binaries which structure his persona, not least because of its moralising simplicity. As Sting himself said of the character he played, 'I didn't have to delve too deeply unto myself to excavate him. He's definitely an exaggerated version of me' (Sandford 1998: 132). The film's narrative is framed by the church. Martin emerges from a church at the beginning along with a group of choirboys, and will be accosted by a man at the end who says that the Bishop will be pleased to see him again. Martin is a fallen angel, however. He is framed against a gargoyle at the beginning of the film, a low-angle camera making him look threatening. Mr Bates says early on 'you could be the Devil himself', and the theme reappears in the dialogue towards the end when Mr Bates has been won over: 'I could have been the Devil himself', says Martin, to which Mr Bates replies, 'That's what I thought you were'. There are occasional shots of a standard portrait of Christ as the Sacred Heart, which functions in counterpoint to Martin as the Devil; this is associated with the credulous and all-forgiving Mrs Bates, whom Martin wins over through deceit. Martin pretends to love Pattie, but as soon as the opportunity presents itself he tries to rape her.

The film's narrative attempts to blunt the severity of this Angel/Devil binary in two ways. First, and most obviously, it suggests that good can come out of evil, since the rape causes Pattie to emerge from her catatonic state, just as Martin's attentiveness to Mrs Bates, whom he calls 'Mumsy', and whom he relieves of tedious housework, gives her purpose and resolve. Secondly, the film suggests that Martin's is not the only problem in moral terms, since we learn through Mr Bates's dream flashbacks that Pattie ran into the path of a lorry after seeing her father making love with his secretary. Mr Bates, then, who runs an ecclesiastical publishing business, has in a sense been punished for his adultery, and Martin is the devilish outsider who has the double function of punishing him even more for his lechery (we see Pattie riding Martin in the same way as the secretary rides Mr Bates in one of his dream sequences, suggesting that his lechery involves incest fantasies), but at the same time causes his daughter to return to consciousness. Martin is simultaneously a rebellious son and criminal lover pitted against an Oedipal father, and an attentive son and healing lover associated with a very motherly Mrs Bates. It is a configuration which occurs elsewhere: in *Plenty*, Mick is a shady black marketeer, but his role in the plot is to provide Susan with the child she so desperately wants.

Eye and voice

The previous section reveals that Sting's film star persona is anchored in simplistic binaries. He is at one and the same time a lover and a criminal, at one and the same time surface goodness and hidden evil; in *Brimstone and Treacle* this combination is supported both by dialogue and *mise-en-scène*. This section considers how Sting's body is used to convey the binaries, most particularly the tension between eye and voice.

The first sequences of *Brimstone and Treacle* construct Martin as a voyeur. He is constantly watching potential prey, from a distance at first, before circling towards the victim, and then finally bumping into him and pretending that he knows him. This initial manoeuvre always happens outside and always happens with men. When he goes to the Bates's house, a similar pattern occurs: we see him watching the house from a distance, gradually getting closer and closer, until he is just outside a window looking in, and startling Mrs Bates. The same pattern occurs once he is inside the house in relation to Mrs Bates and Pattie; his dialogue emphasises the way they look to him, and he works towards intimate contact with both, ending in rape for Pattie. Many of his roles reprise that of the voyeur associated with violence. In *Dune*, during his first extended appearance, he beams as he watches his uncle crushing a young manservant. In *The Bride* he watches Eva, his creation, constantly, before trying to rape her. In *Julia and Julia* he is a photographer whose pictures of Julia play a key role, and whom he watches from afar before raping her. Even in *Stormy Monday*, we are given the impression of a character who watches others before making his move, most obviously when he traps those out to force him to sign away his club, and ends up breaking the arm of one of the thugs. When combined with Sting's physiognomy, the gimlet eyes often referred to in film reviews, it is not difficult to see that in Sting's films his eyes are linked to aggression and violence. Although it is an over-simplification, we could suggest, remembering that in films the gaze is usually constructed as male, that Sting's eyes construct his persona as the macho male, the outsider trying to penetrate a domestic interior through deceit before unleashing his aggression. The aggressiveness implied by the eyes is all the more menacing (a word frequently found in relation to Sting's film performances) because Sting does not look masculine. Commenting on his androgynous look in the mid-1980s, the fashion editors of *Cosmopolitan*, interviewed by one of Sting's early biographers, are reported to have said that Sting 'looks like he could be cruel ... he has no outstandingly masculine features ... he's delicate and sinister' (Cohen 1984: 90).

Sting is above all else a singer, however, whether for fans or non-fans in the film audience. Consequently, the issue of how his voice functions is of primary importance. His speaking voice like his singing voice is high and strained which, it has been suggested, is a way of avoiding the unnaturalness of an intimate male voice (Frith 1988: 155). In other words, Sting's high-pitched voice is both intimate and feminine. If Martin's eyes staring through the window frighten Mrs Bates, his words of comfort soothe her in her sorrow. 'Love conquers all', says Martin, his facial expression suggesting total sincerity despite the banality of the statement; 'you speak so beautifully', says Mrs Bates. Sting himself has said that he tried to model himself vocally on female singers such as Cleo Laine and Flora Purim (Clarkson 1995: 37).

Nevertheless, suggesting that a high-pitched voice such as Sting's connotes feminine intimacy is an essentialising generalisation (Moore 2001: 45). Another way of conceiving of such a voice is to relate it to the same strained and high-pitched voice of the *cheb*, or inspired young lover typical of the North African Rai song tradition. It is no coincidence that on the 1999 album *Brand New Day*, the best-selling single 'Desert Rose' begins with music in this tradition, sung in Arabic by Cheb Mami, followed by Sting singing in English. The collocation makes clear the similarities in their vocal styles, the inspired lover aspect of the vocals being emphasised by the song lyrics which establish a simple binary between fire/desert/ desire and rain/garden/woman as aim of the desire, desire being symptomatic of the Fall: 'Sweet desert rose/This memory of Eden haunts us all/This desert flower, this rare perfume/Is the sweet intoxication of the fall'.

Thus it may be that behind or underneath what is said and how it is said, there is always (and this is the attraction of Sting's voice) a 'grain' which connotes intimacy and affect, as Richard Middleton has remarked of pop music more generally: 'It is common for the vocal "grain" to remain a constant but veiled underside of the syntagmatic and semantic flow' (1990: 263).[8]

Feminised intimacy, when taken with the physiognomical formation of the eye, helps us to understand the corporeal components of the binaries suggested above. Sting's body, no less than his roles, constructs a fractured persona: he is the lover, full of goodness and nurturing, Helith, Angel of Love in *Artemis 81*, his voice feminine and intimate; but he is also, as the final stanza of 'Desert Rose' suggests, a fallen angel, a fallen lover, a criminal, quintessentially evil, the Devil himself, who watches like a snake before he pounces.

I have so far artificially separated different elements so as to analyse the persona: an eye coming from the outside and a voice emanating from the inside. In bringing them together, it can be asserted that the function of Sting's persona for audiences is the creation of *dangerous intimacy*, where aggressive evil eye and bedroom voice vie for supremacy. It is an intimacy directly related to Sting's introspective songs, his hallmark until the beginning of his solo career in 1985. That intimacy is also dangerous because it is unstable for other reasons, not just because it threatens to disintegrate into violence. The first of these is connected to Sting's pronunciation/intonation, and the second is loosely connected to the issue of pronunciation/class and what it might signify to the perceiver.

Sting's speaking voice, no less than his singing voice, has been a transatlantic drawl ever since his arrival in London in the late 1970s. Sting's different film roles required different types of pronunciation and vocal performance, or 'impersonation' rather than consistency of vocal performance which one can see in some stars. In the case of Arnold Schwarzenegger, for example, there is much more vocal consistency over different films, and this 'foregrounds the continuities of the star's image over and above differences of character' (McDonald 1998: 185). Variety of pronunciation emphasises the fact that Sting wished to be an actor, to 'impersonate' rather than to 'personify (himself as star)'.[9] But Sting's vocal performance is usually characterised by reviewers as either excessive or wanting in some way. It is middle-class and over-eager in *Brimstone and Treacle*; one reviewer commented that Sting was 'lucky that he is asked to act as though he must always be seen to be acting' (O'Brien 1982: 34). It is posh and hectoring in *The Bride*, reminding fans no doubt of his first career as an English teacher in St Paul's First School, Cramlington; *New Musical Express*'s reviewer described the performance primarily in vocal terms as 'shrill, insufferable' (Cook 1985: 25). It is a slightly false Cockney in *Plenty*. Even in *Stormy Monday*, acknowledged by more than just *The Sunday Times*' reviewer as Sting's 'most impressive performance yet' (Perry

1989: 3), the Geordie accent is not consistent: 'his Newcastle accent raised a titter or two in the preview' (Romney 1989: 18) although it is unclear if this is because of unfamiliarity with that accent or an awareness of its inconsistency.

The intimacy connoted by Sting's voice therefore is destabilised not simply by what some might consider a bewildering if necessary heterogeneity of accents, but also by what one could call *fractures in vocality*, whether intonation (the over-eagerness of *Brimstone and Treacle*) or accent (unstable Cockney or Geordie). Sting's persona is thus *vocally* dislocated in a variety of ways; I shall approach the additional dislocation between film actor and rock star in the concluding comments.

(Dis)location

A final issue, connected to dislocated voice, is that of class. A common theme of star studies is that stars must at one and the same time show conspicuous consumption, out of the reach of audiences, and yet appear 'ordinary', the same as their audiences. Bound up with this is the myth of success. As Richard Dyer points out, the myth tries to reconcile often contradictory elements, which some stars – like Sting – manage to hold together: 'that ordinariness is the hallmark of the star; that the system rewards talent and 'specialness'; that luck, 'breaks', which may happen to anyone, typify the career of the star; and that hard work and professionalism are necessary for stardom' (1998: 42). If press coverage tends to emphasise Sting's 'specialness', often occluding the labour which stardom involves, his biographies tend to emphasise the other points. It has been argued that the most important factor in the American myth of success, which holds together the basic contradiction between ordinariness and specialness (and which may be true for rock stars more generally) is 'the belief that the class system, the old-boy network, does not apply' (1998: 42). In other words, anyone can be a star; class matters less than the combination of hard work and lucky breaks. This is an issue of which Sting is very aware: 'My background made me grateful; it gave me a motivation to escape. Social mobility isn't a fact of life in England – if you're in a certain class, you stay there' (Getz 1985: 10).

Sting's choice of roles are exemplary in this light. First, his roles underline his principal occupation as a musician but, crucially, they are *aspiring* musicians (the guitar-playing garage attendant; the jazz-club owner who nostalgically plucks at his bass when everyone has left). Secondly, his roles underline his superstar status by their association with nobility or higher beings (Ace Face, Helith, Baron Frankenstein, Feyd, the son of Baron Harkonnen). Thirdly, his roles frequently tend to be upwardly-mobile when they are not associated with the second category

(Martin, Mick, Fledge). As he said commenting on his role as Feyd, thus relating that character to 'his Steerpike side': 'I identify with villains ... I like the way they worm themselves into society' (Brown & Sky 1983: 15). Sting's roles, then, are carefully chosen to uphold his rock star persona, and also to legitimise it by emphasising upward mobility from humbler origins.

It is for this reason that *Stormy Monday* is not only perhaps the best film amongst those in which Sting has a major role, but also the most interesting. This is because his work on it comes at a key moment in his career, not long after he had established himself as a solo artist and also, crucially, in the year when both of his parents died from cancer (1987). Clearly this is something which Sting could not have foreseen when he took on the contract for the film; nevertheless, the combination of events signify a return to roots. Indeed, during this period, Sting 'became a familiar figure on the streets of Newcastle' (Sandford 1998: 181), made well-publicised 'pilgrimages' to places where he had played as a young jazz musician, even filming 'one scene of *Stormy Monday* at a bus stop where he'd stood waiting to go to St Cuthbert's' (Sandford 1998: 181), his old grammar school. The many press reports of this type construct a nostalgic return to roots which at one and the same time confirm success (the trope 'he has travelled so far'), and authenticity (the trope 'he is the same as he ever was, Geordie working-class').

In other words, such material *locates him and dislocates him* at one and the same time, doing the same to fan audiences. Fan audiences locate themselves phantasmatically in the star who is beyond their reach, but they are also dislocated. They are dislocated first, and most obviously, because they are not the star into whose location they fantasise themselves; and secondly because, to the extent that the fantasy might nevertheless work, they are ejected from it as the star manifests his lack of stardom by returning to configurations of ordinariness, which was a necessary condition for the fantasy in the first place. In other words, fan audiences may be working through a phantasmatic circular syllogism such as this: 'Sting is the star I adore from a distance; but Sting is just an ordinary bloke; so I can be Sting the star; but Sting is a working-class Geordie; so I can't be Sting after all; Sting is the star I adore from a distance.'

Selfishness and the Self out of place

So far I have played down the difference between rock star and film star in methodological terms. To conclude, I shall consider the specificity of the rock star as film performer, and bring together the various issues focusing on Sting's binary persona.

It is tempting to assume that there is very little difference between the rock star and the film star in methodological terms, that the charisma manifested in both is of the same type. Speaking of *Quadrophenia*, Sting commented 'I was basically doing what I do onstage, being "charismatic"' (Cohen 1984: 118). Clearly though, for fan audiences and ordinary audiences alike, a rock star (or for that matter a sports star) in a film role involves a dislocation which does not hold for the film star. To relocate the star, and thereby diminish difference, will involve mapping the film roles onto the more usual star persona; hence, as has been noted, the possibility of reading Sting's roles as a support for his on-stage persona. Dislocation nevertheless remains a prominent feature of audience perception, usually marked by the same type of observation made of film stars, that they 'cannot act', they are 'themselves', that they personify rather than impersonate. For the fan audience, the fact that the rock star remains 'himself' is of crucial importance, because it makes identification based on feelings of closeness that much easier.

Sting's film roles, impersonations associated with character acting, are therefore problematic for both the fan audience and other audiences. Fans look for the confirmation of the star-image, but this is more likely to be tarnished by the characters Sting has chosen to play. A 'character' is literally a sign etched into or onto something, in this case etched onto the 'purity' of the star body. Non-fans will be equally disappointed, because they will see imperfect impersonations, given that the image of the star will always disrupt the pleasure of character. This argument hinges on the notion of authenticity, which for the fan is the reaffirmation through performance of a pre-existing image (very literally through it, as in 'seeing through' the performance to the image which lies before or underneath). For the non-fan, on the other hand it is a performance which makes one forget the pre-existing star image.

The film personae of rock stars will therefore always already be fractured, whichever type of audience is being targeted. They are always 'out of place', disjointed, disarticulated. Bowie or Madonna constantly play with their personae, thereby affirming the impossibility of (re)location; stars inhabit a different space to ordinary mortals. By contrast, the reason that Sting presents such an interesting case is because his persona is itself predicated on the issue of authenticity; he is a star who has, much more forcefully than Bowie, fallen down to earth. He has frequently reflected in public on his awareness of stardom and the kind of schizophrenia it involves (Cohen 1984: 132), and even some of his songs ('Nothing About Me') speak of it, constructing an authentic self, more often than not associated with Newcastle and/or domesticity, at odds with the globe-trotting star.

His film star persona works to endorse the binary thus constructed, constantly reaffirming fracture through various types of destabilisation. On the one hand, there is the roaming aggressive sexualised male voyeur associated with the evil gimlet eye; on the other, there is the husky persuasive voice of the lover, feminised and caring, at least in appearance. This binary establishes Sting's key characteristic as dangerous intimacy. It is an intimacy which constantly threatens to collapse through its own internal contradictions. Instability also fissures Sting's defining feature, which we might wish to use to define who Sting is, in relation to other stars: his voice. That voice, like his characters, is mobile and Protean in intonation and accent, obscuring the 'grain' (breathily dangerous intimacy).

Arguably, then, the most 'authentic' moments in Sting's film roles, the moments when he is most 'himself', are not those where he is trying to be someone else, but where he is posing as surface, true to the iconic nature of stardom: Feyd emerging from the shower in *Dune*, almost naked, stretching, glistening with moisture; Daniel in *Julia and Julia,* lying naked on the bed after their love-making. What both of these moments have in common is that Sting *does not say anything;* the singer-star whose iconicity we have identified as a mixture of eye and voice is seen, but remains mute, a problematic object of consumption.

The true nature of the star is supreme selfishness. It is perhaps no surprise that Sting's best-known and best-selling song 'Every Breath You Take' (see the epigraph to this chapter) is about a stalker, where Sting sings the role of the stalker stalking a celebrity (himself, one might argue), reaffirming the key binary of eye/voice: who is singing about whom? who is watching whom? This is perhaps what the *New Musical Express* reviewer meant in his comment on *Brimstone and Treacle*: 'Sting seems an ideal embodiment, cuddly and mischievously sinister by turns. Yet it's his very 'naturalness' that undoes the balance of the central triangle. Sting's bumptious air looks so cunning and fulsome it drips with a familiar selfishness' (Cook 1983: 27). Sting proposes his body and his voice for our consumption, and rejects us ironically while doing so. The irony is generated precisely because he is not a film star, but a rock star in a double and mutually self-destructive performance. He is an icon de-iconising and re-iconising himself in the same moment, anchored in the off-screen which is the on-stage, the on-screen persona always already out of place.

Notes

1   Bowie's other film roles include appearances in *Just a Gigolo* (David Hemmings, 1979), *Labyrinth* (Jim Henson, 1986), *The Last Temptation of Christ* (Martin Scorsese, 1988),

The Linguini Incident (Tony Shepard, 1991), *Twin Peaks: Fire Walk With Me* (David Lynch, 1992), *Basquiat* (Julian Schnabel, 1996), *Il Mio West* (Giovanni Veronesi, 1998) and *Everybody Loves Sunshine* (Andrew Goth, 1999).

2 'A family of losers [which] I've rejected as something I don't want to be like' (Sting quoted in Sandford 1998: 240).

3 His films, including television films, are as follows: *Quadrophenia* (Franc Roddam, 1979), *Radio On* (Chris Petit, 1979), *Artemis 81* (Alastair Reid, 1981), *Brimstone and Treacle* (Richard Loncraine, 1982), *Dune* (David Lynch, 1984), *The Bride* (Franc Roddam, 1985), *Plenty* (Fred Schepisi, 1985), *Bring on the Night* (Michael Apted, 1986), *Julia and Julia* (Peter Del Monte, 1988), *Stormy Monday* (Mike Figgis, 1988), *The Adventures of Baron Munchausen* (Terry Gilliam, 1988), *The Grotesque* (John-Paul Davidson, 1996), and *Lock, Stock and Two Smoking Barrels* (Guy Ritchie, 1998).

4 One or more songs by Sting can be heard on the soundtracks of the following films; the list includes features, shorts and documentaries: *Urgh! A Music War* (Derek Burbidge, 1981), *The Last American Virgin* (Boaz Davidson, 1982), *48 Hours* (Walter Hill, 1982), *The Secret Policeman's Other Ball* (Roger Graef & Julian Temple, 1982), *Cat's Eye* (Lewis Teague, 1985), *Stars and Bars* (Pat O'Connor, 1988), *Resident Alien* (Jonathan Nossiter, 1990), *Regarding Henry* (Mike Nichols, 1991), *Man Trouble* (Bob Rafelson, 1992), *The Gun in Betty Lou's Handbag* (Allan Moyle, 1992), *Lethal Weapon 3* (Richard Donner, 1992), *Demolition Man* (Marco Brambilla, 1993), *Three of Hearts* (Yurek Bogayevicz, 1993), *The Three Musketeers* (Stephen Herek, 1993), *Terminal Velocity* (Deran Serafian, 1994), *Leon* (Luc Besson, 1994), *Ace Ventura: When Nature Calls* (Steve Oedekerk, 1995), *White Squall* (Ridley Scott, 1995), *Copycat* (Jon Amiel, 1995), *On the Edge of Innocence* (Pat Werner, 1996), *The Truth About Cats and Dogs* (Michael Lehmann, 1996), *The X-Files Movie* (Rob Bowman, 1998), *The Wedding Singer* (Frank Coraci, 1998), *The Mighty* (Peter Chelsom, 1998), *Runaway Bride* (Garry Marshall, 1999), *Dolphins* (Greg MacGillivray, 2000), *Bossa Nova* (Bruno Barreto, 2000), *The Red Planet* (Antony Hoffman, 2000), *The Emperor's New Groove* (Mark Dindal, 2000), *Greenfingers* (Joel Hershamn, 2000). The most common song to feature (six times) is 'Every Breath You Take', Sting's best-seller worldwide. Sting performs covers of other people's music on the soundtracks of *Sabrina* (Sydney Pollack, 1995), *Leaving Las Vegas* (Mike Figgis, 1995), *The Object of My Affection* (Nicholas Hytner, 1998), *Prelude* (Fabrizio Ferri, 1998; a short in which Sting plays Bach's Cello Suite No. 1), *The Thomas Crown Affair* (John McTiernan, 1999).

5 'When we asked him what his favourite film was, he answered without hesitation: "*Spinal Tap*, I've seen it more than twenty times".' (Bruch 1996; my translation).

6 The same company had also produced two documentaries: *Boys From Brazil* (John-Paul Davidson, 1993) about male prostitutes exported to Europe; and *Moving the Mountain* (Michael Apted, 1995) about the student democracy movement emerging from the Tiananmen Square uprisings in China.

7 He had bought the film rights for the trilogy and was actively looking for a director in 1982. When this fell through, he accepted the part of Steerpike in a two-part BBC radio version (December 1984). He clearly identifies with Steerpike's ruthless upward mobility, and has called not only his dog and his horse by that name, but also two of his many holding companies.

8 This is borne out by Christopher Sandford's characterisation of Sting's 1987 album 'Nothing Like the Sun' as 'a jumble of maudlin dirges ... and cloying Valentine-card lyrics ... self-obsessed words ... Sting's voice was again the unifying link: a rich, slick and full-toned instrument, achingly irresistible on the ballads and bluesy on the belters' (1998: 189).

9 The distinction between impersonation and personification is made by King (1985).

Chapter Four

THE MUSIC IS THE MESSAGE: THE DAY JIMI HENDRIX BURNED HIS GUITAR – FILM, MUSICAL INSTRUMENT, AND PERFORMANCE AS MUSIC MEDIA

Anno Mungen

Performance study and musicology

This chapter seeks to argue that the close relationship between music, performance and music media is intrinsic for an understanding of the music itself. Music has no relevance beyond live performance or recorded sound. The existence of music-*as*-text (in a score of many hundreds of pages or a sketched melody written down on a piece of paper) does not ensure that this music – which might be called 'intended' music – may finally come to life and be heard. Music is dependent on performance, either live or 'mediatized' (Auslander 1999: 5).[1] To the extent that this is true of Western art music, it is even more pertinent for music which is not primarily dependent on a score but which is based in large portions on improvisation – jazz, rock or non-Western music.[2] Music needs a media framework for its sounding existence. It never exists purely through its own 'material', as other art forms do.

Painting, sculpture, literature and film are linked to one major medium, which contains the information and delivers it at the same time. The media for these art forms all rely on a certain 'material': the screen for a painting, the stone or wood block for a sculpture, the book for literature. Film functions somewhat differently, although the film's material too – the celluloid strip – contains and delivers the information.[3] This material cannot, however, be 'read' by itself, as is the case with sculpture, painting or literature. The performance of a film also needs the equipment for the actual projection. And even art-works like paintings and sculptures, which are more autonomous than film, still rely on a certain mediatized context or environment: in order to be accessible to an audience, they require a space in which they are exposed, such as a gallery or other forms of exhibition setting.

Since music is not strictly linked only to a single medium, it functions very differently. While a painting or sculpture is represented primarily by its own material (which can be touched and felt), the 'material' of music (the sound) is transitory. Paintings, sculptures and books continue their existence through their own tangible and visible material. Music only proves its existence while we hear a performance or a recording. Again, film is also different in this respect, since it too is dependent on the performance of its own material. But the media framework of film is more defined than that of music; the media context of music can shift.

In former times the live performance was the only way in which people could listen to music, but over the last 150 years many music media have emerged which have changed dramatically our approach to music in general. Immense diversification has come though new technologies: from nineteenth-century self-playing musical instruments, through the gramophone and phonograph, record player, radio, film and television to the multimedia personal computers of the twenty-first century. Music today exists in many different ways, a diversity which is linked to its (relatively new) ability to be reproduced endlessly. Both the variety of the media context of music and the ability of endless reproduction are based on the transitory character of this art form. Although music is always performative, today's music does not necessarily have to be performed. In fact, live music performance has become the exception of music perception (Auslander 1999).

There are three different media approaches to music I want to distinguish in order to characterise music perception today.[4] First, music exists in the written text, in the score. This remains particularly relevant for the tradition of (studying) Western art music. Historically this approach determined a certain mode of music listening in the Western world and created prejudices against music not based on these models, such as popular or non-Western music. Secondly, music exists in performance. The (very complex) study of the performance of music is central to the analysis of music in general, but because of a paucity of appropriate methods and sources, historical investigations of music performance are extremely difficult to reconstruct.[5] I will return to the phenomenon of music performance when I consider the discipline of musicology. Thirdly, music is delivered through recordings. We possess sound recordings and – most pertinent for this discussion – music exists in audiovisual recordings. Such recordings may be understood as 'mediatized' performance where the availability of the actual sound is combined with a visual experience. In mediatized performance the music is presented in a visual context, which may be natural (the musical performance itself is revealed) or artificial (freely 'invented' images are added). In both cases, images are directly linked to the sound and synchronised with the music.

In recent decades, music media has gained an extraordinary diversity of forms, technologies and aesthetic strategies for combining sounds with images; in fact, the major media delivering music today are all audiovisual – film, video or television.[6] Such diversified and flexible patterns have introduced a new facet in the practice of music listening: at no other time in history has music been so widely or frequently accessible as it is today through media images. The advent of specialised television music channels since the 1980s is just one example of the immense and dramatic impacts that these developments have had on music itself: 'the televisual has become an intrinsic and determining element of our cultural formation' (Auslander 1999: 2).

Following McLuhan, who argued that a 'new medium is never an addition to an old one, nor does it leave the old one in peace' (1964: 158) it might be concluded that the audiovisual media's (especially television) impact on the old media encompasses the status of music-as-text, music-as-performance and music-as-recording. The fact that music today is largely produced and consumed in mediatized performance – as visual music – indicates a new stage in music perception. Furthermore, the increased academic and documentary attention to the symbiotic relationship between vision and sound (music in film, filmed musical performance, music video) means that the iconography of music has never been easier to study.

Ironically, in spite of these shifts, the field of musicology has only recently started to acknowledge the new options. Musicology was – and to a certain degree still is – preoccupied with one medium (and source) of music history: the score (Bowen 1999: 425, 429). Other relevant media contexts have only occasionally been considered. Musicology devoted its energies to developing methodologies for the analysis of 'text' in Western art music, while music based on performance (popular, non-Western, even classical) was largely overlooked. This devotion to the score has had two results: there is an elaborate methodology to describe and analyse structural models and patterns of Western art music; there is no major methodology to describe and analyse music-as-performance. This chapter proposes an approach which examines music not as text, but through performance delivery.

There are three meanings of the term 'performance' within the context of musicology. The first one relates to a sub-discipline in traditional musicology. The study of performance practice history (Bowen 1999: 429) received attention as musicologists explored authentic ways of performing 'old' (pre-1800) music. The revelation of historical aspects in music performance created a history of the interpretation of musical scores by concentrating on music-as-text, but neglected the performative character of music as such (Cook 1999: 244).[7] The second use of the term performance refers to the most basic and literal sense of the word. Performance on this level describes the situation where any music is played by somebody in front of somebody else (an audience). Although the phenomenon of performance in this literal sense seems to be rather basic – and almost natural – to music, the live performance must be recognised as distinct from the predominance of the audio and audiovisual media. Taking this definition one significant step further brings us to the third meaning of performance. Music performance usually takes place under very particular circumstances. Concert, opera and theatre performances are events planned and designed as social and communicative acts (Frith 1996: 205). This use of the term performance is thus related to its significance in the visual arts, where it has received major attention since the 1960s. Performance, in this context, of a precisely designed live-act situated in a specific space has itself the quality of a medium: 'In terms of art theory what mattered here was the *medium*: art became something living, moving, and, by its nature, changing' (Frith 1996: 204). Traditional borders between the visual arts, theatre and music were challenged, and music (or sound-related features) very often became basic elements of what was presented.

Although musicology has touched on this field of performance occasionally, when considering artists like John Cage or Maurizio Kagel, I want to argue that the conception of performance as a specifically designed live-act can be applied to music in a much broader sense. Any concert event presenting classical or popular music is not just a performance in the second sense discussed above. Concerts – especially rock concerts – are designed in a specific way, which follows certain models and offers a particular production involving theatrical elements (Heister 1996: 703). To approach performance as an art form is to emphasise the visual experience and the interaction of artists and audience. Notwithstanding the explanation of the term performance as live-art-act in high culture, Frith's recognition that 'performance itself ... has a history in low cultural spaces too, and I'm sure that performances in popular places and genres (in the music hall and vaudeville, popular song and comedy) are much more akin to performance art than to "legitimate" art or theatre' (1996: 206) is an important insight.

From these preliminary reflections on the manner in which musicology relates to the conception of performance, two major observations may be drawn which might assist us to develop an understanding of the relationship between film, performance and music in the example to be discussed below. Firstly, the perspective on music taken in this essay has its basis in the concept of theatricality (Munz 1998). Music performance is a carefully designed act such as one finds with any theatre production. This aspect of the performative in music is difficult to study because of its transitory character. The 'reading' of a film as a document of mediatized music performance might help to overcome this problem and is intended to develop methodological ideas to deal with this special quality of music. Developing a method to analyse the way in which music is delivered at the moment in which we hear it and see it will help us to understand music differently. Secondly, this essay argues that the media context of music – in this case based on a live-act performance – is important and fundamental to the very act of the creation of music in general. As will be demonstrated, the other major medium involved – film – is not separate from music, since the music is not just an acoustic phenomenon. Music is visual, and certain aspects of the film are musical. To paraphrase McLuhan, the media of live-act-performance and film do not 'help' the music to come to life, but are part of the musical message itself.

I hope to show that in the example of Jimi Hendrix's performance at Monterey, the audiovisual medium of film is the only adequate way through which his music can be perceived. The four stages of my analysis are structured in a particular order to open up the media framework in which the music appears, and to help in decoding the complex relationships between the different media. Although the film itself is the major focus of the analysis, there are further media or media-like tools that are significant for the music: the concert, the musical instrument, the human body and the performance. Together, they add to the overall assertion that music is indeed visual.

Film and concert

Monterey Pop (D. A. Pennebaker, 1967)[8] is a documentary film of the International Pop Festival held in June 1967 in Monterey, California. It was originally scheduled to be broadcast on television but ABC changed its mind after viewing Hendrix's appearance. The film was eventually released in cinemas (Selvin 1992: 103). It opened in December 1968 at New York's Lincoln Center and was screened in New York afterwards at the Kips Bay Theater (Adler 1968).

Pennebaker's film is first and foremost a documentary record of the concert event in Monterey, which had particular significance for popular music history.[9] From a more formal perspective it was influential in the creation of a new film genre in the late 1960s, linking musical film and musical documentary:

> Some of the most successful documentaries in recent decades have been about music. *Monterey Pop* (1967), *Woodstock* (1970) and *Gimme Shelter* (1970) were the progenitors of the genre of 'rock concert' films ... These films, as well as films of operas and concert performances of art music, mix the genres of documentary and musical film and greatly enrich the connotations of the term 'film music'. (Steiner & Marks 1986: 124)

The *New York Times*'s film critic also referred to its innovative qualities, branding Pennebaker's work a 'contemporary music film', and suggesting that 'it is possible that the way to a new kind of musical ... may begin with just this kind of musical performance documentary' (Adler 1968: 44).[10] A quarter of a century on, in today's MTV age, dominated by the audiovisual of pop culture, it is hard to reconstruct the impact of the combination of the visual and the musical. *Monterey Pop* was widely classified as cross-genre; and in order to relate its presentation of a rock concert to more conventional film genres and film music analyses and to illustrate its radical character at the time of release, it is important to recall a general characteristic of 'film music'.

The analysis of film music usually devotes its general focus to the question of the functionality of music: how does the music work within the context of the images with which it is combined, and what does the music express in relation to the film? This implicit hierarchy reflects the fact that music, in fictional and documentary films, is considered as the supporting feature; it illustrates the image (but not vice versa). In film-making the visual part of the movie is usually generated first, and music and sound are added later. It is not only because of the technical aspects of film-making, but also because of the differences in our perceptions of the aural and the visual, that we usually think about music *for* the images if we consider film music. Perceptually, the visual is predominant; sound – especially if it is not related to semantics, as in instrumental music – is perceived more subconsciously.

Nevertheless, in the history of film music there are examples to be found where the approach to film and music works the other way round. Images have been crafted in order to 'illustrate' the music, and pictures have followed what the music 'dictates'. In the first generation of 'sound films' from the early beginning of the twentieth century, gramophone recordings of operatic arias were synchronised with a short film of the singer in performance, and Walt Disney's *Fantasia* (1940) famously used classical pieces like Beethoven's 'Pastoral Symphony', Stravinsky's 'Rite of Spring' and Bach's 'Toccata and Fugue in D Minor' as inspiration for stories which were narrated by cartoon images (Steiner & Marks 1986: 123).

Neither visually-inspired audio approaches nor an audio-inspired visual approach to film and music capture the relationship between sound and image in Pennebaker's film correctly. However, although *Monterey Pop* certainly belongs to the documentary field, since it authentically reflects live performances by rock musicians, it still cannot be analysed with those tools typically employed for a standard (non-musical) documentary. And the fact that it is also not a fictional film therefore excludes it from the two general categories available for research in film music. It is a special case: a documentary 'about' music.

Whereas non-musical documentaries are faced with having to make a decision about what music to add to the images, this is a question which need not trouble the makers of concert documentaries: the images we see and the sounds we hear are created during one act. Music and image are, therefore, not just very closely related, but together with the theatrical aspects of the performance, they establish a symbiotic relationship, with particular consequences. The semantics of the visual are only fully understandable through the sound; the music receives its 'meaning' only through the image. That is why *Monterey Pop* cannot be integrated in the image-focused tradition of film music history and cannot be analysed with the common methodological tools of film music criticism. Yet the function of film as a medium of music is crucial for the interpretation of the material.

Concert and musical instrument

Rock and pop concerts of the second half of the twentieth century are public performances of popular music in front of large audiences. Historically and structurally they are based on settings of similar events presenting music of the nineteenth century (Heister 1996). Common to both periods and genres is the general arrangement of the concert, whereby the musicians on stage are facing an audience who is listening to the music and watching the musicians perform. To a certain degree the audience is able to interact and communicate with the musicians. Applause, screaming and other reactions to express approval or disapproval are the 'answers' to the musicians' performance.

It is not only structurally, but culturally, that the modern rock or pop concert can be compared with similar settings of the nineteenth century. In that period, public music performance in concert arrangements had become accessible to mass audiences for the first time in music history (Heister 1996: 698). Industrialised landscapes and democratised societies had created an expanded interest and a new desire for cultural/leisure activities in general. As music began to be a matter of broader public interest, its popularity grew. In particular, a certain type of soloist's concert reflected those developments; sociologically, there are obvious connections to the rock or pop concert setting of recent years. In both cases, the focus of attention is the 'star', sent on tour to perform in front of different audiences in various cities. Renowned performers of classical music in the nineteenth century, such as Swedish soprano Jenny Lind and French pianist Henri Herz, gave recitals in huge auditoriums all over Europe, even touring North and South America. Lind's visit to the United States in 1852 was carefully planned and executed to make her a star in the New World by the entrepreneur P. T. Barnum. Although his major interest was financial, his strategies to promote the soprano also had particular effects on music and the music market; he made Jenny Lind a household name across the United States, and he made the music she performed popular.

There are other similarities that are especially relevant to this discussion. Some famous instrumentalists in the nineteenth century captivated their audiences visually. Virtuosos such as Paganini, Liszt and Herz attracted their audience not just because of the actual sounds they created, but also because of particular aspects of their playing, which were only visually available. Audiences were fascinated to watch the star manipulate his instrument (violin, piano) and see him execute the difficult parts of his music. The relationship between the instrument and the performer that emerged at this time, and its consequent significance for the visual aspects of music performance, helped write a story which would be so effectively retold decades later at Monterey.

Jimi Hendrix is celebrated as one of the most influential musicians of the twentieth century; in performance and on record, he is seen as a key figure in the history of rock music: 'His revolutionary guitar technique and his innovative use of the recording studio as a compositional environment have had a greater impact on rock music than the work of any other musician. His songs and instrumental numbers are not easily separated from his individual style of performing them' (Piccarella 1986: 372). Although his creativity in the studio may have been paramount for Hendrix's music, his live stage performances were equally memorable. Hendrix himself described one particular aspect of his performance, pointing out the theatricality of his music:

Sometimes I jump on the guitar. Sometimes I grind the strings up against the frets. The more I grind, the more it whines. Sometimes I rub up against the amplifier, sometimes I play the guitar with my teeth or with my elbow, I can't remember the things I do. (in Trampert 1994: 111)

To what extent are these techniques necessary to the sound of his music?

There are two broad categories related to visual performance aspects of special treatments of the musical instrument: one which has no particular effect on the music as sound, and one which is highly significant to the musical message. As will be discussed (and as Hendrix describes it himself) actions like jumping on the instrument while it is still connected to the amplifier were introduced to impact on the music directly and significantly, while techniques like playing the guitar with his teeth or playing the guitar behind his back had no direct effect on the sound. But both serve as a visual demonstration to the audience.[11]

Lothar Trampert provides an intriguing example of the first category, which reveals the virtuoso aspects of Hendrix's playing. During a session when Hendrix performed with British guitarist Jeff Beck at New York's 'Scene' club, there was a moment of the performance when the guitarists suddenly transferred instruments: Hendrix caught Beck's bass, and Beck caught Hendrix's guitar. Not only was the actual exchange very fast, but each was also stylistically flexible enough to immediately adopt the other's playing style. The recording leaves no audible 'record' of that switch. It is an example of purely visual virtuosity without any impact on the sound. In fact, the lack of any discernible effect on the sound is a crucial part of that virtuosity.

A similar example can be seen in *Monterey Pop*. During 'Hey Joe', Hendrix gives two guitar solos, one executed behind his back, one played with his teeth. In both cases, the 'sound' of the solo passages contain no differences from a conventional performance. This is reminiscent of the virtuoso displays of the star pianists and violinists of the nineteenth century, through which musicians demonstrate(d) complete sovereignty over their instruments. They not only play the music, but they also 'play around' with their instruments while making music.

Musical instrument and sound

In contrast to the above examples of virtuosity, the visual incorporation of instrument and sound is relevant for a proper appreciation of Hendrix's performance at the Monterey Festival and is also crucial to the status of *Monterey Pop* as a contemporary 'musical film'. Unlike 'virtuosity for its own sake', visual elements within the conception of theatricality serve to define Hendrix's musical 'message' in a very specific way.

His performance of 'Wild Thing' in Monterey is carefully choreographed and executed in several steps. Nothing is left to chance.[12] The act can be regarded as a 'production' of theatre *for* music, where all elements of performance are meant to have their own significance. The focus of this stage act is the relationship of the musical instrument to the performer's body. More precisely, the music as part of a theatre-like setting and the interaction between the bodies of musical instrument and performer in an almost dance-like arrangement are the foundations of the performance.[13] Hendrix's guitar and Hendrix himself are media for the music.

There are different levels at which the instrument can be described as a medium for the music. At the most basic level, the guitar (with its equipment) is the tool – an 'instrument' – to create sound. Since it is an electric, not an acoustic, instrument the guitar itself does not contain the actual sound; the guitar's external 'machines' (as the amplifier might be called) are the extension of the instrument, where the sound is generated. In this way, the guitar (with its supporting tools connected directly to the instrument) can be seen as a sort of 'keyboard' to the instrument, which is used to initiate the music rather than craft the sound.

The guitar as a body therefore gains a significant flexibility to be used for purposes other than musical ones. In a very general sense it reflects the sexual impact of the rock musician's performance and functions as the symbol of a phallus – or a 'technophallus' (Waksman 1999: 189). This can be verified through numerous photographs of Hendrix holding the guitar between his legs with the fingerboard protruding in a particular way, or it can be observed in his performance at Monterey (especially during 'Foxy Lady'). The title of Waksman's book on the electric guitar – 'Instruments of Desire' – emphasises the relationship of musical instrument as body to the sexual meaning of the rock musician's performance.

These correspondences between sexuality, music and performance are intrinsic to Hendrix's art, as is evident from the next level of understanding that can be applied to the guitar. Hendrix treats the instrument as a theatrical tool in order to identify it with/as a female human body. At the beginning of 'Wild Thing' he performs a dance with this body; at the end he simulates intercourse with it. The music is created in the intervening space/time, and seems to have the power to push the performer to further actions: the sexual drive is becoming a part of the music.

The final level of the musical instrument's use as a theatrical tool with symbolic impact is the most disturbing feature of the performance. The moment when Hendrix destroys his instrument symbolises the music itself which is – in a figurative sense – burned to death. The relevance of any music, and of culture in general, for humanity is challenged at this point: 'Through the medium of the electric guitar, Hendrix was able to transcend human potential in both musical and sexual terms' (Waksman 1999: 188).

Similarly, the performer himself is a medium for the music or, as Frith explains it, 'the musician's body is also an instrument' (1996: 219). Music seems to come from the inside of the performer's body, representing his feelings and experiences; simultaneously, the sound of the music pushes him further, encouraging more self-expression. The music he creates and hears makes him move, dance, sing and play. Thus, 'Hendrix's music cannot be considered as separate from his physicality' (Waksman 1999: 188). The musical energy, as well as the relationship between musical instrument and performer, originates from his dance-like act. Although it is the performer who creates this relationship (the musical instrument is still a 'dead' body) it appears that the instrument possesses its own will and existence, and that the performer and the musical instrument's body are interacting. And it is the music that maintains this relationship by continuing the dance. The 'interaction' might be interpreted as a choreography for a love-dance. The musical performance in Hendrix's act develops the choreography in several steps, whose sequence can be ordered for analysis in four major sections.[14]

(1) Hendrix introduces the performance of 'Wild Thing' with a short address to his audience.[15] He declares the following song to be the 'English-American combined anthem', a remark which could be related to his status at the time. The Seattle-born Hendrix with his British band 'The Jimi Hendrix Experience' had become extremely popular in the UK but was less well known in the US. His appearance at Monterey was meant to change this – and did (Selvin 1992: 3). His short speech might also have been an attempt to moderate the effect of the show to come. Although his warning, 'Don't get mad! I am not losing my mind!' might express his own ironic distance to the act he is about to deliver, the remark also implies that the show is not merely based around some effective stage-tricks made up spontaneously, but contains an idea. Pennebaker's film of this address is from an unusual perspective. While he is talking to the audience, we see Hendrix at a distance and in profile, mumbling his words; whereas before and after the introduction to 'Wild Thing', he is typically presented from the front, his face and body in full size or close-up.

(2) The beginning of the musical performance is designed to capture the audience's attention. Pennebaker's film communicates this visually. Initially, Hendrix's face is shown in close-up pointing with both hands to his ears and

repeating this movement a couple of times, telling the audience by gesture, 'Now, open your ears, and listen to this!' Then, Hendrix is shown with his guitar while producing noisy and screaming sounds. Only the instrument is presented in full size; Hendrix's body remains a torso. Pennebaker's employment of close-ups to show particular details of the instrument, and its handling by Hendrix, underlines its significance as a musical tool. He wants the audience's full attention. This part has – strictly speaking – no immediate musical basis: there is no melody, harmony or rhythm involved. It might be musically considered as a sort of 'avant-garde' fanfare, introduced to open up acoustically the frame of the special performance to come. In fact, at the end of the performance of 'Wild Thing' this electronic 'music-as-noise' is (after the destruction of the instrument) revisited.

(3) The actual performance of 'Wild Thing' now begins. Although broadly similar to the performance of his previous songs on stage, it differs in some ways. Hendrix exaggerates his physical motion more than before, adding a higher dynamic impact to the act. Both his playing and singing are closely linked to the dynamic features of his dance-like movements. He employs one of his show tricks and plays the guitar behind his back; this is perfectly integrated within the sequence of his movements. While these dynamic features are based on body movements and gestures, the quotation of another song in this performance refers to music itself. Hendrix plays the melody from Frank Sinatra's 'Strangers in the Night' on the fingerboard of his guitar with his left hand. Without any further comment, or indication of the significance of his musical quote, he rises his right arm while playing. The gesture seems mainly to ask for attention for what is a very unusual moment within the overall performance.

(4) The transition into the final segment of Hendrix's performance is indicated by his move away from the audience towards the back of the stage. What follows contains the more theatrical part of the show, including two provocative acts: the sexual allusion and the destruction of the musical instrument. All of this is musically accompanied by a long and extensive drum solo and by noises created by Hendrix on guitar:

'Wild Thing' descends into a fit of electronic noise as Hendrix turns away from the crowd to simulate intercourse with his guitar and amplifier, aggressively thrusting his hips at his 'equipment'. He then moves back toward the audience and, after straddling his guitar for a moment, retrieves a can of lighter fluid from the back of the stage, which he proceeds to 'ejaculate' onto his instrument. And next comes a match – the guitar is on fire at the foot of the stage, and Hendrix, kneeling over it, flicks his tongue and motions with his hands to conjure the flames higher. Picking up the tortured still-burning instrument, he smashes it to pieces, and proceeds to fling its scorched bits into the crowd before stomping off the stage, amplifiers still squealing with feedback. (Waksman 1999: 188)

Steve Waksman's description refers only to the stage performance. Pennebaker's film additionally reflects briefly and significantly on some of the audience reactions to these events. The faces of two women are shown in separate close-ups during Hendrix's destruction of the guitar. They express mixed feelings of shock, surprise and fear. This first visual interruption to the stage show is followed by a second, with a rather different 'meaning': an uplifted arm holding and playing a tambourine. While its sound is unheard, its movements imply a joyful, happy response. The musical background to this sequence is still dominated by the aggressive drum solo to which is added the shrill noises of the amplifier. Finally we are listening to one screaming tone, until the equipment is turned off. Hendrix and his band leave the stage. The show is over.

Sound and vision as film

This chapter's exploration of the genre of film as mediatized performance in the context of music perception, through the investigation of the particular media frames discussed above, now returns to its main thesis: that the 'message' of Hendrix's music in *Monterey Pop* is only fully understandable by considering both the musical and the visual aspects of his act. In other words, the music is perceivable to full degree only in mediatized performance, where all features of the theatrical act prove their significance.

In distinction to other art forms, film depends on performance but retains – unlike music – the information within its own material. Any performance which is based either on pre-existing material (film) or on artistic expression to be created during the act (music) is primarily time related; performances of both music and film therefore need a certain space to expand their material. The actual concert environment at the Monterey Festival, as Pennebaker (re)creates it in *Monterey Pop* – the space in which the music 'takes place' – is relatively insignificant. While Pennebaker's principle cinematic focus remains the stage, he occasionally (and significantly) pans into the audience in order to capture aspects of the communicative elements of the concert, such as the women's faces mentioned above. From a cinematic perspective these faces (re)relate the music performed to those human emotions created by the musical performance as a live-act.

Music's ability to reveal and deal with human emotions is emphasised by Hendrix's performance of 'Wild Thing'. The 'meaning' of his performance can only be approached via its visual elements. This analysis of *Monterey Pop* prompts two main observations which illustrate the particular property of music as a visually-grounded medium.

(1) Music is visual

Hendrix uses his instrument in ways which allow the guitar to take an active part within his show – theatrically and musically. The quotation from 'Strangers in the Night' illustrates this point. While Hendrix plays the melody, the musical instrument itself seems to adopt the familiar pose of a singer. The unexpected location of a 'sweet' melody within the context of a rock concert provides the guitar with the opportunity to supply an ironic answer to Hendrix's 'wild' performance. The theatrical interaction between Hendrix and his instrument is set briefly at a musical level.

Hendrix's introduction of strategies of personification (of the electric guitar) prepares the audience for the climax of the performance, the destruction of the instrument. The guitar's noises at the end of 'Wild Thing' are comparable to human acoustical non-semantic expressions, such as whining and screaming. The interpretation of the screaming guitar as human is further emphasised by the artist's 'story' told through the performance images. We can observe how Hendrix relates his human body (and music) to the body of the instrument as human. By reinventing his guitar as human, Hendrix suggests its 'death' – like that of a movie character who dies slowly and painfully after being shot. The association of its 'human' noises at the moment of 'death' would not emerge were we to simply listen to the music. We must see Hendrix's act in order to understand this provocation.

(2) Music in society

The close relationship between sound and vision is fundamental. Hendrix's show is a 'performance' in the sense of a live 'piece' of art whose provocative elements connect it to the 'Happening' culture of the 1960s, where conventional artistic values and traditions were routinely confronted. But we also need to consider the problems of 'reading' this film in the early years of the twenty-first century. Neither the simulated sexual intercourse nor the tortured noises produced by the instrument are as shocking today as the fact that Hendrix sets his instrument on fire. There can be nothing more destructive for music than the burning of an instrument, an act which can only be compared to the burning of books.

Hendrix's performance raises some difficult questions: Why should a musical artist want to destroy his own basis? What did he wish to tell the audience then? What does *Monterey Pop* tell us today? What is the significance of the events' stage setting?

The climax of Hendrix's act may be a symbolic destruction of the music itself. Such an interpretation stresses the significance of this action in a broader social context and in the disciplinary context of musicology.[16] Since the film is not part of the image-focused tradition of film music history but a music documentary, it can and should be read as a 'text' for music performance study.[17] Musicology has to consider sources like *Monterey Pop* in order to understand how music 'works' when it is created and performed on stage. At the same time, media studies need to gain a greater sensibility and appreciation of the questions of sound and music in the multimedia arrangement of film perception. Sound is an essential part of the visual, and the visual is an intrinsic feature of the musical. Both are basic to any cinematic perception. *Monterey Pop* is a source which makes this evident.

The answer to the question 'why burn the music?' might be as follows. On the one hand, the film shows how art forms based on particular media frameworks relate in a symbiotic way to each other (there would be no music without the film, and there would be no film without the music). On the other hand it shows how the media for music connect to the world of our existence (Hendrix's identification of the guitar-as-human relates his art to our lives). In burning the music he reflects on something contrary: on an unthinkable human existence without music. Hendrix's shocking performance thus reveals the political significance of music; indeed, *Monterey Pop* is based around this. The film – like any documentary of musical performance – would lose its *raison d'être* without the music, the musicians, or the instruments.

Notes

1 Auslander derives the term 'mediatized' from Baudrillard, but uses it in a more concrete way, especially when referring to audiovisual media.
2 As I am a musicologist trained in the traditional text-oriented way, with the focus on the score of art music, one major focus will be the musicological. I am aware that the conditions for studying popular music are different from those for studying classical or art music. One of my goals is to deconstruct the traditional borders in methodology in order to inspire some different ways of examining art music too.
3 The media context of these art forms might shift as well to different forms of delivery, in the same way that literature has recently become available on audio media.
4 This classification is similar to Simon Frith's categorisation of different stages in music perception, which he organises historically. First, 'music is stored in the body' and in

musical instruments, which he calls the 'folk' period. Secondly, 'music is stored through notation … it can still only be retrieved in performance'; this is the 'art' period. Thirdly, he distinguishes the 'pop' period: 'music is stored on phonogram, disc or tape … this transforms the material experience of music: it can now be heard anywhere; it is mobile across previous barriers of time and space; it becomes a commodity, a possession. And yet, ideologically – as a matter of interpretation and fantasy – the old values remain (presence, performance, intensity, event), and listening to recorded music becomes contradictory: it is at once public and private, static and dynamic, an experience of both present and past' (1996: 226).

5 Music iconography and performance history are devoted to this field. See Heck 1999.

6 José Bowen discusses the relevance of audiovisual sources briefly, and points out that the options provided by these sources have 'hardly been explored' yet (1999: 443).

7 'According to this language, we do not have "performances" but rather "performances of" pre-existing, platonic works. The implication is that a performance should function as a transparent medium "expressing", "projecting" or "bringing out" what is already "in" the work, with the highest performance ideal being a selfless *Werktreue*' (Cook 1999: 244).

8 Biographical references to Pennebaker seem to be rare, despite the fact that he is one of the best known specialists in concert films; see the introduction to an interview published online by Nathan Rabin at www.theavclub.com/avclub3318/avfeature3318.html. Pennebaker started his career in the 1960s; his most important work from that period, along with *Monterey Pop*, is the Bob Dylan documentary *Don't Look Back* (1967). His work includes collaborations with Norman Mailer, Jean-Luc Godard and David Bowie. His film *The War Room* (1992) documented Bill Clinton's presidential campaign and received an Academy Award nomination.

9 See Heister (1996: 703) for an assessment of developments in concert history; see Steiner & Marks (1986: 124) for its significance for film music; see Selvin for a general overview: 'The Monterey International Pop Festival was not only an unprecedented and unmatched collection of talent, the three-day event was also an axis on which the world of rock music turned. Music would never be the same again' (1992: 5).

10 One implication of this is that *Monterey Pop* and other concert documentaries of the era might be historically linked to today's music video.

11 Trampert argues that these visual aspects are largely irrelevant to Hendrix's music, and considers them as effective tricks to 'entertain' the audience (1994: 115).

12 It has been suggested that the destruction of the guitar was a spontaneous decision (Trampert 1994: 119). However, this cannot be confirmed, whereas there is an obvious and close connection between Hendrix's actions on stage and the 'performance art' of the 1960s.

13 Frith discusses in detail the close relationship of pop music performance to dance and ballet. His main thesis stems from the assumption that listening to music creates movement, and that dance is a 'form of enhanced listening' (1996: 220–5).

14 This idea is based on the first analytical step in approaching a piece of Western art music in musicology. Formal dispositions here – ABA, ABC, or others – are considered basic for the structural understanding of such music.

15 This address goes unmentioned in accounts of Hendrix's performance by Selvin (1992), Trampert (1994) and Waksman (1999).

16 This question became more important within the context of 'New Musicology'. See Cook & Everist: 'In the aftermath of the near collapse of classical music as a form of public entertainment … it is not just the disciplinary integrity of musicology that has become problematic; it is, to put it bluntly, the relationship between musicology and the rest of the universe. (Where does musicology come on anybody's list of global priorities? When we look on our lives, will we be able to justify our career choice to ourselves?)'

(1999: vii).

17 See Bowen: 'There is plenty of scope, therefore, for music in performance as a subdiscipline. While the lack of discographies (roughly akin to catalogues of source material and manuscripts) presents a burden to any new field, the possibilities for future studies are enormous. (And the 'texts' for this field are by no means limited to audio recordings; the use of film or marked scores has hardly been explored)' (1999: 443).

Chapter Five

The Act You've Known For All These Years: Telling The Tale Of The Beatles

Ian Inglis

The neglect of the film biography – or biopic – in academic or historical accounts of film is a surprising but consistent omission. While genres such as animation, science fiction, film noir, the western, comedy and horror have been comprehensively explored and documented in texts both general and specific, there remains a reluctance to engage in any comparable study of the biopic; for example, it goes unmentioned in two recent and widely used introductory readers (Nelmes 1996; Hollows *et al.* 2000).

That this neglect is even more marked in one of its principal sub-categories – the musical biopic – is doubly puzzling, since the musical has long been an important component of the movie industry's output. Through the 1940s and 1950s, such movies as *Night and Day* (Michael Curtiz, 1946) which told the story of Cole Porter, *The Glenn Miller Story* (Anthony Mann, 1953), *Love Me Or Leave Me* (Charles Vidor, 1955) which followed the career of Ruth Etting, and *The Benny Goodman Story* (Valentine Davies, 1955), provided histories of some of the best-known musicians of the pre-rock'n'roll era. This emphasis shifted in the early 1970s to classical performers and composers in movies like *The Music*

Lovers (1970) which examined episodes in the life of Tchaikovsky, *Mahler* (1974), and *Lisztomania* (1975) (all of which were directed by Ken Russell) and *Amadeus* (Milos Forman, 1984), which concentrated on the rivalry between Mozart and Salieri. And from the late 1970s through to the 1990s, the lives of pop or rock musicians were extensively scrutinised in a long list of films which included *The Buddy Holly Story* (Steve Rash, 1978), *Elvis* (John Carpenter, 1979), Loretta Lynn in *Coal Miner's Daughter* (Michael Apted, 1980), Patsy Cline in *Sweet Dreams* (Karel Reisz, 1985), Ritchie Valens in *La Bamba* (Luis Valdez, 1987), Jerry Lee Lewis in *Great Balls of Fire* (Jim McBride, 1989), *The Doors* (Oliver Stone, 1991), Tina Turner in *What's Love Got To Do With It* (Brian Gibson, 1993), Sid Vicious in *Sid and Nancy* (Alex Cox, 1993) and Sonny & Cher in *And the Beat Goes On* (David Burton Morris, 1999).

The popularity of the genre poses questions about the intention of such films. Is it to accurately relate historical events in order to present 'a mechanical reproduction of reality' (Easthope 1993: 8)? Is it to manipulate reality by presenting 'specific materials combined together to fabricate a history' (Tribe 1981: 321)? Or is it to fashion a commercially attractive product in which 'reality matters less than spectacle' (Atkinson 1995: 31)? In passing, it should be noted that this preoccupation with pop or rock stars is not just confined to the cinema, but has been mirrored in recent theatrical productions which have presented musical histories of the lives and careers of performers as diverse as Roy Orbison, Dusty Springfield, Jackie Wilson, Ellie Greenwich, Buddy Holly and Billy Fury. And the enduring success of so-called 'tribute' bands, whose popularity seems to depend not on their own musical expertise but on their ability to reproduce the musical expertise of others, has provided another opportunity for popular music's history to be re-presented.

By comparing and contrasting two movies which have attempted to recount a part of the history of the Beatles, it may become possible to offer some insights into these and other issues which surround the consumption and production of the musical biography in general. *Birth of The Beatles* (Richard Marquand, 1979) and *Backbeat* (Iain Softley, 1993) both examine the group's early years in Liverpool and Hamburg, when Pete Best and Stuart Sutcliffe were still members, alongside John Lennon, Paul McCartney and George Harrison.

The choice of the Beatles for such an analysis is deliberate and governed by three related factors. There is an abundance of documentary material (books, television and radio) about their career, against which the content of the films can be examined. In addition, it has long been recognised that their significance was – and is – far greater than that of a mere 'pop group'; they are widely perceived as musical innovators, as role models for many millions of youngsters worldwide, as 'the most important single event in British popular culture of the postwar years' (Evans 1984: 7). Finally, there is a particular significance to the decade in which they were most active – the 1960s. It has been noted that historical drama of all kinds is likely to be well-received if it can revisit 'times in which the self-image of the society as a whole was buoyant and optimistic' (McArthur 1981: 288); and rightly or wrongly, the decade has managed to retain to this day its 'collective image of modernity, a vision of bright lights and speed and vitality, in which every individual ingredient was simply part of the whole' (Booker 1969: 45).

In many ways, the growth of the pop biopic stemmed from a dissatisfaction with the archetypal fictional pop movie which had developed throughout the late 1950s and early 1960s. British and American performers routinely appeared in films widely seen as 'inanely conformist … their main virtue lay in the professionalism with which once threatening teenage idols are transformed into lovable young men only too happy to be integrated into adult society' (Murphy 1992: 133). Thus, Tommy Steele's initial presentation of the cheerful working-class Cockney lad in *The Tommy Steele Story* (Gerard Bryant, 1957) was seamlessly duplicated in *The Duke Wore Jeans* (Gerald Thomas, 1958) and *Tommy the Toreador* (John Paddy Carstairs, 1959). Cliff Richard repeated his role as a decent, responsible and deeply conservative young man in *The Young Ones* (Sidney J. Furie, 1961), *Summer Holiday* (Peter Yates, 1962), *Wonderful Life* (Sidney J. Furie, 1964) and *Finders Keepers* (Sidney Hayers, 1966). However, it was the career of Elvis Presley, who starred in more than thirty films from 1956 to 1969, which typified most acutely the predictability and complacency of an industry which saw no reason to deviate from a policy of creating movies which were 'poor pop vehicles, all resembling each other, all about having fun, falling in love, boy makes good, with Presley using the same screen persona with a different name in a different setting' (Agajanian 2000: 94).

But in addition to the broad creative discontent engendered by such movies, the structure they had adopted presented two problematic issues, which the biopic was to solve. The first was to discover a way in which music might be appropriately accommodated and presented within the body of the film. As described by Bob Neaverson, many musical sequences in the traditional pop movie were 'inevitably based around the presentation of lip-synched "performances" of songs by a solo singer which, often combined with minimal onscreen backing sources, essentially attempted to articulate the illusion of "real", diegetic performance' (2000: 154). However, these illusions were never convincing, and often absurd. The biopic's strength is that it can replace such obviously unwieldy sequences by making the fictional factual. In seeking to recreate the working life of professional musicians, the decision to show them at work – in rehearsals, on stage, in the recording studio – overcomes immediately and uncontentiously the awkwardness of the non-diegetic performance.

The second major drawback to the traditional pop movie is that within a few years of its birth in the mid-1950s it had become an anachronism; 'its attempts to keep pace were doomed to failure' (Medhurst 1995: 69). In the 1960s, it quickly became apparent that instant and intimate exposure to popular music could be more happily achieved through the increasing number of radio stations, a realisation that was emphasised via the proliferation of discotheques, clubs and concert venues in the 1970s, and ultimately through music television in the 1980s. The move towards the biopic can thus be seen as cinema's attempt to reclaim for itself a position as a legitimate agent of popular music provision by choosing to concentrate not on the present, but on the past.

The issues raised by the two movies relate to three principal components of their design: narrative, and its significance as a vehicle of historical explanation; music, and the ways in which it is selected and employed; nostalgia, and its role within the films' production and consumption.

Narrative

Birth of The Beatles is told in flashback from the point-of-view of the Beatles in early 1964, on the eve of their first visit to the USA. Lennon, McCartney and Harrison are shown initially as truants from school or college in 1959. As their career gathers momentum, we see the recruitment of Stuart Sutcliffe on bass guitar, followed by Pete Best (the film's technical adviser) on drums, a number of disappointing auditions, engagements in various clubs in Hamburg during which Sutcliffe leaves the group to live with his German girlfriend Astrid Kirchherr, their return to Liverpool, Sutcliffe's death, their 'discovery' by Brian Epstein, the appearance of producer George Martin, Best's dismissal and replacement by Ringo Starr, the onset of Beatlemania in the UK and their early triumph in the USA.

Backbeat covers some of the same events in a slightly different sequence. It begins in 1960, and shows Sutcliffe joining a group which already has Best as its drummer. Their appearances in Hamburg and return to Liverpool are followed by more engagements in Germany before Sutcliffe makes his decision to leave in order to study art and be with Astrid. The movie ends with his death. Ringo Starr, Brian Epstein, George Martin, British and American success are still in the future.

That the two versions do not cover the same events in strict chronological sequence is not surprising; few histories, in whatever form, do. But there are some puzzling inconsistencies in the story they tell.

The attack on Stuart Sutcliffe in the summer of 1960, which is widely believed to have triggered the problems which led to his death, is shown in *Birth of The Beatles* after a group gig in Liverpool; the other members come to his rescue. In *Backbeat*, the assault is on Sutcliffe and John Lennon after the two have been drinking in a pub.

When in August 1960, the group makes its debut in Hamburg, *Birth of The Beatles* has them appearing at The Indra Club; *Backbeat* places them at The Kaiserkeller Club.

In November 1960, the group was deported from Hamburg after it was discovered that the 17-year-old George Harrison lacked the necessary work permit. In *Birth of The Beatles*, the arrest takes place on stage, mid-performance; in *Backbeat*, the arrest in is the group's living quarters during the day.

And in their recounting of the crucial events surrounding Sutcliffe's death in Hamburg in April 1962 (after he had left the group) the movies are in disagreement over the whereabouts of the other Beatles and the manner in which they learn of the tragedy. *Birth of The Beatles* places them in Hamburg, preparing to go on stage when they are visited by a distraught Astrid. In *Backbeat* they are still in England, and are only told of his death when they return to Hamburg to find Astrid waiting at the airport.

Of course it would be naive to be surprised at narrative variations like these. The inevitable uncertainty of all historical explanation has been repeatedly exposed by historians. E. H. Carr has pointed to the general unreliability of documentary accounts of the past and has concluded that 'the belief in a hard core of historical facts existing objectively and independently of the interpretation of the historian is a preposterous fallacy' (1961: 12). Others have suggested that what passes as 'history' may be shaped not merely by interpretation, but by imagination and invention: 'the past is an absent object of inquiry ... all interpretations of the past are as much invented as found' (Jenkins 1995: 17–19).

Furthermore, we should be aware that – unlike historians – those who make movies have no remit even to attempt to portray the past accurately. For them, the past is an opportunity for commercial exploitation and presentation; characters and events can be re-created or simply created to assist those objectives. *JFK* (Oliver Stone, 1992), *Wyatt Earp* (Lawrence Kasdan, 1994), *Titanic* (James Cameron, 1997), *Shakespeare in Love* (John Madden, 1998), *Pearl Harbor* (Michael Bay, 2001), *Ali* (Michael Mann, 2001) and *Iris* (Richard Eyre, 2001) are among the many examples of movies which have blended fact and fiction, history and biography, love story and documentary in order to create a marketable commodity. In fact, the cinema's instrumental attitude to history was revealed frankly in the contract between Warner Bros. and Cole Porter in 1946 to film *Night and Day*, in which it was stipulated that 'the studio shall be free to dramatise, fictionalise or emphasise any or all incidents in the life of [Porter] or interpolate such incidents as [it] may deem necessary in order to obtain a treatment or continuity of commercial value' (Maltby 1995: 312).

Where the past is so distant as to have escaped documentation, the cinema may be a main, sometimes the sole, source of our information about a particular topic or period or character. For many, the events and explanations contained in *The Adventures of Robin Hood* (Michael Curtiz, 1938), *Ben-Hur* (William Wyler, 1959), *Camelot* (Joshua Logan, 1967), and *Gladiator* (Ridley Scott, 2000) add to the stock of historical knowledge gleaned from more conventional sources. This is no less true of the musical biopic. James Stewart's role in *The Glenn Miller Story* and Diana Ross's performance as Billie Holiday in *Lady Sings the Blues* (Sidney J. Furie, 1972) provide attractive and accessible representations of a past we come to think we know:

> Films want to make us think they are reality. Yet the reality we see on the screen is neither inevitable nor something natural to the camera, but a vision creatively constructed out of bits and pieces of images taken from the surface of a world. Even if we know this already, we conveniently forget it in order to participate in the experience that cinema provides. (Rosenstone 1995: 54)

These observations remain equally valid when applied to the film biopics of the Beatles, even though the subjects may be closer to us in time and we may have access to many more documentary accounts. But the cinematic discourse in which they are grounded – one which tells history as a story, which places individuals in the forefront of that story, which admits no alternative possibilities, which emotionalises history, which pursues and celebrates the 'period look', and which shows history as process (Rosenstone 1995: 55–61) – can supplant versions of the past perceived as less compressed or less entertaining.

And undoubtedly they have contributed to what one biographer of the Beatles has described as the proliferation of 'myths and rumours, multiplying stronger than ever around this scarcely-imaginable, true story' (Norman 1981: xvi). Furthermore, the consequences of these inclinations have been noted by the Beatles themselves:

Paul McCartney: People are printing *facts* about me and John. They're *not* facts. But it will go down in the records. People will believe it all. It will become part of history. (Davies 1985: 473)

Thus, although not intended as historical records, these films – with their inconsistencies, contradictions and uncertainties – have the capacity to *become* histories. What is more, the histories may prove to be disruptive, to the extent that their differing narratives incorporate myth and rumour alongside historical fact, but fail to distinguish between the two.

Music

Neither film contains music that is performed by the Beatles themselves. In *Birth of The Beatles*, the songs are performed by a California-based tribute band, Rain. For the songs in *Backbeat*, the producers assembled a band comprising members of Nirvana, Sonic Youth, REM and the Afghan Whigs which, according to Pete Best (1995), 'captured the early essence of the Beatles, that rawness'. *Birth of The Beatles* includes group compositions and contemporary rock'n'roll tracks; *Backbeat* features only cover versions of contemporary songs. In both films the selection and presentation of songs contain inaccuracies. In *Birth of The Beatles*, the group is shown performing 'Don't Bother Me' on stage in Hamburg in 1960, although its composer, George Harrison, has recalled that it was 'an exercise to see if I *could* write a song ... I wrote it in a hotel in Bournemouth, England, where we were playing a summer season in 1963' (1982: 84). And Paul McCartney has said of *Backbeat*, 'One of the things I didn't like about the film is the way they gave 'Long Tall Sally' to the John character. I was not amused. I always sang that' (The Beatles 2000: 96).

The songs in both films are seen in performance, and this is significant in several respects. First, it ties music to narrative in a direct and straightforward manner; the films purport to tell us about the lives of the Beatles, and what the Beatles were doing at this stage in their lives (socially and professionally) was playing music. To this end, the musical interludes are neither an unnecessary disruption to a satisfying narrative nor 'a means of entering and leaving a relatively flimsy and predictable plot' (Maltby 1995: 49). Instead, they are an integral element of the narrative or plot. In particular, both films choose to illuminate the personal friction between Stuart Sutcliffe and Paul McCartney by drawing attention to Sutcliffe's poor musicianship, the obstacles this presented to the development of the group's career, and McCartney's growing resentment. The juxtaposition of the early Liverpool audition in *Birth of The Beatles* in which Lennon, McCartney and Harrison defiantly and unanimously resist the promoter's request to perform 'Dizzy Miss Lizzy' without Sutcliffe – 'We don't play without him ... he's a Beatle' – and the Hamburg club sequence in *Backbeat* in which McCartney demands Sutcliffe's removal from the Beatles after his performance of 'Love Me Tender' has embarrassed the group in front of a Polydor executive – 'We're supposed to be a rock'n'roll group, not a charity show ... this group can't carry Stu' – illustrates the specific use of music as a dramatic statement which carries the narrative forward.

Secondly, the songs unambiguously celebrate the musical characteristics of film itself. In recent decades the definition of what may constitute a musical has been expanded from the singing-and-dancing movies of the 1930s, 1940s and 1950s to include films whose musical content may be incidental, additional or peripheral; it is not unusual to find 'soundtrack' albums of films which contain little or no music. However, *Birth of The Beatles* and *Backbeat* belong in that category of movies described by John Taylor as 'film musicals in the fuller sense that music pervades them, dictating their form and colouring every corner of them' (1971: 69).

This is true even for *Backbeat*, which although allegedly about the relationship between Sutcliffe and Kirchherr as much as it is about the Beatles, was forthright in promoting its musical components – the pedigree of the musicians, the release of the accompanying soundtrack. Jonathan Romney and Adrian Wootton's defence of the pop movie as 'a deferred experience, not live but recorded, telling you what you'd missed by not being there' (1995: 4) is thus *quite literally* fulfilled in these two movies, which show cinema audiences around the world just what they *did* miss by not being present in Liverpool or Hamburg. Music – the music that we *missed* – is one of the principal attractions of these films. In their employment of a strategy first seen in *The Jazz Singer* (Alan Crosland, 1927), the films subordinate a pseudo-documentary style and a biographical theme within the conventions of musical entertainment. In viewing *Backbeat* and *Birth of The Beatles*, we are constantly reminded that whatever else the Beatles may have been, it is the music they produced – 'their greatest resource, their most dangerous tool, their last and only resort' (Rosenberg 2000: 243) – through which they are ultimately defined.

In considering the above points, it might be noted that both movies continue a tradition exemplified in many Hollywood musicals from the 1930s onwards, in which music-as-performance has co-existed with music-as-narrative. Faced with a choice between the re-creation of the spontaneity and immediacy of a live show or the third-person narrative of the conventional drama, cinema has frequently chosen to combine the two; one result of this has been the establishment of the backstage musical. And, as in the backstage musical, the cinema audience for *Backbeat* and *Birth of The Beatles* is obliged to shift its perspective – from that of a theatrical audience (where we are positioned among the audience *in* the movie, watching and applauding a performance) to that of a narrative audience (where we are more familiarly located as the audience *of* the movie, to whom a story is being told). This interplay between internal participation and external spectatorship – between 'the theatrical audience' and 'the narrative audience' (Feuer 1992: 23–4) – is more than just a structural aesthetic. It is also one of the commercial strengths of the contemporary popular music biopic, in that it encourages audiences to actively intervene in both the narrative and musical spheres; within and between the dual roles of spectators and participants, our memories and insights have as much currency as those of the film-makers, and we are allowed to confirm or deny the accuracy of what we see and hear with a conviction which few other cinematic genres allow.

Finally, the songs act as signifiers. They help to fix the movies in time. In the same way that the opening bars of 'The Charleston' inform us that we are in the Chicago of the Prohibition era, or the strains of Vera Lynn's 'We'll Meet Again' and 'The White Cliffs of Dover' locate us in wartime Britain, so tracks like 'Good Golly Miss Molly', 'Johnny B. Goode', 'Dizzy Miss Lizzy', 'Long Tall Sally' and 'Love Me Tender' fix us unequivocally in the late 1950s/early 1960s.

But in order for these musical clues to be sufficient, there has to be an understanding that the audience possesses a working knowledge of recent musical history. If this is not the case, additional information is required. Thus, in *Birth of The Beatles* the establishing shot of Liverpool, accompanied by the strains of 'My Bonnie' (the first song to be recorded by the Beatles, with Tony Sheridan, in 1961) is supplemented by the caption 'Liverpool, England 1959'. And the opening scene in *Backbeat*, in a pub where the female vocalist is singing 'Kiss Me Honey Honey Kiss Me' (a hit single for Shirley Bassey in 1959) carries the caption 'Liverpool, England 1960'. In both cases, the music anchors the narrative to a particular place at a particular time and, in so doing, contributes to the 'reality' constructed by the film.

Overall, the functions of music in *Birth of The Beatles* and *Backbeat* correspond with the three functions of film music generally, as defined by Annabel Cohen: 'music interprets and adds meaning; it aids memory; it suspends disbelief' (2000: 361). And because the movies' music is exclusively diegetic, is broadly familiar to its audiences, and is integral rather than additional, these tasks are accomplished in an unusually direct and effective manner.

In her discussion of the distinctions between the composed score (music written specifically for the film) and the compiled score (assembled from existing musical sources), Anahid Kassabian has warned that compiled scores 'bring the immediate threat of history' (2001: 3), by allowing audiences to engage with the film in ways which may be influenced by their previous knowledge of, and interaction with, familiar songs. Ironically, it is this which is one of the operational strengths of these two movies. While it may be true that within film generally the 'affiliating identifications' offered by the compiled score permit a range of reactions and perceptions as broad as the audience itself, the conventions of the pop or rock biopic contest this tendency. Their compiled scores, and the external associations they encourage, direct the audience towards a specific musical and historical environment which helps to articulate and acknowledge the accompanying narrative.

Nostalgia

The functional property of nostalgia is that it allows us to employ symbolic objects of a public or private character in order to exchange the dissatisfactions of the present for the attractions of an idealised past. Further, it has been argued that access to the past can only be gained 'through some such medium as music, dance or poetry ... in other words, via some symbolic medium which ... directly engages our feelings' (Davis 1979: 29).

Whether through painstaking attention to the replication of historical details or through general representations of a familiarly recognised era, film has an unrivalled capacity to show us the past – its architecture, its language, its transport, its costumes. In this sense, one of its primary functions is the stimulation of a form of public nostalgia whereby the collective responses of many millions of audience members can be triggered by recognition of symbolic resources or events from the past, preserved and presented on film – the first moon landing, VE Day, the Coronation. Music, on the other hand, may more readily evoke the intimacies of private memories, unique to individual listeners, by reflecting temporal associations between particular songs and those individuated memories possessed by one person – a first girlfriend or boyfriend, a childhood pet, the eccentricities of a favourite school teacher, a special holiday.

The fusion of these two symbolic mediums – film's depictions of a very public, collective past and music's evocations of the intimacies of personal recollections – is thus an extraordinarily potent device through which the practice of nostalgia is activated. In particular, the popular music biopic's reliance on a recent past to which many audience members have ready access, and the transformation in recent years of the Beatles themselves into objects of nostalgia (aided no doubt by the deaths of John Lennon and George Harrison) have permitted *Backbeat* and *Birth of The Beatles* to satisfy and contribute to 'the widespread nostalgia and pre-occupation with nostalgia' (Lowenthal 1989: 29) that is evident today.

While both movies contain elements of collective and private nostalgia, *Backbeat* emphasises images of a collective nostalgia available to all. Its opening credits utilise old newsreel to display a series of events and people commonplace in the late 1950s and early 1960s, but now largely disappeared – transatlantic liners arriving at Liverpool, a bathing beauty competition, a policewoman directing traffic, the soccer star Stanley Matthews, the singer Frankie Vaughan, a record player on which sits a ten-inch 78 rpm disc – which serve to evoke a general historical period in which popular music merely has a place. By contrast, *Birth of The Beatles* employs specific depictions which may act as catalysts for private nostalgia understood chiefly by those to whom the particular story of the Beatles is familiar – The Cavern Club in Liverpool, the creation (by Astrid Kirchherr) of the distinctive Beatle hairstyle, the early demonstrations of Beatlemania at the group's live appearances – and for whom popular music occupies a central position in their own recent history. Put simply, *Backbeat* assumes and constructs a general nostalgia for an era, *Birth of The Beatles* emphasises a specific nostalgia for the Beatles. And one particular way through which this is accomplished is, as discussed above, through their choice of music: the absence of original Beatles songs in *Backbeat* and their inclusion in *Birth of The Beatles* directs the audience along clearly differentiated routes to the past.

Yet both movies demonstrate that too sharp a division cannot be maintained between the two formulations of nostalgia. *Backbeat* uses its collective images to provide a context for personal recollections, while the private or personal nostalgia for the Beatles in *Birth of The Beatles* leads directly to a parallel nostalgia for the 1960s. Like all movies which create a mythologised past, they 'offer the recovery of lost purity, the attempt to recapture the elemental pleasure of childhood delight in a magical state' (Collins 1992: 260). And these are precisely those strands which occur again and again in the manner in which these movies (and other texts) tell the tale of the Beatles – the purity (of the music), their (and our) childhood, and the seemingly magical way in which they were to enchant the world.

Furthermore, the films possess qualities which allow the audience to engage in differing practices of nostalgia as distinguished by Davis (1979: 16–29). Simple nostalgia, which involves the straightforward and positive evocation of the past typically contrasted with negative or indifferent impressions of the present will, in this context, allow for speculations such as 'I prefer to listen to the music of the Beatles because it's better than the music of today' or 'I prefer to listen to the music of the Beatles because it reminds me of a time when I was younger and happier'. Reflexive nostalgia will permit a more thoughtful review or evaluation of the past against the present, leading to questions which ask 'Are the songs, and the period in which I heard them, how I remember them? Were the Beatles really as good as I think they were? Are things today as bad as they seem?' Interpretive nostalgia invites the individual to objectively question the experience of nostalgia itself: 'Why am I feeling nostalgic? What functions does nostalgia serve for me? Does my loyalty to the Beatles mean that I've lost the ability to critically respond to today's music?'

Alongside the many other relics of the Beatles' career, the two films thus provide fertile environments where simple, reflexive and interpretive nostalgia can take root and flourish. Through the questions they pose and the explanations they favour in their (apparent) documentation of the group and exploration of a period, they lend themselves – theoretically and substantively – to nostalgia.

Of course, the mere existence of films cannot determine how and why they are employed. It has been argued that the conditions under which nostalgia will emerge are 'a secular and linear sense of time, an apprehension of the failings of the present, the availability of evidences of the past' (Chase & Shaw 1989: 4). That each of these requirements is present today has been confirmed and expanded by a postmodernist doctrine that the only certainty is that there are no longer any certainties. And in an age of uncertainty, attempts 'to cling to the alleged certainties of the past' (Chase & Shaw 1989: 8) clearly become even more potent.

There is, however, an irony which is made all the more acute in the particular case of the Beatles. Despite commerce's re-creation and celebration of the past and our own apparent readiness to re-enter that past, it remains a territory to which few would willingly return: 'Nostalgia expresses longings for times that are *safely* rather than *sadly* beyond recall ... its features are prettified and its virtues exaggerated ... [but] *the past is false*' (my emphases) (Lowenthal 1989: 28–9).

Thus, although *Backbeat* and *Birth of The Beatles* sketch out the prologue to a romantic, even heroic, odyssey in which four working-class provincial boys, rejected for years by the musical establishment, struggle against heartbreak and tragedy to become the world's most successful performers, the Beatles themselves have made it clear that it is a past which they are glad to have escaped. That past too is a false past.

George Harrison: We got in a rut. There was no satisfaction in it. Nobody could hear. It was just a bloody big row. We got worse as musicians, playing the same old junk every day. (Davies 1985: 232)

Paul McCartney: We were fed up with being the Beatles. We really hated that fucking four little mop top boys approach. We were not boys, we were men. (Miles 1997: 303)

Ringo Starr: There were good nights and bad nights ... but they were really all the same. (Davies 1985: 224); Four years of Beatlemania was enough for anyone. (Clayson 1991: 108)

John Lennon: One has to completely humiliate oneself to be what the Beatles were. It was awful, all that business was awful. It was a fucking humiliation. (Wenner 1971: 20)

Their comments remind us that the history of the Beatles as retold in these two films is a history that has been re-shaped, re-written and re-located to 'a never-never land that is available neither in the present nor the past, but in an imaginary pre-history or originary moment' (Collins 1992: 289). While such nostalgic revision might stem from a real or fancied discontent with the present, the inevitable ageing of those associated with the Beatles' story, or partisan attempts to offer alternative explanations, the strategies through which these films' perceptions of the past are produced and consumed illustrate the more general insight that any past will cease to be attractive 'if we tarnish it with verifiable fact' (Lerner 1972: 246). While their typification of the past both embodies and stimulates nostalgia, it has to be remembered that these pasts are not sites for *histories of* the Beatles, but for *stories about* the Beatles. Nostalgia is not a tool with which we can really discover the past, but a perspective from which we comfortably view the past.

One essential pleasure inherent in cinema viewing is that it provides us with the illusion of looking in on a private world. When that private world is one in which we have an interest or knowledge or membership, the pleasures derived begin to multiply as our beliefs are either confirmed or challenged by what we witness. The popular music biopic is thus a remarkably apt arena in which these pleasures may be experienced, offering a unique combination of narrative, musical and nostalgic attractions. Moreover, *Birth of The Beatles* and *Backbeat* tell stories which are not yet complete. John Lennon's murder, the group's 'reunion' in 1995, the knighthood awarded to Paul McCartney, the death of his first wife and his subsequent re-marriage, the attempted murder of George Harrison and his death from cancer have all added new chapters to the tale of the Beatles during the 1980s, 1990s and the early years of the twenty-first century. To the extent that these additions to the group's story allow for re-evaluations of the events and circumstances of previous decades, the movies themselves become texts to be consulted and scrutinised for clues and commentaries they may contain.

The contemporary pop or rock biopic therefore accomplishes a variety of tasks, existing as historical drama, musical entertainment, period documentary and biography. *Birth of The Beatles* and *Backbeat* may be seen as possessing an additional significance in that through their exploration of the early career of the Beatles, they are able to inform many of the perspectives (historical, musical, sociological) through which popular music's most celebrated performers have been studied, and to illuminate many of the issues (group membership, career strategy, personal relationships) with which those studies have been concerned. Given the group's continuing presence in the public domain, the enduring popularity of its music, and the familiar points of its narrative history, we might, as the title of this chapter suggests, choose to think of the Beatles as an act we have all known for many years. In fact, it may merely be the tales told of the Beatles with which we are familiar.

Chapter Six

THE SOUND OF A NEW FILM FORM[1]

Anahid Kassabian

Throughout the literature on contemporary film sound and music, debates abound about volume. Routinely, one sees complaints about how sound, and especially music, are so loud that dialogue cannot be heard. Arnt Maasø has observed that 'for the general public, loudness and dynamics are one of the few issues concerning television sound that are discussed and commented – for instance in letters to newspapers and feedback to broadcasters' (2000: 1).

Unfortunately, such comments rarely provide an opportunity to think about sound and contemporary sound design. The issue here is not about volume, but rather about the evaporating boundaries and hierarchies between sound and music. From the mixing of instruments in talk-show bands to the volume of music in restaurants, distinctions between foreground and background sound are slowly disappearing and, with them, the distinctions among noise, sound and music.

David Brackett notes that many new forms of music are labelled as 'noise'. His comparison of the discourses surrounding the advents of rock and rap shows that both were received as noise in their early years and, from this, he suggests that music is defined by the displacement of social fears onto aesthetic criticism:

The dominant beliefs of the early 1950s that excluded rhythm and blues from consideration as 'Music, Music, Music' and the point-of-view that dismissed rap as non-music (even rappers celebrated its noisiness) may be fading, but covert assumptions about what music is and is not continue to play a crucial role in how social groups associated with particular types of music are portrayed in the mass media. (1999: 139)

With Jacques Attali (and R. Murray Schafer, and others), Brackett argues that noise and music are embedded in – that is, both define and are defined by – relations of power.

When power wants to make people *forget*, music is ritual *sacrifice*, the scapegoat; when it wants them to *believe*, music is enactment, *representation*; when it wants to *silence* them, it is reproduced, normalized, *repetition*. Thus it heralds the subversion of both the existing code and the power in the making, well before the latter is in place. (Attali 1985: 20)

Attali's well-known argument is that music has a singular capacity to signal power relations in the making: we can, if we choose to listen, hear power before we see it or feel it. According to that logic, therefore, Brackett's argument might well also be inverted. Perhaps rock and rap *are* noise, in that they ask us to hear the history of music in the twentieth century as an increasing absorption of noise into music. Perhaps they herald new relations of power. Certainly, a range of examples – from John Cage's writings to guitar feedback to scratching – support such a contention. Sampling takes this a step further, however. In providing the raw material of both hip-hop and techno, sampling technologies have turned music into sound and back again, treating previously recorded music as the functional equivalent of industrial sounds and noises for composers of *musique concrete* and for groups like Kraftwerk. And, from a different direction, the growth of Muzak through the twentieth century has turned music into sound or noise for most of us at one point or another.

The evaporating segregation of sound, noise and music has had a pronounced effect on film sound editing and scoring practices. For example, Daniel Falck (n.d.) has argued that speech in *The Thin Red Line* (Terrence Malick, 1998; music by Hans Zimmer) is often de-privileged and/or mumbled; it can be thought of, after Michel Chion (1994), as 'emanation speech ... a line of contour of a speaking body ... in the same way as a silhouette is a line of contour of a visual body'. Falck makes the case that music, speech and sound in *The Thin Red*

Line are levelled out and used together to create a world not dependent *a priori* on the images.

His observation is one among many examples of the dissolving boundaries among kinds of sounds in which I am interested. For example, the soundtrack of *The Cell* (Tarsem Singh, 2000; music by Howard Shore) is not primarily, or even substantially, musical. *The Cell* projects the interior world of its characters in sound as much as it envisions it in images. The opening sequence of the film takes place in a desert, with sweeping vistas of dunes. The instrumentation includes *ghaita* (an Arabic double-reed instrument), *lira* (a bamboo flute), and double-headed Moroccan drums. The music uses quarter-tones as is typical of Arabic musics. Thus, the basic musical materials are 'Middle Eastern' (actually North African – Moroccan Jajouka), even though we eventually learn that the landscape is located in the mind of Edward, a psychotically disturbed young boy. But while the markers signifying the Middle East are clear, there are other musical sounds as well. On top of the Jajouka is another layer of composed music that has no particular direction or shape; the sounds signify alienness and tension, but without any suspense. In this way, the overall effect is of layers of sounds rather than a through-realised cue. The invocation of West Asian or North African music serves an environmental rather than a narrative purpose.

The same timbres and textures appear again alongside a sweep of dry, brown fields in central California, and follow a cut to our first view of serial killer Karl Rudolph Stargher. It re-appears when Catherine dreams of Edward's internal scene and again, later, when she enters Stargher's mind for the first time. That cue begins with a throbbing, bass string sequence that clearly signifies 'ominous'. Layer upon layer is added to it: tympani, mid-range strings, horns, a cash register, a baby crying, birds, the distorted sounds of a baptism, machine sounds. The sounds recede layer by layer, and are replaced by extremely distorted sounds matched by surreal images: a drop of blood falling in water, a grasshopper jumping, a dog shaking off water and blood. Catherine finally confronts Stargher in a tiled room with a horse and a clock, with extreme echo in the ambient sound, pronounced ticking of several clocks, and increasing layers of sounds and instrumental timbres.

This is neither music nor not music, but rather a textural use of sound that disregards most, if not all, of the 'laws' of classic Hollywood film-scoring technique. (On the basic rules of this practice, see, for example, Gorbman 1987: 73.) The sound music is foregrounded for attention, not 'inaudible' as is standard. It is not a signifier of emotion, nor does it provide continuity or unity. It is not subordinate to the narrative or the visuals, but on par with them in creating an affective world. *The Cell* initiates a soundtrack of the unconscious, where the familiar boundaries recede in favour of a different logic.

Mary Ann Doane argues that synch sound in film is an important ideological force, asserting that:

> The drama played out on the Hollywood screen must be paralleled by the drama played out over the body of the spectator – a body positioned as unified and nonfragmented. The visual illusion of position is matched by an aural illusion of position. The ideology of matching is an obsession which pervades the practice of soundtrack construction. (1985: 60)

But *The Cell* actively strives to break that illusion, to mismatch visual and aural position by using a range of techniques such as sound close-ups to signify perceived rather than objective sound. This is a soundtrack of the unconscious, although we cannot distinguish between the unconscious sound worlds of the psychologist and the patient, or of the cop and the patient.

Much of the film takes place inside the mind of Stargher, the serial killer, who has Waylon's Infraction[2] and whose mind Catherine has entered through an experimental technology in order to find his imprisoned, soon-to-be-next victim. As she meanders through the rooms and corridors of his strange unconscious mind, we are led through it by richly textured terrains of both aural and visual materials not organised by principles of narrative.

Similarly, on occasions when Stargher is on his own earlier in the film, we hear a garble of sounds. While he is watching his next victim from his car, a passing motorcycle engine sounds as if it is in the car with him, then it is layered with high whines (possibly synthesised strings) and a distorted male voice that is extremely slowed down. It is clear that the voice (or voices) is speaking, but no words are comprehensible. When Stargher is in the bathtub – his last conscious moments – we hear a faint high drone, to which the same morphed voice is added, then factory sounds, and a sound like a car starting. On a cut away from his interior soundscape to the police arriving at his house, repetitive string figures are added – the first overtly musical sounds in the cue.

The most recognisable film music accompanies comparatively ordinary sequences, such as when the SWAT teams break into Stargher's house, although even this cue has thick machine drones underneath it. Many other cues are simply pedal points – long, extended single notes or layers of notes – with no melodic or horizontal motion whatsoever. All of these decisions add up to a new approach to sound, one in which sound materials are no longer treated according to clearly established hierarchies of voice over music over sound over noise.

I want to suggest that *The Cell* is one touchstone in the development of a new film form that is slowly pulling away from linear narrativity, as we know it from novels and classical Hollywood films. In its place, the piecemeal, iterative narrativity of videogames is developing a film language of its own. And in this shift, narrativity is subordinated to sensory experiences, with a new emphasis placed on soundtracks created from very different aural and musical materials.

Two other films that proclaim these shifts are *The Matrix* (Wachowski Brothers, 1999; music by Don Davis) and *Lara Croft: Tomb Raider* (Simon West, 2001; music by Graeme Revell). Each participates in this 'new narrativity', taking it in very distinct and gendered directions, but there are additional, and striking, similarities between the two. Each focuses on an action hero; *The Matrix* generated comic book art and *Lara Croft: Tomb Raider* began as a now-classic computer game, first released in 1996. Each plot demands that its hero save the world; and each hinges on the fact that s/he is uniquely equipped to do so.

It is important to remember that saving the world does not mandate narrative closure. While serials have long been an important part of film history (*Flash Gordon* (1936/1938/1940), *Indiana Jones* (Steven Spielberg, 1981/1984/1989)), sequels are becoming more and more expected. For instance, as the news media unanimously reported, all three *Lord of the Rings* films (Peter Jackson, 2001/2002/2003) were made before the first was released. Serials and sequels follow the logic of comic books – an unending but nonetheless linear logic; thus, the *Star Wars* films are referred to in the order of their chronology in the story world, not the order in which they were produced.

But in the case of *The Matrix* and *Lara Croft: Tomb Raider*, something else, something more, is at work – a logic of endless iteration. They have little devotion to linearity. Even within the stories themselves, moving back and forth through time is thematised. This move away from linearity and between realities is announced clearly in *The Matrix* and *Lara Croft: Tomb Raider*, heralding a new film form born in videogames and dance culture and based on iteration. And that form is established significantly through music.

While each film uses contemporary popular music in its score, there is very little overlap in the styles and genres. *The Matrix*, grounded in a future technological dystopia, does not use techno but a mix of shock rock (including Marilyn

Manson) and rap metal (including Rage Against The Machine). *Lara Croft: Tomb Raider*'s plot centres on ancient mysteries and a once-every-5,000-years planetary alignment, but despite its mythical content, the soundtrack is techno/electronica (Chemical Brothers, Fatboy Slim, Moby), full of machine and electronic sounds. Moreover, while *The Matrix* released two soundtrack albums – one of songs, the other of composed material – it only uses three of the songs noticeably in the film. *Lara Croft: Tomb Raider*, however, makes ample use of its techno songs, using them for at least eight cues, to score everything from establishing shots to action sequences.

The Matrix
Soundtrack albums tracks vs songs listed in film credits:

Title	Artist
'Dissolved Girl'*	Massive Attack
'Dragula' (Hot Rod Herman Mix)	Rob Zombie
'Leave You Far Behind'	Lunatic Calm
(Lunatics Roller Coaster Mix)	
'Mindfields'	Prodigy
'Prime Audio Soup'	Meat Beat Manifesto
'Clubbed To Death' (Kurayamino Mix)	Rob D
'Minor Swing'*	Django Reinhardt
'Begin the Run'*	(from *Night of the Lepus* aka *Night of the Lupus*, 1972)
'I'm Beginning To See The Light'*	Duke Ellington
'Spybreak'	Propellerheads
'Wake Up'	Rage Against The Machine
'Rock Is Dead'	Marilyn Manson
'Bad Blood'**	Ministry
'My Own Summer'**	Deftones
'Ultrasonic Sound'**	Hive
'Look To Your Orb For The Warning'**	Monster Magnet
'Du Hast'**	Rammstein

*   song appears in film credits but not on CD
**   song appears on CD but not in film credits

Lara Croft: Tomb Raider
Soundtrack albums tracks vs songs listed in film credits:

Title	Artist
'Elevation' (Tomb Raider Mix)	U2
'Absurd'	Fluke
'Speedballin''	Outkast
'Terra Firma' (Lara's Mix)	Delerium, featuring Aude
'The Revolution'	BT
'Lila'*	Vas
'Piano Concerto in F Minor'*	J. S. Bach
'Satellite'	Bosco
'Devil's Nightmare'	Oxide & Neutrino
'Illuminati'	Fatboy Slim
'Get Ur Freak On' (Remix)	Missy Elliott, featuring Nelly Furtado
'Song of Life'	Leftfield
'Ain't Never Learned'	Moby
'Deep'	TrenT Reznor
'Inhaler'*	Craig Armstrong
'Edge Hill'	Groove Armada
'Galaxy Bounce'	Chemical Brothers
'Where's Your Head At'	Basement Jaxx

*   song appears in film credits but not on CD

And finally, the musics have very different textures and vocabularies. Both soundtracks use songs whose musical vocabularies depend on repetition more than on development. Most of Western music, at least since the late 1600s, has been organised by a logic of development in which a goal is projected and then reached. This is certainly truer of concert-hall music than other forms, but it has some power in describing most popular musics as well. It does not, however, describe the musics used in *The Matrix* and *Lara Croft: Tomb Raider*. One might be tempted to suggest that they are cyclical as opposed to linear, but the repetitions are different from standard strophic song forms; there is more emphasis on repeated fragments than on a shape and its returns. Overall, they share a break from more traditional Western musical patterns of goal-oriented motion.

Their styles of repetition, however, differ in significant ways. The techno musical world of *Lara Croft: Tomb Raider* is almost completely devoid of directionality. The tracks use a number of gestures to create this sense. First, and most obviously, there is the omnipresence of sampled loops. In almost every cut, we hear not merely repetitions of the same phrase, but iterations of the same performance of the same phrase. There is no development, as there is in restatements of a phrase or theme in concert-hall music or even in rock. Secondly, and relatedly, there is a very high profile of mechanical intervention. The loops certainly mark that, as do many of the sounds themselves. But in addition, the samples are often cut off at the beginning and end, so that we can only hear the middle of the sound. All sounds can be described as having a beginning, middle and end – usually referred to as attack, sustain and decay. Many sampled sounds in *Lara Croft: Tomb Raider*'s songs have clipped off the attacks and decays to leave only the sustain – in other words, they are all middle, with no beginning or end. This forecloses the possibility of a sense of narrative or development. And finally, the rhythmic patterns are often unaccented or less accented, so that they emphasise something like presence or immediacy over drive.

It might be tempting to imagine techno as an opposition to a more phallic, directional model. Much writing on music and gender, at least since Susan McClary's *Feminine Endings* (1991), has relied on the notion that narrative is structurally masculine, as is indicated in Robert Scholes' insight:

> For what connects fiction – and music – with sex is the fundamental orgastic rhythm of tumescence and detumescence, of tension and res-olution, of intensification to the point of climax and consummation. In the sophisticated forms of fiction, as in the sophisticated practices of sex, much of the art consists of delaying climax within the framework of desire in order to prolong the pleasurable act itself. When we look at fiction with respect to its form alone, we see a pattern of events designed to move toward climax and resolution, balanced by a counter-pattern of events designed to delay this very climax and resolution. (quoted in de Lauretis 1984: 108)

Certainly much music can make the same claims. Tonality itself requires the kinds of diversion and completion that Scholes describes. Thus, in comparison to such clear linearity and narrative development as sonata form, and even in comparison to most rock, techno is certainly not narrative, developmental, masculine. But if techno opposes phallic directionality, is it therefore feminine? It does not offer itself as a cultural expression of care, which is one strong thread of contemporary feminist thinking. Nor is it significantly produced by women – men far outnumber women as DJs. Nor is techno circular or recursive in structure, which are the most commonly posited feminine alternatives to phallic linearity.

The very technicity of the musical materials refuses any of the romantic harkening back to pre-Enlightenment times or matriarchies that often undergird such arguments. Narrativity is no longer the defining characteristic of gendered cultural forms. Techno is forging a new space of gender, in which directionality is inconsequential.

The Matrix soundtrack, however, is full of directionality, but not of a traditional kind. Neither the songs nor the composed score unfold according to a necessary logic – in fact, most of the songs stop rather than end. 'Wake Up' by Rage Against The Machine is one of many songs on the album that simply fades out at the end. Rather than reaching an obvious developmental conclusion, there are a series of phrases of different textures and tempos, which simply stop at some point. Even the fan guitar tablatures online struggle to notate how this song closes:

OUTRO
kind wiggle back and forth on fret
WAH
G:-17-|
Transcribed by: Kevin Dole (kdole@provide.net)
http://www.ratm.net/tabs/guitar/selftitled/wake_up_tab.html

BRIDGE 1 (screaching part)
RIFF 1 ('WAAAAAKE UUUP!')
SECOND SOLO (not tabbed)
OUTRO
that's it!
Transcribed by Marcel
http://www.ratm.net/tabs/guitar/selftitled/wake_up_tab2.html

The rest of the song is parts that I have written, just put em tagether. I'm sorry, I am havin trouble tabbin the second solo. If you write me, i'll help ya tha best I can – just use tha harmonizer?
http://www.musicfanclubs.org/rage/tabs.htm
byrnesb@elmo.nmc.edu

And while the *Lara Croft: Tomb Raider* songs rarely have accented rhythmic patterns, these songs rely on highly repetitive patterns in the bass, percussion and/or vocals to motor them forward. The patterns repeat throughout the songs, often in subtle variations of, for example, percussion against vocal line, to create a sense of direction and expectation. This kind of song structure is widespread in *The Matrix* and, in combination with the lack of closure in the songs, the patterns that propel this music amount to forward motion without a goal or endpoint.

The songs of *The Matrix* comment on existing sound worlds in other ways. First, as noted above, they betray their own directionality by refusing it a *telos*. Secondly, they blur the distinctions between voice and instrument, and between noise and music, altering and morphing voices in all kinds of ways. In ways that are reminiscent of Stargher's internal soundscape in *The Cell*, many of these songs alter voices to signify threat and rage; the mutated voices mark affects of alienation and anger that are central to the sound world of *The Matrix*. And arguably, this is an important register for blurring the boundaries between human and machine, which is the central thematic of the film.

The Matrix stops without ending; after the resolution of the plot line, we inexplicably find Neo back in the Matrix. This is the identical gesture set up repeatedly by the songs, and echoed in the songs on the soundtrack CD that were not used in the film. This is not a closed narrative of the kind to which we are accustomed; something else is going on here.

What I wish to take from these textual details is the sense of a new film form: one that is not linear but iterative, one shared by techno and videogames but not symphonies and novels. A new film form in which narrative is not primary, but equal, if not subordinate, to the sensory experiences of sight and sound. And in this new form, some possibilities, such as traditional character development, are foreclosed in favour of some new ones.

Lara Croft herself provides an all-too-tempting example. She is an Oedipal daughter, in a struggle with her dead father to both be him and beat him. Her success is defined by completing his work. And the story does not really resolve, much less deliver her to another man and pack her away into a relationship, as would be demanded by traditional narrative form. Once the regime of linear narrativity is opened up, phallic order is no longer a given. But lest that sounds ambitiously utopian, I want to emphasise that not all the outcomes of this shift will be pleasant or simple.

For example, *Lara Croft: Tomb Raider* gives feminists an unpleasant heroine – should I celebrate her strength, her prowess and the legacy of her father, or should I bemoan her violence, the absence of other women and any sexuality? Should I cheer her for being a narrative agent, or call her a man in drag? These questions are no longer easy to answer – if they ever were – because they are born of a framework that no longer applies. Instead, Lara Croft is one among many new women and men and others made possible by the strange new world of videogame films.

In this new film form, with its emphasis on iteration rather than development, music serves as a guide. In both *The Matrix* and *Lara Croft: Tomb Raider*, it is possible to hear the coming of a different regime of narrative. In its iterations, this form radically shifts the marks of gender. And, again using music as a guide, new forms of gender may be heard as well. Directionality without a goal as a trope of an inventive masculinity? Non-directional machinic sounds as a trope of an innovative femininity? It is possible to see these as belonging to longstanding regimes of gender, but that would be a mistake. The soundtracks of *The Matrix* and *Lara Croft: Tomb Raider* are early markers of an important shift in our understanding of gender, in which narrativity and sexuality may finally be unhinged, and difference may become audible.

Notes

1 Thanks to David Schwarz, the members of my Fall 2001 Film Theory seminar at Fordham University (especially Brandi Fanning, Duane Loft and Beatrice LaBarge) and to my research assistants, Missy Pinto, Edwina Hay and Maral K. Svendsen, for their important contributions to this essay.
2 According to the film, Waylon's Infraction is a form of severe schizophrenia that presents as catatonia.

Chapter Seven

CASE STUDY 1: *SLIDING DOORS* AND
TOPLESS WOMEN TALK ABOUT THEIR LIVES

Lauren Anderson

'Music is the glue of the world, man. It holds it all together'
– Eddie, in *Empire Records* (Allan Moyle, 1995)

On 28 December 1895 the Lumière brothers presented, for the first time ever, a series of short films to an audience at the Grand Café in Paris. At this screening a pianist also provided the first musical accompaniment for a film, and from that moment on films have had a not-so-silent partner of musical accompaniment.

Today one is as likely, if not more so, to hear a score compiled from contemporary popular songs as a score of 'classical' music composed specifically for the film.[1] Not only do contemporary movies increasingly utilise popular music, but such films are routinely complemented by the simultaneous release of high-profile soundtrack albums. Furthermore, popular music does not merely pervade credit sequences – where many believe it made its cinematic debut in *The Blackboard Jungle* (Richard Brooks, 1955) – but often plays through much of the film as well, albeit in a variety of styles and settings: compare *American Graffiti* (George Lucas, 1973) or *Forrest Gump* (Robert Zemeckis, 1994) with *Moulin Rouge* (Baz Luhrmann, 2001).

In addition to providing a significant percentage of sales per annum for record stores (see Baillie 1999), the almost obligatory soundtrack album serves to advertise a film, often well before it reaches cinemas. The high level of marketing activity surrounding such albums (intense advertising, frequent promotional give-aways, radio airplay) makes popular music in movie soundtracks almost impossible to ignore. It often seems as though the popular music soundtrack has displaced the 'classical' film score. In order to compare the uses and functions of popular music with those considered to be conventional in 'classical' Hollywood film music, this chapter analyses some of the textual relations between the narrative, characterisation and themes of two recent films, and the popular music they contain: *Sliding Doors* (Peter Howitt, 1997) and *Topless Women Talk About Their Lives* (Harry Sinclair, 1997).

Although critics generally seem to agree on the established conventions of musical accompaniment, there are considerable differences in the broader conceptions of music's operation within the cinematic apparatus. The analyses I propose to employ are grounded in the neoformalist approach which, in contrast to the suture theory that has been a significant trend in film music criticism,[2] does not prescribe one specific methodology: 'Each analysis uses a method adapted to the film and the issues at hand, and interpretation will not always be used in the same way' (Thompson 1988: 13). The goal of neoformalist analysis is to examine 'devices' within the filmic text (camera movement, theme, music) to attempt to discover their functions (in various contexts) and the motivation for their presence, while also paying attention to the historical circumstances of the text and its viewing.

Film music conventions

Authors have drawn attention to the key conventions of 'classical' Hollywood film music (Carroll 1988; Kalinak 1992; Flinn 1992; Brown 1994; Burt 1994; Smith 1995, 1996). Generally, the music must 'serve' the narrative, and will not usually distract viewers from their involvement in it (Gorbman 1987: 78). Its primary function is to illustrate explicit and implicit narrative content (it may reflect something viewers see on-screen, tell them something they cannot see, or provide a commentary on the action). Secondly, music's form is often dictated by the narrative – it is usually considered to be 'inaudible' (the viewer is not supposed to be directly aware of its presence lest this threatens the dominance of the narrative), appropriate (matching the mood, action and so forth), and able to connote something (a particular setting or era). Thirdly, music can also be used to signify emotion – either by suggesting specific feelings, or imparting a sense of 'epic feeling' which suggests that the happenings in the film possess greater importance and deeper significance than those of everyday life (Gorbman 1987: 81; Levinson 1996: 258; Frith 1996: 118). Finally, music may be used formally to sustain structural unity through repetition of leitmotifs[3] and musical themes, and to enhance continuity at points where this may have been challenged (Gorbman 1987; Kalinak 1992; Smith 1995; Levinson 1996). It is important to note however that these conventions which developed around 'classical' Hollywood film scoring are not set in stone: 'a given principle may violate any of the principles ... provided the violation is at the service of the other principles' (Gorbman 1987: 73).

Meaning in popular music[4]

In order to discuss the ways in which popular music works in film soundtracks, a brief examination of the way meaning is constructed out of popular music in its normal listening environment is necessary. Explaining 'the meaning' of popular music is not a simple task; there are as many different potential interpretations as there are listeners. Four factors are relevant: sound, lyrics, secondary connotations and context.

The general 'sound' of the song (tone of voice, instrumentation) is arguably the first thing a listener will notice, and will often have differing sets of associations related to mood, attitude and so on. 'Sounds' are often grouped according to genre,[5] which is a common and basic, yet useful way to obtain an initial insight into the meaning of a song. Lyrics are usually analysed according to the semantic rules of language. A crucial issue here, of course, is whether the lyrics are intelligible, but even if they cannot be fully understood, factors such as genre and sound allow the song to carry meaning.

More detailed semiotic approaches which approach the meaning of popular music involve the examination of secondary connotations of its primary elements (such as lyrics or tempo) and the broader social codes that influence the reading or 'decoding' of a text.[6] Such analyses may reveal divisions and dichotomies within popular music and its evaluation, such as a belief that pop is escapist and essentially commercial, while rock displays tradition, originality and truth (Harron 1988: 209). The context of the music (actual or ideal listening environment) also plays a significant role in the formation of meaning, particularly when popular songs are used in films. The original context of any song comprises a part of the meaning that is frequently associated with that song; when the song is used in a new context (such as a film) meanings from the original context will be applied to the new situation. And, while the area has not been explicitly addressed here, a consideration of varying levels of listening activity (from automatic toe-tapping to conscious deliberation) within the audience is a critical factor. The concept of an active audience underpins the analyses; the meanings I may describe are by no means exhaustive and it is essential to remain alert to alternative ways of reading a song/image relation.

By relating some of the perspectives through which meaning is assigned in popular music to the conventions of film music, the following case studies will examine the musical 'devices' in two recent films in order to clarify and further understand their 'functions' and the 'viewer responses' that are 'cued' by the text.

Sliding Doors

While not possessing an obviously 'youth' or 'teen' related storyline, *Sliding Doors* does contain a significant amount of popular music on its soundtrack. These songs are generally used in similar ways to 'classical' score and cues.

Following events in the life of Helen, a recently-fired London publicist, the film shows the potential consequences that catching, or not catching, a morning train back to her apartment could have for her. In one storyline, she misses the train, is mugged on her way home, arrives at her apartment moments after her partner's mistress has left, and carries on a fairly mundane existence as a waitress and delicatessen assistant. In the second story, Helen catches the train, arrives home to find Gerry and Lydia in bed together, walks out, meets and falls in love with James, and starts her own PR business. The two parallel stories are cleverly edited together throughout the film, eventually converging into a fateful ending.[7]

Just under half of the fifty minutes of music in *Sliding Doors* is popular music.[8] The beginning and end of the film, points where music is typically considered to be especially prominent (Kalinak 1992: 97), are accompanied by popular songs. The pop cues are generally longer than the composed cues.[9] In these ways, popular music makes a significant contribution to the *Sliding Doors* soundtrack.

Each song performs one or more of five main functions: providing setting information, functioning as source scoring, explicating characters' thoughts and moods, providing commentary on the narrative, and maintaining continuity between story-lines. Jamiroquai's 'Use The Force' is one song in *Sliding Doors* which carries out each of these functions in a very broad sense. Its inclusion initially is as 'period wallpaper' of sorts, locating the film in the late 1990s. While a viewer might not specifically notice the 'era' of the music/film when watching it on its release in 1997, the inclusion of these songs suggests that when viewed again some years later, *Sliding Doors* will be recognised as belonging to a specific point in time. Several other, less audible, tracks – not quite mainstream, but not quite alternative – provide connotations of the 'fashionable' and 'trend setting', which can then be linked with the characters and the world they inhabit.[10]

'Use The Force' also provides an example of source scoring. This refers to those occasions when a diegetically motivated track is employed to perform some additional non-diegetic functions.[11] Jamiroquai's lively song plays at the opening of Clive's restaurant and bar – shots of which are intercut with shots of Helen 1 working at the restaurant while Gerry is away with Lydia in Dorset. The implication is that the song is diegetic (its volume increases as the camera enters the bar, and the volume is altered later for inside/outside changes). However, in much of this sequence, the song is dominant over most diegetic sound: no dialogue is heard even when close-up shots of people talking are shown (although camera flashes and a hum of conversation are audible). Moreover, 'Use The Force' (along with the ambient sound of the party) carries on playing over the cuts to Helen 1 working at the restaurant.

The lyrics of the track are very clear at first, but reduce later so that the dialogue between Helen 2 and Gerry can be heard. The vocalist sings 'I must believe I can do anything, I can be anyone, I must believe' – words which reflect the thoughts of both Helens. For Helen 1, they serve as a kind of 'mantra', recited to herself in order to persevere with her menial waitressing job. For Helen 2, who presents herself as being well in control of the seemingly successful party, they imply some lingering feelings of self-doubt. In fact, the lingering instability in Helen 2's suggested thoughts becomes more obvious when Gerry turns up; the music mix becomes muffled and 'woozy', and the filming slows down as if Helen 2 has become dizzy or faint. The lingering shot of a camera flash reflects the shock that she apparently feels at seeing him in Clive's bar. Its sound-effect is heard on the line 'I've got to get myself together', reinforcing her determination to be strong when she talks to Gerry (to resist his charms and maintain her new independent status rather than going back into a familiar, if ultimately dishonest, relationship). At this point, the music becomes more explicitly diegetic and more closely related to the narrative as the audience hears what Helen 2 is presumed to hear (this also happens when the two Helens have their simultaneous dizzy spells and stumble).

That the mixing of the song reflects what Helen 2 is hearing also implies a link between the theme of the lyrics and her own character. Presented as reflecting her thoughts, the upbeat, energetic sound indicates her buoyant mood and sense of achievement at the busy party. Thus, while 'Use The Force' is diegetically motivated, it clearly performs some functions of non-diegetic accompaniment through its fulfilment of the established Hollywood film music function of explicating or modifying the viewers' understanding of characters' thoughts and mood. An additional similarity to the 'classical' tradition is in its formal provision of continuity to the editing between the different story lines of the two Helens (particularly when they both have a dizzy spell). A further non-diegetic – and 'classical' – function that 'Use The Force' performs is creating 'spectacle'. The volume of the music, dominating most other elements on the soundtrack, allows this sequence (which depicts an important event in the narrative) to become much more significant than it would have been without musical accompaniment.

Peach Union's 'On My Own' similarly performs multiple functions. The song was a minor hit in the UK at the time of the movie's release, and was re-issued in the US in late 1997 to coincide with the film. The song begins on the cut to a 'morning after' shot (both Helens are suffering from the after-effects of the previous evening in a bar). Anna wakes Helen 2; Gerry wakes Helen 1. The song continues to play over a sequence that portrays Helen 1 looking for a new job, and Helen 2 getting a radically new haircut with Anna's encouragement. Here the track functions as a non-diegetic accompaniment: the mix is 'close' and most diegetic sound is reduced. Some significant dialogue is heard: Helen 1 laments, 'There are no PR jobs', while Anna tells Helen 2, 'What you need is a change of image', but most is muted under the music. Moreover, the song spans a significant period of diegetic time in the space of a few minutes. The track is louder, faster and livelier than the songs that were playing in the bar scene of the previous evening. The instrumentation is amplified – drums and piano are particularly audible. The strength of the female vocalist's voice and the clarity of the lyrics focus attention on their key theme – 'moving on' – as she sings 'It's right for me to go, I'm on my way' and 'I've got to do this on my own'.

The song relates to the situations of Helen 1 and Helen 2: both are moving on from setbacks. The upbeat, positive feel of the song better reflects Helen 2's circumstances; she seems to be reasonably happy with her changes. Helen 1 is struggling to come to terms with her new position as a waitress, a job she has to take in order to make ends meet (her stressed state is emphasised in a scene where she encounters a particularly rude customer); indeed, her situation seems all the more unfortunate to the audience, who are aware of Gerry's infidelity. 'On My Own' thus illuminates the contrast between the two women's success/failure in their attempts to move on, through its literal commentary on the narrative experiences of Helen 2 and its ironic commentary on those of Helen 1.

The track also maintains continuity between and over the two stories and the montage of shots. Music has been commonly used in montage sequences in Hollywood films; it maintained continuity over potentially disruptive shot changes and provided a sound that was easier to listen to than constantly changing diegetic sounds. In its accompaniment to a moderately rapid montage of shots, 'On My Own' clearly fulfils the task of achieving unity: the song plays through a variety of settings (Anna's flat, the hairdresser's salon, Helen 1 and Gerry's place, the restaurant). The montage serves to describe a length of story time in a few minutes of film time; in 'real time' the scenes would demand much more than a few minutes of screen montage. And the selection of an upbeat popular song also means that the sequence can be seen as a 'spectacle', which is quite distinct from the rest of the 'normal' narrative development. The significance of the actions depicted (Helen 2's haircut as a sign of moving on from her relationship with Gerry, while the deceived Helen 1 remains with him) are highlighted by the song's inclusion.[12]

Overall, the *Sliding Doors* popular music soundtrack functions effectively in very similar ways to a 'classical' composed soundtrack and also contains additional levels of meaning available to 'informed' viewers.

Topless Women Talk About Their Lives

Topless Women Talk About Their Lives is a New Zealand-made film that premiered at the Cannes Film Festival in 1997. Its soundtrack is also 'New Zealand-made', featuring songs by performers largely unknown outside that country. However, despite their idiosyncratic style and unfamiliarity to international audiences, the tracks are still largely used in similar ways to 'classical' Hollywood film music cues.

The multi-faceted plot of *Topless Women Talk About Their Lives* is the continuation of a twenty-part television series of the same name; the four-minute episodes used to screen at 11.00pm on Friday nights in New Zealand and soon picked up a cult following. Their movie derivative centres on a group of twenty-something adults living in Auckland. Liz is disturbed to find she may be about to face motherhood on her own, as her cute but tiresome boyfriend Geoff seems to be more concerned with ravishing her pregnant body and knitting, than dealing with his previous girlfriend's imminent return from overseas. Liz's best friend Prue has problems of her own in her marriage to Niuean-born Mike. Neil, who is Liz's former partner and the apparent father of her baby, is trying desperately to figure out what role he is going to play in the child's life.

Finally, there is the neurotic Ant, an aspiring film-maker who presents his debut feature film 'Topless Women Talk About Their Lives' to a less than impressed audience. Harry Sinclair's 'slice of life' film examines all the characters' trials and tribulations, not quite tying up the loose ends before the birth of Liz's baby at the end of the movie.

Music accompanies approximately one third of *Topless Women Talk About Their Lives*; all of it is made up of pre-existing popular songs. Unlike *Sliding Doors*, it is not the lyrics which are the key site of meaning formation; frequently, the words of the songs are indistinct and it is the overall 'sound' of the track that performs the major musical functions. All of the tracks are clearly audible and mixed closely; most of them function as non-diegetic accompaniment and only a few are motivated within the diegesis. This audibility (of sound rather than words) increases audience recognition which, in turn, increases potential soundtrack album sales. Indeed, Cushla Dillon, the film's music supervisor and editor, expressed the hope that the film's soundtrack might open the door for New Zealand music in overseas markets (Aldworth 1997: 7).

At a very general level, the music in the soundtrack provides information about the setting of the film: it represents 'New Zealand-ness' to both local and international audiences. All of the songs in *Topless Women Talk About Their Lives* come from the catalogue of the New Zealand music label, Flying Nun,[13] a record label which has since the 1980s promoted an independent sound in New Zealand and which has developed something of a cult following overseas. However, Dillon noted that they 'never set out to make a grand statement about New Zealand music … [it was] just a compilation' (ibid.).

Several songs reflect or explicate mood. Dillon and Sinclair searched the Flying Nun archives and chose songs which 'honoured and conveyed the emotions and energies within the story' (ibid.). A prominent example is 'North By North' by the Bats, which is heard initially after the opening credits as Liz tries to get to her appointment at the abortion clinic, and is heard again near the end of the film as she tries to get to the hospital to deliver her baby. In both cases, the song's guitar introduction begins as Liz gets into the elevator in her flat telling Geoff that he needn't come with her. As she rushes outside the bass and drums begin, both at a fairly fast tempo. The lyrics of the song are largely indistinguishable, but its pulsing beat emphasises Liz's hurry and frustration as she tries to reach her destination: on her way to the abortion clinic she misses the bus, then has trouble hitching rides; on her way to the hospital, she walks as fast as she can gripping onto lamp-posts as her contractions begin. In both sequences, the song stops at Liz's arrival at her destination (signified by a cut to the abortion clinic receptionist nonchalantly filing her nails, and a cut to the interior of the vet clinic where she ultimately delivers her baby); this synchronisation serves to further strengthen the link between 'North By North' and Liz's situation and mirrors the 'urgency' depicted in the narrative.

'Waves' by Superette illustrates the otherwise ambiguous mood of a particular scene. The track begins over a shot of Mike watching Prue lead a somewhat distraught Ant away from the crowd at the unsuccessful film premiere. It continues over the shots of Liz's taxi ride (which Geoff invades) and then further over the friends' plane flight and arrival at Niue. The track's slow, gentle sound and simple guitar-based melody is melancholic and introspective and illustrates Mike and Liz's moods (which would be slightly ambiguous without the accompaniment). Mike's concern about Prue's level of commitment to their relationship (referenced in an earlier scene) increases as Prue dismisses him in order to save Ant from the potential embarrassment of facing reporters (or lack thereof) at the premiere; the tone of the song indicates his disappointment. And when Liz's taxi journey home (with a well-meaning driver who is chatting about solo motherhood) is interrupted by the appearance of an apologetic Geoff who climbs in at a set of traffic lights, she leaves the cab to the accompaniment of the same music which serves to sum up her low-key sadness and annoyance.

Because 'Waves' also plays over the scenes of the group's arrival in Niue (for Mike and Prue's wedding), the song provides an additional level of information not present in the visual elements of this sequence. While the characters appear happy and are smiling as they meet Mike's family, the continuation of the slow, melancholy song implies that the issues that developed on the night of the film premiere will become significant again at some point during their stay. The implication is confirmed in the narrative: Liz confides in her friends about her worry of being alone during her pregnancy, and Ant finds out that, contrary to what Prue told him, no-one really liked his film.

In a similar way, Chris Knox's 'Not Given Lightly' also provides extra information and insights into the scenes it accompanies. The song starts on a cut to Liz talking to Prue on the telephone just after she has told Neil that she loves him (and he has admitted that he feels the same way about her). A medium-paced love song with guitar and acoustic percussion accompanying the vocals, its familiar lyrics – 'It's you that I love, and it's true that I love, and it's love not given lightly' – contrast pointedly with what Liz is telling Prue on the telephone: she confesses that she does not love Neil, but told him that she did to avoid being alone. The romantic lyrics provide an ironic counterpoint to or commentary on Liz's situation; the words may describe an idyllic romantic situation, whereas she regrets the fact that she has lied to Neil. Alternatively, Liz's admission may modify potential understandings of the song, her convincing lie to Neil suggesting that many professions of true love which abound in popular culture (such as in this song) are in fact false. 'Not Given Lightly' also continues over a shot to the other end of the phone call, depicting a reconciled Prue and Mike in bed together. In their case, the song seems to relate more literally to their situation: they have apparently discussed the problems that had separated them for a time, and their relationship appears to be stronger again.

Topless Women Talk About Their Lives is characterised by an episodic structure which results in a need for devices – musical or otherwise – to create unity across the narrative segments. To this end, some songs maintain continuity by playing 'around' a scene (they begin, stop for the key action, then play again at the end) or playing over a significant scene change or narrative development. 'Ugly Things' by Superette plays first when Liz finds out about Geoff's girlfriend, and secondly as she walks away from her office after being fired from her job. The repetition of the song serves to link the despondent moods of both scenes. 'Spooky' by the 3Ds plays over a moment of significant narrative development (the agreement between Liz and Neil to be together for the sake of the child). When the song stops for their conversation, their dialogue is thus highlighted as crucial. Its connotation of melancholy implies that their feelings have not changed to any great extent, despite the fact that they have agreed a momentous decision.

Some tracks in *Topless Women Talk About Their Lives* play over several different scenes but fulfil similar functions each time they are heard. In this sense they resemble the leitmotifs of 'classical' film music, which aim to create unity by repetition. The 3Ds' 'Animal' accompanies Liz rubbing oil onto her pregnant belly, and later lying on her bed playing with a child's toy; in both cases it suggests her thoughts about the baby. Superette's 'Saskatchewan' evokes intense or extreme emotion: first, as Ant rushes away to get dressed having unwittingly stripped in the street (whilst arguing with a billboard), and secondly, when Liz gives birth to her baby. The reappearance of 'Spooky' – a song already used within the film to signify melancholy – over the end credits emphasises the poignancy inherent in Liz, Prue and Mel's ignorance of Neil's fate. Through their repetition, these songs become associated with particular ideas or feelings, and work as leitmotifs to structurally unify the plot (Kalinak: 1992) and its episodic narrative structure.[14]

Thus, much like the more mainstream and bigger-budget *Sliding Doors*, the soundtrack in *Topless Women Talk About Their Lives* still functions in similar ways to 'classical' Hollywood film music.

Popular music's functions in film soundtracks

The examples outlined from *Sliding Doors* and *Topless Women Talk About Their Lives* both show that popular music can be, and is, used to fulfil functions traditionally carried out by a 'classical' composed film score. However, it is important to note that popular music fulfils these functions in slightly different ways to 'classical' film music. The compilation score draws on some features particular to popular music: in particular, the lyrics (which also make the songs more audible than 'classical' score), the songs' structural independence, and the wealth of extra-textual meanings that popular music inevitably carries.

As Jeff Smith maintains, the linguistic elements of popular songs (titles and lyrics) provide an 'associational potency'; these elements are the aspects of songs that most often confer referential meaning on music (1995: 346–51). As noted earlier, a song's words are an important element of its overall 'meaning', and are based in commonly accepted rules of language rather than an understanding of musical convention. The specificity of meanings afforded through lyrics is in contrast to 'classical' music, which tends to rely on 'a more nebulous parallelism between the emotive connotations of particular musical textures and the content of specific image sequences' (Altman 1999: 249).

Unlike 'classical' fim music's subordination to dialogue, popular music's lyrics can replace or substitute for dialogue. In a filmic context, lyrics often perform tasks such as 'speaking' for a character, thus establishing or underlining character traits. Lyrical relation to character and action is seen particularly clearly in *Sliding Doors*, in which the songs' words frequently reflect Helen's thoughts or aspects of her character. Like dialogue then, the lyrics can assist in the movement and development of the narrative.

Song lyrics also contribute to the greater structural independence of popular music. Smith (1995: 348) and Rick Altman (1999) both insist that popular music exhibits greater independence than 'classical' music, in relation to the film as a whole:

> Because it has an obvious coherence, with each line clearly connected to the overall structure and a universally expected musical cadence and linguistic conclusion, popular song never allows listeners of the song's individual parts to escape from the whole. As such, the popular song always remains a coherent block that appears to be authored separately from whatever images it accompanies. Quite to the contrary, the meandering capacity of 'classical' music makes it able to lead listeners away from any overall

structure and into a realm where the music seems to be generated not by some global vision, but by the image at hand. (Altman 1999: 252–3)

Thus, even when only a brief snatch of a popular song is heard in a film, it automatically alludes to the presence of the rest of the song as a separate entity existing outside the soundtrack.

On the other hand, this structural independence can prevent popular songs from being used for some of the 'classical' film music functions (Kalinak 1992: 187; Smith 1995: 348). One principle that is difficult to maintain when using popular music is direct synchronisation of music and image. Because a popular song is not usually composed for a specific sequence, as a 'classical' cue is, it is unlikely that its rhythm and inflection will exactly match the action. This autonomy can also alter the way music is used to accentuate the dramatic build-up of a scene: this tends to be achieved through variations in the popular music's volume and the prominence of diegetic sound, rather than through compositional changes in key or tone, or through conformity to Western musical codes which call for 'closure', as might occur in a composed cue.

In addition, the formal autonomy of popular music can sometimes lessen its chances of being used to maintain structural unity or continuity (Kalinak 1992: 187; Smith 1995: 333). In 'classical' soundtracks, unity and continuity are usually maintained through repetition of short musical themes, or leitmotifs. Smith suggests that because popular songs cannot be segmented in the manner of leitmotifs, they are unlikely to be used to fulfil this function (1995: 348). Instead, he maintains that compilation scores tend towards functions that maximise rock and pop music's sociocultural specificity, rather than towards maintaining structural continuity and unity. While this is probably the case overall, the two examples studied here do show that popular music can be used to maintain continuity and unity, though reduction to short themes or leitmotifs is not necessarily required to achieve this. In *Sliding Doors* the music frequently functions to assist in sustaining continuity between the two concurrent storylines by playing over shot changes; in *Topless Women Talk About Their Lives*, the music functions to maintain unity by repeating long segments of certain songs over different sequences in the film. The two films do provide useful counterexamples to illustrate the notion that popular music is not necessarily as limited in its potential for formal use as Smith has asserted.

The prominence of lyrics and the greater structural independence or autonomy that tends to be exhibited by popular compilation scores also mean that these soundtracks elicit greater attention than 'inaudible', 'classical' film music. This audibility is linked to the marketing of the soundtrack as a 'tie-in' item that the viewer can purchase; because the soundtrack is designed to generate additional revenue, it must be sufficiently noticeable and memorable to secure extensive radio play and promote the sale of albums. Although film scores were available for purchase in the early days of film accompaniment (often as sheet music) this focus on the soundtrack-as-commodity became a major aspect of film marketing in the 1960s, when pop aesthetics took hold in film scoring (Smith 1995: 62).

Another feature of popular music frequently observed in compilation soundtracks is its strong extratextual associations. In conveying setting and character associations, popular music tends to maximise the music's special sense of socio-historical specificity: 'Because of the compilation score's heavy reliance on pop and rock tunes, its meaning within a film is often dependent upon the meaning of pop music in the larger spheres of society and culture' (ibid.: 333). The extramusical associations that are brought about by rock history and culture are then used by film-makers to cue settings, character traits, and dramatic situations.[15]

Because popular music in compilation soundtracks fulfils functions of 'classical' film music and conveys meanings that are related to the music's social and historical contexts, it can be considered as a two-tiered system of communication. Such a system exists when one device (such as a popular song) can be read on two different levels, according to how much the viewer knows about that device and its associations.

The concept of the two-tiered system was developed by Noel Carroll (1982) in relation to films of the 1970s, in which directors frequently drew on devices from film history to make quotes or allusions that increased a film's depth of meaning (the reworking of genres or particular shots). Film directors could thus simultaneously appeal to the 'uneducated' viewer who simply wanted to be entertained, and also send obscure/witty messages to any film buffs in the audience (a practice that has been enthusiastically embraced by directors such as the Coen Brothers). Smith developed this concept in his work on film soundtracks from the 1950s and 1960s, and I have followed him in using it to inform my analyses of these two films. He provides a succinct summary of the way the two-tiered system works:

> On one level, an audience of uninformed viewers may interpret the song as background music pure and simple. As such, they may make judgements regarding the overall style and its appropriateness to considerations of setting, character and mood. However, an audience of informed viewers

will recognise the song's title, lyrics or performer, and will apply this knowledge to the dramatic context depicted on screen. (ibid.: 353)

The popular music in both *Sliding Doors* and *Topless Women Talk About Their Lives* sits comfortably within this paradigm. In both films, the music functions as 'soundtrack', working to reflect narrative or characterisation, but also provides a wealth of differing meanings to those viewers with prior knowledge of the music, whether it be the contemporary chic of the *Sliding Doors* soundtrack or the cult 'underground' status of the Flying Nun music in *Topless Women Talk About Their Lives*. Romney and Wootton have commented that films using pop songs today 'appeal to specific areas of knowledge, to the viewer's adherence to distinct genres of music or film – as if each film exclusively addressed the habitués of one particular rack in a megastore whose clientele is fragmented as never before' (1995: 5). And yet, as shown above, this specialist appeal of much pop and rock music does not prohibit the compilation score from successfully fulfilling the functions of 'classical' film scores for an 'uninformed' audience. Alongside the inescapable, extratextual, socio-historical meanings of popular music is a definitive capacity to engage effectively – though differently – in the delivery of many of the traditional functions of film music.

Notes

1 Throughout this chapter, the term 'classical' is placed in quotation marks following Royal S. Brown (1994: 38–9) to indicate that the term is not used to designate two centuries of musical tradition, but only the styles commonly used for 'late silent films and through-composed sound films' (Altman 1999: 248).
2 The process of cinematic suture is believed to work as follows: the filmic discourse presents the spectator with structures considered to be marked by absence. The spectator fills these absences in, momentarily completing them, and thus deriving a sense that the film is coherent, unified and homogenous; these qualities are in turn appropriated by the subject him/herself, who is apparently encouraged to identify his/her own perceptions with those of the film. The suture theorist examines the film and its features/devices to find out where this process occurs. See Gorbman 1987; Flinn 1992; Kalinak 1992.
3 The leitmotif is a principle developed from Wagnerian opera whereby a musical phrase becomes identified through repetition with a particular character, place or idea; leitmotifs served to unify lengthy and often convoluted material (Kalinak 1992: 63).
4 Defining the term 'popular music' is not a particularly straightforward exercise (Shuker 1998). For the purposes of this analysis, 'popular music' is distinguished from the 'composed film score' according to whether a cue is recognisable as part of a song; that is, if a musical cue is a few bars or verses of a song (with lyrics implied, if not necessarily heard) it is considered to be 'popular music', while if it is a few bars of music that are not obviously 'song' based, then the cue is considered to be 'classical' film music.

5　Anahid Kassabian defines genre as a set of intramusical features (such as rhythmic patterns and tone of voice) and extramusical associations (for example, 'trendy' clothing and youthful, energetic performers) that combine to give meaning to a name, for example 'teenybop' (2001: 174).

6　One problem with text-based approaches such as semiotics is the implied concept of a meaning that is 'locked in' by the text's producers, with the listener's task being to 'unlock' these meanings. The idea that musicians communicate unambiguous meanings by expressing themselves is considered questionable by many theorists: Malcolm Budd, for one, notes in his work on music and emotions that the feelings or meanings that the composer 'put in' to the text, or the feelings or meaning that the performer 'put in' as he or she performed the text, are not necessarily the ones the listener will read out of it (1985: 18).

7　In this chapter, the Helen who misses the train and hence remains unaware of Gerry's infidelity (and also remains brunette) will be referred to as Helen 1, while the Helen who catches the train and thus finds out about Gerry and Lydia's affair (and who later dyes her hair blonde) will be referred to as Helen 2.

8　The style of popular music used in the film might broadly be classified as 'adult contemporary pop' – it is not quite 'alternative' but also not quite 'mainstream'.

9　The average length of the popular music cues is 15 seconds longer than the average length of the 'classical' composed cues.

10　A simple way to see how tracks that play in the background like this work to convey meaning is to mentally substitute them for other tracks and imagine how this would alter the meaning of the sequences. For example, if 'Miracle' (which plays at Clive's newly-opened restaurant) were replaced by a piece of classical music, or a track by Kenny G, the viewer's resulting impression of the restaurant's image and its clientele would be significantly different.

11　The term 'diegesis' refers to the world of the film. Thus, diegetic, or diegetically motivated, music comes from within the film (for example, a character switches on a stereo and the audience hears the same song the character hears) while non-diegetic music is from outside the film (the traditional soundtrack music, of which the characters are not aware).

12　Abra Moore's 'Don't Feel Like Crying' is another song in the *Sliding Doors* soundtrack which functions to highlight the significance of the action it accompanies by working with the device of montage to create spectacle (it plays over the scenes which show Helen 2 setting up her own PR company).

13　By sticking with one label the film's producers saved problems associated with copyright, production and distribution. Winston Aldworth has commented that 'Flying Nun seemed a logical choice given the amount of talent on its books' (1997: 7).

14　Dillon also notes that the average length of each episode in the first television series was about four minutes, which is similar to many pop songs; moreover, she asserts that 'Harry's narrative style in those early episodes seemed to be quite well suited to the verse-chorus-verse format' (Aldworth 1997: 7). She thus implies that the popular music aesthetic has been an implicit part of *Topless Women Talk About Their Lives* from its inception.

15　A significant aspect of the workings of extratextual associations is to do with audience recognition of a particular song and its contexts. If the song is well known, it will allow for a wider range of individual inflections than one that has only been released for a short time. Moreover, audience identification with music also plays a crucial role. For a comprehensive discussion of audience competence and identifications with popular music, see Kassabian 2001.

Chapter Eight

RIDICULOUS INFANTILE ACROBATICS,
OR WHY THEY NEVER MADE ANY ROCK'N'ROLL
MOVIES IN FINLAND

Antti-Ville Karja

In around ten films made between 1957 and 1962, there was some kind of
rock-related fervour ... mostly in the form of jesting or dance scenes.
   – Bruun *et al.* 1998: 23

Since the era of television began in Finland in the late 1950s and put an end
to the use of feature film as the main promotional vehicle for popular music
performers, films with explicit narrative content concerning popular music have
been relatively rare. Only in the late 1990s did that pattern change and in recent
years, Finnish cinema has – somewhat surprisingly – produced a number of films
devoted to popular music in one form or another.
   These have included 'fictitious documentaries' or biopics of some of the central
figures in Finnish popular music's history. *Kulkuri ja joutsen/ The Vagabond and
the Swan* (Timo Koivusalo, 1999) tells the story of two icons of Finnish *iskelmä*,
lyricist Reino Helismaa and performer Tapio Rautavaara. *The Real McCoy* (Pekka
Lehto, 1999) is a film about Andy McCoy, the guitarist and former member of the
rock group Hanoi Rocks. *Badding* (Markku Pölönen, 2000) presents a 'fairytale'

version of the life and times of Rauli 'Badding' Somerjoki, a rock'n'roll/*iskelmä* star. *Rentun ruusu/Rotter's Rose* (Timo Koivusalo, 2001) is a homage to the quintessential *iskelmä* rebel, Antti Hammarberg (aka Irwin Goodman).

A little earlier in the decade, some more traditional fictional movies dealing with, or at least touching upon, popular music were released. Markku Pölönen directed a number of 'tango nostalgia' films, including *Onnen maa/Land of Happiness* (1993), *Kivenpyörittäjän kylä/The Last Wedding* (1995) and *Kuningasjätkä/A Summer by the River* (1998). *Sairaan kaunis maailma/Freakin' Beautiful World* (Jarmo Lampela, 1997) told the tale of three juveniles growing up in an urban environment, to the accompaniment of techno music. *Pitkä kuuma kesä/A Long Hot Summer* (Perttu Leppä, 1999) was a film about the formation of a fictional punk band.

In fact, it can be argued that all but two of the films mentioned above are tied together by their theme of nostalgia. *Kulkuri ja joutsen*, *Onnen maa* and *Kuningasjätkä* are located mainly in the 1950s and concentrate heavily on the dance pavilion culture of those days. *Badding, Rentun ruusu* and *Kivenpyörittäjän kylä* draw on the styles and manners of the 1970s. *Pitkä kuuma kesä* is set in the early 1980s, when the Finnish punk scene was particularly active. And *Badding* includes several scenes recounting the events and circumstances of the mid-1980s. Only *The Real McCoy* and *Sairaan kaunis maailma* can be said to deal with contemporary reality – or surreality, in the case of the former.

Most of these nostalgia-oriented films are predominantly concerned with different forms of *iskelmä* music. For those unfamiliar with the genre, a brief explanation may be useful. In general terms, as Pekka Jalkanen describes it, there are basically two versions of *iskelmä*: a sentimental love song and a humorous narrative. In each case, the lyrical and the musical world-view of *iskelmä* is 'regressive, escapist and nostalgic' (1992: 15). In specific terms, the music is stylistically old-fashioned and formulaic, following a strict verse/refrain structure with a tonal melody and occasional sequences of fifths. Modulations are minimal (1992: 16; see also Jalkanen 1996: 221–8).

Of the films mentioned above, only *Pitkä kuuma kesä*, with its emphasis on early Finnish punk, and *Badding*'s momentary attention to the rise of revivalist rock'n'roll in Finland during the early 1970s (Somerjoki was one of its leading figures), are exceptions. The reference to rock'n'roll here is significant since, as a specific genre of popular music, its audiovisual representations are relatively rare in Finnish film and other audiovisual media. And this is not just a question of temporal distance. Even in its heyday it was treated, as I hope to demonstrate, in quite specific ways, and through particular representational strategies. But before I engage in that discussion, a brief consideration of the major vicissitudes of Finnish popular music and its relationship with the audiovisual media is necessary.

An extremely truncated history of Finnish popular music and audiovisual media

Film historian Sven Hirn has argued that in the early days of cinema, its 'patterns of international progress' were replicated in Finland, although in a somewhat 'primitive' form and to a delayed schedule (1981: 7). The first Lumière-style film show in Finland was presented just six months after the original Paris show, on 6 July 1896, at the House of Societies (now the City Hall) in Helsinki. In the late 1890s, various film exhibitors toured Finland and, as noted by Hirn, the new medium had its breakthrough year in the country in 1899 (1981: 146). From 1905 onwards, proper film theatres were established in major Finnish cities and, as elsewhere, exhibiting films turned out to be a lucrative business in the next few years. Music too was present at those early screenings; phonograph recordings were at first used as an equal attraction, film clips and songs following each other in turn. Later, during the cine-palace era of 1910–30, movies were accompanied by regular film music orchestras, often containing up to thiry members on opening nights. The music performed was often a varied selection – cue sheet tunes, stage music overtures, and 'light classical' excerpts.

The same slightly delayed replicative tendency prevailed in later years, too. Sound in the cinema came to Finland in 1929, with the screening of short sound films of Finnish origin and several full-length Hollywood talkies; it was the latter that were chiefly responsible for the breakthrough of sound films in Finland (Honka-Hallila 1995: 59). It is interesting to note, however, that American and Finnish films alike were inextricably tied to the field of popular music: the big American hits were *Sonny Boy/ The Singing Fool* (Lloyd Bacon, 1928) and *Broadwayn sävel/ Broadway Melody* (Harry Beaumont, 1929), and the Finnish ventures were reproductions of dancing and musical performance. The very first sound film screening in Finland, on 9 September 1929, at the Kinola theatre in Turku, was advertised: 'Misses Vuorisola and Hahl dance to the accompaniment of music, T. Weisman sings.'

As feature-length Finnish sound films emerged in the early 1930s, they too drew from popular music. Two of these, *Aatamin puvussa ja vähän Eevankin/ In Adam's Clothes and a Little Bit in Eve's Too* (Jaakko Korhonen, 1931) and *Jääkärin morsian/ Soldier's Bride* (Kalle Kaarna, 1931) were originally shot as silent films, but in the light of the increasing popularity of soundies, were enhanced with a background which contained songs and some dialogue. *Sano se Suomeksi/ Say It in*

Finnish (Yrjö Nyberg, 1931) has been celebrated as the first completely authentic Finnish sound film, as it lacked subtitles and was lip-synchronised. However, this (now lost) film was not in fact a dramatic movie, but a 'revue' which included a couple of short plays, dance, and singing (Honka-Hallila 1995: 65).

By this time, it had become obvious that the Finnish audience wanted to hear its own native language spoken and sung while watching moving pictures. Finnish society was at the same time gripped with 'gramophone fever', and people were spending more money on leisure activities than ever before. This strengthened the appeal of sound films with musical content – a development which was reinforced by the decision of the recently-established national radio broadcasting network to concentrate on the 'highbrow' in its musical selections. Thus, people increasingly turned to the cinema for their preferred music. As a consequence, a symbiotic relationship was formed between the film and music industries; films benefited from the popularity guaranteed by the latest hit songs, and record manufacturers gained more visibility for their products.

The 1930s and 1950s were profitable for the Finnish film industry; even the despair and poverty of the Second World War and its aftermath did not quash movie production. In fact, because of strict legislative measures (including dance prohibition) the popularity and productivity of cinema entertainment was guaranteed. Although the supply of raw materials for all kinds of products was severely depleted, documentary and fictional films were made. The raw film needed was imported from Germany, with whom Finland was a wartime ally. Films were produced not least for purposes of war propaganda; they were seen as important in their delivery of anti-Soviet messages, and as a source of escapist entertainment which provided audiences with temporary respite from the traumas of war.

After 1945, film production continued in larger quantities than ever. The early 1950s were an especially buoyant era with up to thirty new Finnish films per year (by comparison, in 1974 only two Finnish feature films were made; currently around a dozen titles appear per year). It was customary for the film companies to split their production across two categories: one of light comical farces with plenty of popular musical numbers, and another of 'serious' films with more artistic ambitions. The former were almost without exception more popular with the audience, and their profits were partially used for the production of the latter. This was certainly true of the largest of the studio companies, Suomen Filmiteollisuus (or SF), which produced almost half of the total number of Finnish films made between 1930 and 1963: 234 of 474.

SF's films are indeed a major source of material for those interested in the phases of Finnish popular music in audiovisual media. *Iskelmä* music played a central role in many of them, and the plots for some were frequently based merely on the lyrics – or simply the titles – of contemporary hit songs. One particularly important genre were the so-called *rillumarei* films; the name derives from an onomatopoeic phrase in the title song of the first of them, *Rovaniemen markkinoilla/At the Market of Rovaniemi* (Jorma Nortimo, 1951). These films, as well as the music that sprung out of them, created a substantial amount of controversy. Social historian Matti Peltonen believes that *rillumarei* represented such a different world-view, value system and mentality that it was bound to create disagreements (1996: 13–15). These conflicts stemmed from the tensions between the prevailing sentiments of 'high culture' which brusquely dismissed *rillumarei* and some of *rillumarei*'s own direct references to the absurdities of modern high art. It is interesting to note, however, that while *rillumarei* films were defended by their producer T. J. Särkkä, the way in which rock'n'roll was deployed in later films can hardly be seen as positive.

The triumphant years of Finnish film studios came to a halt during the latter half of 1950s. The reasons for this were many, and similar to those experienced elsewhere. The challenge posed by the new medium of television was clearly important. In addition, the 1956 general strike in Finland and the consequent economic decline, and the growth of leisure activities such as dancing and travelling reduced potential audiences and potential profits. Moreover, the success of *Tuntematon Sotilas/Unknown Soldier* (Edvin Laine, 1955), the most popular Finnish film of all time, created problems of its own. On the one hand, it overshadowed all other releases; on the other, as the huge profits gained from it were injected into the making of new films, the film industry was soon facing a period of overproduction. Finally, a new generation of film critics and 'activists' emerged during the 1950s, whose pro-art film sentiments became dominant by the end of the decade.

However, in its relation to popular music, one group of films from this period is of particular interest: *iskelmäelokuvat* or 'hit song films'. The number of these films is disputed, but there are seven or eight films made between 1959 and 1966 that are usually assigned to this category. *Suuri sävelparaati/The Great Tune Parade* (Jack Witikka, 1959) was the first, quickly followed by *Iskelmäketju/Hit Song Chain* (Hannes Häyrinen, 1959) and *Iskelmäkaruselli pyörii/The Hit Song Carousel is Spinning* (Harry Orvomaa, 1960). There is agreement over the inclusion of *Tähtisumua/Stardust* (Aarne Tarkas, 1961) and *Toivelauluja/Favourite Songs* (Ville Salminen, 1961) but the status of *Nuoruus Vauhdissa/Youth Going Fast* (Valentin Vaala, 1961) is less clear since it revolves around a more recognisable plot. *Lauantaileikit/Saturday Games* (Maunu Kurkvaara and Aarre Elo, 1963) and

Topralli/Top Rally or *Top Ditty* (Yrjö Tähtelä, 1966) brought the sequence to a close. Because they are basically chains of popular music performances which resemble the way in which the early MTV presented its videos, these films have been described as 'music video compilations of their time' (Juva 1995: 163).

Following the consolidation of television in Finland through the 1960s, the tight relationship between film and record companies was disrupted as the stars of popular music found a new place in the ephemeral flow of various television programmes. Of course, films of subsequent decades did continue to use popular music and its performers in different ways, especially those directed by Aki Kaurismäki, which featured several documentary-like scenes of Finnish popular musicians of the 1980s. And the re-emergence of Finnish film during the 1990s revived the model of mutual benefit for the film and music industries, as contemporary hit songs were routinely included in film soundtracks and soundtrack albums; and both the pop stars and the films in which their music is played are widely seen in music videos which thus fulfil a double promotional function.

Rebels with a cause

It can be reasonably argued that there is no musical genre which is not embedded in audiovisual media. Rock and pop have their music videos, classical music and jazz their concert footages, techno its demos. Of course, different sub-genres or styles possess their own audiovisual conventions which, to a great extent, determine how a particular type of music may be visualised. One only needs to compare the music videos of, for example, Britney Spears, Puff Daddy and Metallica to see the difference. While the boundaries between these conventions are not completely rigid, on a general level they cannot be overlooked.

Thus, it is interesting to note how rock has been entangled in various 'audiovisual crises'. The unwillingness of Sonic Youth to make music videos, for example, is an apparent indication of the band's tendency to avoid accusations of 'selling out'. The video career of Bruce Springsteen is a similar case; it was some three years after the launch of MTV that he agreed to make his first music video; and when he did ('Dancing in the Dark') it presented an imitation of a concert performance. Gareth Palmer has suggested that his 'reluctance to use video may express his fear that the new medium would detract from the authenticity of the true Springsteen experience' (1997: 110).

Within rock, this relationship between a live performance and a pre-recorded and manufactured audiovisual footage has been a persistent problem. As music video today is an established and beneficial way to promote popular music, the issues raised may no longer be as sensitive but at different stages in the evolution of popular music, historical precedents for these tensions can be seen. Frequently, these have concerned television; in the late 1960s, surrounded by the counter-cultural atmosphere of an emerging rock 'underground', the television series *The Monkees* (and the group itself) represented for many the most crass example of popular music's commercialisation and domestication. Similarly, the audiovisual performances of Pat Boone, Frankie Avalon, Fabian, Bobby Rydell and other 'teen-idols' in the late 1950s and early 1960s were widely perceived as inappropriate, sanitised and tamed versions of the original, raw and rowdy rock'n'roll stars of the mid-1950s. Paul Friedlander has described them as 'mostly cute and nattily attired young men [who] sang ersatz rock music that contained little or no beat, saccharine string arrangements, and a multitude of nonsexual, romantically safe messages' (1996: 71). Their performances were epitomised in the television show *American Bandstand*, where 'popular music favorites lip synched their hits while regular Bandstand dancers ... strutted the latest steps – the well-dressed, well-behaved side of rock music' (ibid.).

Hollywood's so-called rock'n'roll films of the late 1950s were, for their part, interpreted in an ambiguous fashion. Initially, they were not seen as proper films with cinematic ambitions, but dismissed as 'a succession of numbers and acts together with barely a pretext of a plot' (Mundy 1999: 110) which formed 'an endless stream of contrived "jukebox musical" quickies' (Shore 1984: 41). In this sense, their reception is very similar to that of the Finnish hit song films. However, this reading has been challenged by John Mundy's assertion that the 'revue structure' was more the exception than the rule, and that such films articulated the 'oppositional resonance of the rock'n'roll performer' which was 'rapidly replaced by images of normative characters "working" within a narrative' (1999: 110).

There was at the same time a certain amount of concern expressed about representations within rock'n'roll films of the morally suspicious behaviour of delinquent youth. From the perspective of the entertainment industry however, these films were more likely to be regarded as Hollywood's attempt to profit from the emergent new musical phenomenon. The films of Elvis Presley have been seen in just this way; in his identification of them as 'the pinnacle of show-biz exploitation, the adulteration of rock rebellion', Michael Shore suggests that their success was due to the stardom of Elvis Presley rather than their connection to rock'n'roll. In fact, he argues that Presley's films had no relationship to rock'n'roll at all (1984: 43).

How does Kekkonen rock'n'roll?

The contest for the first Finnish rock'n'roll recording is an exemplary indication of the domesticating tendency that was prevalent in the 1950s. The three candidates for the title are male vocalists Göran Ödner and Reijo Kallio, and the female vocal group the Harmony Sisters, all of whom recorded 'Tunnista Toiseen' ('Rock Around The Clock'). What makes this confusing is that none of these artists is a rock'n'roll performer; the Kallio and Harmony Sisters versions in particular can be regarded as sterling evidence for the rule that one cannot build a rock'n'roll song on a clean melody and elaborate harmonics.

One reading of the transformation of rock'n'roll to *iskelmä* performances is to regard it as symptomatic of a certain kind of moral panic. Seppo Bruun *et al.* remind us that in the Finnish press, rock'n'roll was deemed inferior 'by musical as well as racial, moral, medical and judicial criteria' (1998: 19). Undoubtedly, economic interests were at stake here; the commercial potential of any kind of *iskelmä* recording was, in the mid-1950s, significantly greater than that of a new and unknown genre like rock'n'roll, which was in general treated as a passing fad. Nevertheless, to interpret these objections solely on economic grounds is to disregard the socio-cultural and ideological implications of economic decisions.

It is customary for people to treat all things new with a certain amount of suspicion. In medical or environmental examples (where evidence and arguments are often in conflict), this might be wise, but with cultural products the situation is less straightforward. Nonetheless, there is a considerable amount of historical evidence showing that various forms of music have been received with apparent caution and distrust. This has been especially true of popular music, although the grounds for anxiety have changed over time. The early moments of 'Western' bourgeois popular culture during the first half of the nineteenth centrury were surrounded by value and moral judgments, which reflected the attitudes of a class-based society; hence the division between elite/high art and popular culture for the masses. Since then, similar criticisms have been made about the alleged deficiencies of diverse forms of popular culture. In Finland during the 1920s, jazz came under fire from nationalist and racist claims about the style and origins of the music. And in the immediate post-war decades when, amplified by a generation gap greater than ever before, the fear of Americanism was articulated in different forms of cultural protectionism, the emergent rock'n'roll was an obvious target.

Furthermore, the cultural climate of the immediate post-war decades was characterised by additional factors. First, the ban on public dancing – in restaurants, pavilions, or elsewhere – which had been in force during the war years was gradually relaxed, leading to a real and widespread 'dance craze'. Secondly, because of the general poverty which resulted largely from the war compensation payments Finland was obliged to make to the Soviet Union, many things were severely rationed. Plenty of daily commodities were 'on the card' and could only be purchased by those who possessed a permit to do so. Thirdly, these factors were intermingled with a strong protective attitude in social politics, one of the most manifest forms of which was the regulation of alcohol distribution (and therefore, hopefully, also of alcohol consumption).

Moral marketing devices

It is a matter of conjecture whether or not this protective attitude influenced the way in which popular music was used in films of that era. Nevertheless, the particular examination of rock'n'roll in Finnish films does seem to indicate that, at the very least, its consequences for the audiovisual media were problematic. To begin with, there is no such concept as a Finnish rock'n'roll film; if one is to believe film scholar Mervi Pantti, the 'hit song films' are just that – films with hit songs (1998: 112). The actual rock'n'roll performances (which ultimately are a matter of definition, of course) are sparse and, in fact, they are equally likely to be found in any other 'entertainment film' of that era.

But let us concentrate for a moment on these hit song films. As the name (given by later generations) implies, the dominant musical form of the series is *iskelmä*. With this historical burden, the films did not specifically question the values of dominant adult culture; instead, as Pantti suggests, they can be reasonably considered as careful experiments in promoting new, youthful, popular music through the medium of film (1998: 112–13). More evidence for the 'careful' character of the films is provided by the fact that – judging by the featured performers – they were not targeted exclusively at young people.

Understandably, the motivation of Finnish studios to make hit song films was never far away from the intentions of their models on the other side of the Atlantic; the reasons were mainly economic. As noted above, one central factor was that the increasing prominence and popularity of the hit song star cult actively encouraged the production of films which would compensate for the losses made by other kinds of movie; to this end, a compilation of favourite hit song performances was seen as more than suitable. Ironically, as it turned out, only a few of the films were profitable.

The musical material of the films relied strongly on the *iskelmä* tradition, although in some of the later ones, other contemporary popular musical forms appeared. These included some performances of 'steel wire' music – instrumental electric guitar music with massive tape echo, influenced heavily by the Shadows – and more 'rockish' performers, such as the Cadillacs. A peculiarity of its own kind in *Iskelmäketju* were the appearances of the Delta Rhythm Boys, who were immensely popular in Finland at that time.

But rock'n'roll is by no means absent from these films. As this music represented a clear indicator of the activities of an emerging youth culture, it was repeatedly appropriated in films that were concerned with that particular demographic group. It has been argued that the first youth film in Finland was *Kuriton sukupolvi/ The Reckless Generation* (Wilho Ilmari, 1937), remade in 1957 by Matti Kassila in the wake of an apparently rebellious post-war youth culture. In the later version 'the guys were rocking with their hussies even a bit too existentially' (Uusitalo 1981: 134). It should be noted, however, that both versions of the film have been excluded from the 'hit song film' category – for being too clearly plot-oriented.

Analysis of the ways in which rock'n'roll was employed in both the hit song films and other entertainment films of that time reveals three strategies. First, films which included rock'n'roll scenes were defined and constructed as comedies. Even if the hit song films are considered as a genre of their own, they cannot escape a comical treatment. This can be illustrated by the example of the song 'Mustat Silmät' ('Black Eyes') in *Iskelmäketju*, performed by Onni 'Grazy' Gideon And His Gipsy Rockers. During the performance, the song is transformed from a traditional Russian-flavoured folk song to an almost acrobatic rock'n'roll act, during which Gideon is lying on the floor on his shoulders, holding his upright bass upside down between his legs. According to Bruun *et al.* such depictions were a part of the second phase of societal reaction to rock'n'roll in Finland, which was to ridicule it (1998: 19, 22). (The first phase had been an automatic fascination with the novel and bizarre.)

The acrobatic manoeuvres point to the second strategy. Rock'n'roll was repeatedly represented as a form of dancing, whose acrobatic dimension was further enhanced by the various jumps and tosses. Dance can be approached either as a social ritual that is governed by tradition and authority resulting in a representation of 'the triumph of discipline and restraint', or as 'the very model of social disorder' because of its connections to 'passionate impulses which threaten social stability' (Straw 2001: 158–9). In addition to its unequivocal situation in the latter category, it is also easy to characterise rock'n'roll dancing as silly or funny 'jerking' and, indeed, 'rocking'. In *Yks' tavallinen Virtanen/ One Ordinary Guy* (Ville Salminen, 1959), perhaps the most active characters are a motorcycling couple whose objective is to train for the world record in rock'n'roll dancing.

In *Toivelauluja*, an interesting juxtaposition is made between wild rock'n'roll whirling and delicate ballet manoeuvres. And in *Isaskar Keturin ihmeelliset seikkailut/The Fantastic Adventures of Isaskar Keturi* (Aarne Tarkas, 1961), the dancing is performed by two children.

The presence of children is the central component of the third strategy. It might be justifiable for the performers and dancers in rock'n'roll scenes to be young, but the example of *Isaskar Keturin ihmeelliset seikkailut* goes beyond this convention, and reduces it to the infantile. Not only are the rock'n'roll dancers identifiably pre-teen, but the song to which they are dancing is performed by a child: Vesa Enne, who became famous through his renditions of rock'n'roll songs in the late 1950s and early 1960s. The song he sings in the movie – 'Jöröjukkarock' ('Grumpy Jack Rock') – is filled with references to traditional children's songs. The same song is also performed in *Iskelmäkaruselli pyörii* in its 'original' arrangement by its composer and lyricist Saukki (aka Sauvo Puhtila), accompanied by two little hand-doll squirrels – for whom some of the lines are recorded in double speed. Rock'n'roll is thus defined as a childish activity, not meant to be taken seriously. The tendency is also visible in *X-Paroni/X-Baron* (Risto Jarva, Jaakko Pakkasvirta & Pertti Pasanen, 1964), in which a group of peasant children are seen twisting.

An additional characteristic of the representations of rock'n'roll to be found in Finnish film is the speech used by its practitioners. Conventionally, the language used in the movies of that era follows rigidly the correct grammar and pronunciation of 'official' Finnish. Traces of dialect are rare. However, within these films, rock'n'roll performers, musicians and dancers frequently use – or rather, imitate – the slang of the Helsinki city area. This is equally true for the youngsters in *Kuriton sukupolvi* (1957 version), the dancing motorcyclists in *Yks' tavallinen Virtanen*, Vesa Enne in *Isaskar Keturin ihmeelliset seikkailut*, and the dancing couple in *Toivelauluja*. In this way, the representations of rock'n'roll participate effectively in the creation of tensions between young and the old, between urban and rural. The urban/rural confrontation is forcefully present in *Yks' tavallinen Virtanen* and *X-Paroni*, as both films are partially situated in out-of-city environments. In their own peculiar way they depict the intrusion of rock'n'roll to the Finnish countryside, (a major source of traditional conceptions of Finnish-ness) and the awkward consequences of this. In *Yks' tavallinen Virtanen*, rock'n'roll is literally an intrusion and a nuisance to be eliminated. The example provided by *X-Paroni* is more complicated: there the country folk appear to be quite content to twist, but the circumstances in which the dancing takes place reduce it to the absurd. How else to describe a rhythm orchestra walking around the countryside, the drummer being pushed along in a milk cart with only a snare drum and a crash cymbal, entering a farm courtyard and performing – by the farm-owner's request – 'Heinähanko Twist' ('Hayfork Twist'), which induces the leather-booted farm-owner to dance around too?

There is an additional question about the role and nature of music in these scenes. I have been referring generally to rock'n'roll without exploring its defining characteristics. But of course, 'any attempt to isolate a definitive or core style of 1950s rock'n'roll is a highly problematic enterprise' (Keightley 2001: 114–15); there are, for example, certain ethnic, commercial and age-related factors which determine whether or not a piece of music can be (and has been) labelled as rock'n'roll. My decision not to employ a specific definition of rock'n'roll has the advantage of relying on common conceptualisations of the music, thus ensuring that my rock'n'roll will not differ too much from other people's rock'n'roll. The question therefore concerns the manner in which the music in these films departs from the musical characteristics usually attached to rock'n'roll.

From the above discussion of hit song films it might be expected that rock'n'roll in Finnish film would be musically modified along the *iskelmä* tradition. Yet this is hardly the case. To the extent that the music has been modified, it has been achieved through the use of jazz flavours. In fact, this applied to early Finnish rock'n'roll in general, as it was 'probably closer to up-tempo swing boogie, accompanied by more or less snotty tenor saxophones' (Bruun *et al.* 1998: 21).

The songs that are assigned here as rock'n'roll have some prototypical qualities, such as three-chord harmonies, sometimes even a full twelve-bar blues chord progression and guitar accompaniment. The beat is generally straightforward and simple, but is slightly obscured by the excessive use of crash cymbals, which tends to create an atmosphere resembling swing. Horns and woodwind are frequently used, principally saxophone and trumpet; again, especially the presence of the latter points to jazz, rather than 'pure' rock'n'roll. The lead clarinet on 'Heinähanko Twist' acts in the same way. Thus there is a certain amount of generic ambivalence inscribed to the music, and listeners are likely to find it disturbing since it is neither 'really' rock'n'roll nor 'really' jazz. Indeed in *Toivelauluja*, the dancing couple add to this ambivalence by speaking of their destination (where several youngsters are subsequently seen twirling and tossing each other around) as 'a jazz club'.

The music's generic uncertainty can be largely explained by productional factors. Since rock'n'roll was treated as a passing fad, it was not taken too seriously by the record companies, and Finnish rock'n'roll songs were mostly cover versions of international hits, although arranged and performed differently. On many occasions, the younger generation's new music was played by trained jazz musicians from exact note sheets. A general, rather mythologising assessment is that they therefore lacked a substantial amount of the relaxed feeling and drive that underpinned the original rock'n'roll hits. Hence the emergence of rock'n'roll songs in the guise of *iskelmä* or even jazz.

The end

It would appear therefore that one cannot satisfactorily base the definition and investigation of rock'n'roll in Finnish films on mere musical components. In fact, the various ingredients I have discussed above are instrumental for the definition of rock'n'roll in this context. It is rock'n'roll – but only because its themes are ridiculous, its performers are juveniles, it is linguistically abused, its postures are deviated, and its sonorious conventions are indecisive. And to define rock'n'roll in this way is also to present a denial of a definition. That is why they never made any rock'n'roll films in Finland; there is no such thing as rock'n'roll in Finnish films.

I would not claim, however, that rock'n'roll's audiovisual representations in Finnish films necessarily and exclusively follow the pattern outlined above. As the 1960s unfolded, the depiction of rock'n'roll, and youthful popular music in general, was released from its comical treatment. *Jengi/ The Gang* (Åke Lindman, 1962) is an early case in point; it includes scenes from a dance venue where twenty-something people are dancing both the tango and the twist. There is little 'excessive existentialism' here, but 'a realistic and striking depiction of the working-class youth of the early 1960s Helsinki' (Uusitalo 1981: 258). In very general terms, films from this point on do begin to depict the social conditions of young people more realistically.

It has been claimed that audience reaction in the USA and Europe to *Rock Around the Clock* (Fred F. Sears 1956) demonstrated 'a distinctly youth-oriented and oppositional stance' that popular music acquired with the advent of rock'n'roll. Evidence of this comes from assertions that the film inspired 'unruly behaviour', as movie theatre aisles were used as dance floors, cinema seats were ripped out, cars were turned upside down, shops and street signs were vandalised, and street demonstrations organised. Governments participated in the creation of turmoil by banning the film, and police attempted to control the rioters with water cannons (Bennett 2000: 34–5).

Compare these images with those following the premiere of *Tunnista tuntiin/ Rock Around the Clock* in Finland. Arguably, it was the country's first large-scale rock event, and news about the violent audience responses in London and elsewhere had already reached Finland. And yet:

... the anticipated reaction never came. The audience was clapping its hands, stomping its feet and whistling; after the show, some rowdy youngsters were baiting the police in the streets and urging each other to turn vehicles upside down. Direct action reached its dramatic climax when one Moskvitsh automobile was moved by a metre or so. (Bruun *et al.* 1998: 19–20)

In relation to the representations of rock'n'roll in Finnish films this report carries a certain resonance. Rock'n'roll is indeed funny; and the history of Finnish film offers apparent evidence of this.

Chapter Nine

CONSTRUCTING THE FUTURE THROUGH
MUSIC OF THE PAST: THE SOFTWARE IN *HARDWARE*

K. J. Donnelly

While today the film musical is at best a rarity and at worst a moribund form, films like *Hardware* (Richard Stanley, 1990) demonstrate a form of cinema where music still can be a central aspect. Rather than integrating music, *Hardware* coheres music as a semi-independent discourse running through the film, unencumbered by the requirements of narrative development. In films that are not musicals, music usually is conceived and theorised as an afterthought to the important matter: the film's images, dialogue and narrative development or the diegetic world on screen. Yet plenty of films seem to contradict this notion to a greater or lesser extent. *Hardware* is not alone, although in some ways it is a very singular film. It was a British-made science fiction film set in a post-catastrophic future, where there is a desert 'zone', a continuous war, and constant radio broadcasts about dangerous radiation levels. It was made cheaply, costing only $1 million to produce over an eight-week shoot (Jones 1992: 25). *Hardware*'s story is as follows: in the future, fragments of a robot are found in the desert. Mo gives them to his lover, Jill, who welds them onto a sculpture. The robot pieces turn out to be part of a prototype military machine (called Mark 13) that has malfunctioned during tests; the robot regenerates itself by welding various household utensils together and goes on a killing rampage through Jill's flat.[1]

The film includes a foregrounded discourse about pop/rock music, which runs throughout as a parallel text to the narrative. The music consists primarily of songs from the 1980s, some of which are then articulated as if they were songs from the film's diegetic world's past. While they may be songs from the past of *Hardware*'s time of production (1990), in the film they fail to be constructed as if they were music from the distant past, and thus they contradict, or at the very least undermine, the film's sense of being set in the future. In addition to the songs, the background score for *Hardware* references an elsewhere, including musical objects that seem to ground the film away from its futuristic representations in the image track. Overall, *Hardware* figures the present (including the recent past) in 'the future' of the film's diegesis through its articulation of music – not only through the songs themselves and references in the background score, but also through the figuration of an MTV-like channel on the television, as well as the film's structuring of two sequences using a pop video aesthetic, all of which firmly place a contemporary understanding of pop music within the futuristic world portrayed in the film.

Pop/rock music in *Hardware* constitutes a semi-autonomous channel, providing another dimension for the film – both in aesthetic terms, and as an esoteric parallel text that is largely independent of the film's narrative development. Pop music appears as a discourse in its own right, rather than as part of the film's narrative, or as an agent of nostalgia, or as a connection to the conventions of traditional film music in science fiction films. At times the film seems less interested in devising a scenario about the future than it is about other things, such as employing pop music as an internal logic of the film. It is used for both its material and referential levels, where music is both discursive, discussing itself, and the material flesh of the film, setting up its own temporal structures within the film's bounds.

The future of music: genre music and history

How might it be possible for music to construct an idea of the future? There has been a tradition of music representing the future that probably has been most concrete in the music written for the science fiction film genre. The option open to musicians broadly appears to have been either to frame the film's visual representations of the future with music that is in a contemporary style, or to become part of the film's construction of the future, as a 'futuristic' effect in itself.

After the advent of synchronised sound, one of the first significant science fiction films to build an image of the future was the British film *Things To Come* (William Cameron Menzies, 1936). It utilised a musical score by a highly reputable British concert hall composer, Arthur Bliss, yet never asked its music to do anything to construct an idea of the future itself. Instead, it used a contemporaneous idiom, thus framing the film's construction of the future in a musical bath of the present's (1930s) style. The late 1970s and early 1980s saw the success of the Star Wars trilogy – *Star Wars* (George Lucas, 1977),[2] *The Empire Strikes Back* (Irvin Kershner, 1980), *Return of the Jedi* (Richard Marquand, 1983) – and Steven Spielberg's *Close Encounters of the Third Kind* (1977) and *E.T. The Extra-Terrestrial* (1982). All of these films had incidental music composed by John Williams, and carry a distinct similarity in terms of their musical style and melodic drive. Williams' manipulation of orchestral resources marked something of a return to the style of film music in classical Hollywood films of the 1930s and 1940s (Kalinak 1992: 189; Donnelly 1998a: 142). In a similar vein, conventional action film music, lacking the 'futuristic' aspirations of much synthesizer music, is embodied by science fiction films such as *Star Trek: The Motion Picture* (Robert Wise, 1979) and *Total Recall* (Paul Verhoeven, 1990), both with traditional orchestral scores by Jerry Goldsmith. Similarly, *Robocop* (Paul Verhoeven, 1987) uses orchestral music by Basil Poledouris, including a heroic theme for the eponymous hero, while the television series *Star Trek* (Paramount/NBC, 1966–69) had also predominantly used familiar orchestral sounds that did not detract from (nor add to) the programme's future setting.[3]

More 'futuristic' music appeared in science fiction films of the 1950s, encouraged by the increasing availability of electronic instruments. *The Day the Earth Stood Still* (Robert Wise, 1951) had a score by Bernard Herrmann that used the cinema's traditional orchestral resources, but additionally utilised the eerie electronic theremin as a sound effect, a sound source that aurally represented the alien Klaatu and his unfamiliar advanced technology. A more extreme musical score, that lacked any continuity with film music traditions, was produced for *Forbidden Planet* (Fred M. Wilcox, 1955) in which Louis and Bebe Barron edited together recordings of experimental and self-regulating electronic sound devices, creating a sonic fabric that destroyed any distinction between traditional non-diegetic scores and diegetic sound effects.

The success of *The Terminator* (James Cameron, 1984), which had a pulsing electronic soundtrack by Brad Fiedel, was testament to the effective and 'futuristic' sounding film scores that could be achieved relatively cheaply and easily by using keyboard synthesizers. John Carpenter had made his own synthesized music something of a trademark in the films he directed. His remake of *The Thing* (1982) used synthesized music by Ennio Morricone that was much in the same vein as Carpenter's own musical style. Both of these films used the newer breed of integrated preset synthesizers that replaced the previously complex modular amalgam of knobs and wires, and that became more widely available by the early 1980s. These offered a simplicity of operation at a non-exclusive cost and allowed the flowering of a whole zone of film and television music that was not only cheaper and more versatile than the established orchestral tradition, but also by necessity was concerned more with the specific instrumental colour, sound effects and musical texture. The possibilities offered by electronic timbres have been noted by Kathryn Kalinak: 'Synthesizers ... are often exploited in sci-fi and futuristic genres to create an other-worldly effect ... [while in] more conventional genres, synthesizers can give a film that much-sought-after contemporary edge' (1992: 188). Synthesizers have dominated the musical scores for low-budget films and television programmes. For example, the potential of new electronic technology was exploited by television in the music for *Dr Who* (BBC 1963–89), and Dudley Simpson's theme music for *The Tomorrow People* (Thames Television 1973–79). Indeed, the unconventional sounds of synthesizers offered a crucial futuristic dimension to television programmes severely restricted by budget. Probably the most successful use of synthesizers as a 'futuristic' sound to complement images of a future world was Vangelis' music for *Blade Runner* (Ridley Scott, 1982), although some of the film's music sounds fairly conventional.

Science fiction film music generally has either adopted a strategy of framing the cinematic vision of the future with traditional or contemporary music which allows it to work effectively as a conventional film score, or positioning it as an essential part of the film's construction of the future through the adoption of self-consciously 'futuristic' aspects. *Hardware* uses a synthesizer score that tends to provide a futuristic tone for the action, but significantly uses pop/rock music as a more traditional contemporaneous musical frame to the representations of the future. However, pop/rock music appears in *Hardware* as a seemingly autonomous discourse in its own right rather than being part of the film's futuristic representations; indeed, the film is arguably less interested in the future than it is in articulating pop/rock as the spine of the film. Pop music represents an insistent strand in *Hardware* that cannot be accounted for by reference to the film's narrative and representations.

Music as software: Pop music and pop music culture in Hardware

Pop/rock music has an evident and important place in *Hardware*. Its position may to only a small degree be accounted for by commerce, as more significantly it provides cultural co-ordinate points for the film. While *Hardware* embodies the increased integration between the music and film industries, it is also a product of the interaction, in aesthetic terms, between the cinematic medium and the pop music discourse. It features, or rather showcases, two pop songs, 'The Order of Death' by Public Image Limited and 'Stigmata' by Ministry, both of which appear for significant durations. In addition to this, the songs are foregrounded in the film in a manner directly reminiscent of pop videos. *Hardware* also features a largely electronic musical underscore (incidental music) composed and performed by Simon Boswell, who has been associated with the independent fringes of pop music as well as film scoring. The film contains cameo appearances by three pop performers and *Hardware* presents a discourse concerning pop music which, while not being of any real importance for the film's narrative development, seems to have a high degree of prominence.

The development of MTV and the frantic exploitation of record label back-catalogues in the late 1980s and 1990s both are vividly inscribed across *Hardware*. Cultural recycling was endemic in popular culture in the mid-1980s, and record companies were keen to exploit other markets. R. Serge Denisoff and George Plasketes described the industrial strategy called synergy, involving the mutual publicity of co-ordinating record releases from a film's soundtrack (1990: 257) while Jean Rosenbluth pointed to the accommodation where 'studios and record companies began to work together regularly to maximize their products' financial potential' (1988: 4). In the first part of the 1980s, the industry's rhetoric about 'home taping is killing music', added to dwindling profits through lower record sales, led to a retrenchment of the international music industry, which towards the end of the decade was boosted by the CD 'revolution' (Eckstein 1993: 45). This was the conclusion of a strategy that allowed record companies to reanimate and resell all their back-catalogues with equal, if not greater, energy than that with which they were promoting and selling contemporary artists.

MTV and pop videos became increasingly important throughout the 1980s, both as marketing tools and as cultural objects in their own right. Richard Stanley (*Hardware*'s director) had attained a certain reputation as a director of pop videos for independent non-mainstream pop/rock groups, including The Fields of the Nephilim, Public Image Limited, Renegade Soundwave and Gallon Drunk. He also directed *Brave*, an extended 'concept film' for Marillion.[4] *Hardware* stands as an example of a particular type of film that melds the form of the pop video with the format of the cinematic feature (Lapedis 1999: 367). A common accusation levelled at film directors who have come from a background in pop video production is that their films are aesthetic failures because they resemble pop videos and do not or cannot sustain cinematic drama. The review of *Hardware* in *Monthly Film Bulletin* noted these characteristics, although it presented them as virtues rather than negative aspects:

> Richard Stanley's feature debut is an impressively glossy high-tech thriller which eschews narrative intricacy in favour of pop-promo production values. Contributing greatly to the movie's impact is the droning, mechanical soundtrack which underscores much of the action ... *Hardware* is a palatable exercise in trash aesthetics whose flashy visuals and seamless soundtrack belie the relatively low budget. (Kermode 1990: 297)

The film clearly exhibits the pace of action that had become commonplace for pop music and its associated images since the proliferation of pop promos on music television. MTV began broadcasting in the USA in August 1981, Euro-MTV started six years later, although European terrestrial television shows were already showing pop videos and exhibiting the 'MTV style'. What pop video makers bring to feature films is a sense of style and detail, geared to short spectacular sequences and consequently a neglect of the macro-level of the film, specifically the traditionally dominant levels of narrative sustenance and character delineation and development.[5] The intrusion of micro-narratives weakens the authority of the central narrative drive. *Hardware* is an example of a form of textuality where there are a number of micro-narratives (music, spectacle, special effects, foregrounded technology, coloured lighting/filters, etc.) whose autonomy has arguably replaced the all-important story of traditional films. However, Stanley (1993) denies that pop video making has been a significant influence upon the style of his films, maintaining that many pop video makers instil a cinematic mode into their pop videos. He sees no essential difference of aesthetic between the narrative film form and the pop video, just a difference of scale. Despite an initially low prestige status (Kirby 1991: 20), the boundary between pop video and film directors is now easily transversed. David Fincher and Spike Jonze have crossed from being pop video makers to acclaimed film-makers, while respected film directors have made pop videos, including John Landis and Martin Scorsese (both for Michael Jackson) and Derek Jarman for the Pet Shop Boys and the Smiths.

Certain forms of film textuality are prone to subsuming the narrative level into a succession of spectacles, and the science fiction genre is often one of these. If film structures traditionally are built around a strong narrative drive, then films that have a weakened narrative allow a situation where other discourses can adopt the foreground. In the case of *Hardware*, like many other science fiction and horror films, spectacle has partially replaced developmental narrative and, additionally, discourses like that of music can function within the film as a structuring device as well as an attraction in its own right (Gorbman 1987: 162). *Hardware* fits the pattern of narrative prevalent in spectacle-based films, where the film's conclusion is a 'pay-off' (in terms of spectacle) for the audience while the exposition of the film lacks sustained pace and action because it establishes the characters and the (thin) narrative that frames the action spectacles. Its two sequences that are distinct pop video-like spectacles cued by the music can therefore be seen to function as attractions in the exposition to balance the concluding section's extremity of action.

While *Hardware*'s soundtrack album features some of the film's pop music – the songs by Public Image Limited and Ministry – the album predominantly consists of Simon Boswell's electronic score, and also includes an adapted excerpt from Rossini's 'Stabat Mater'. The two pop songs were not released as singles tied-in with the film, a common strategy at the time. They were also not contemporary with the film's release, both appearing on relatively poorly-selling albums a number of years earlier. The pop/rock music featured is marginal to the field as a whole and its function for the film is to forge intertextual references to that marginal *milieu*, that which self-consciously is beyond the mainstream. That the soundtrack album includes only the Ministry and Public Image Limited songs is probably because of an inability to gain licence to use the two additional songs that feature less conspicuously.[6] *Hardware* was produced as a product that was never going to have appeal much wider than the ghetto of violent horror and action films and the pop music that appears in the film reflects the film's situation as a marginal product in itself. Instead of symbiotically marketing a number of licensed songs through/alongside the film, *Hardware*'s soundtrack album undoubtedly was conceived as an experience that is very directly an adjunct to the film. Its status as an annexe was confirmed by one review of the album, which noted 'you can almost smell the burning shrapnel as you load the tape' (Black 1991: 31). The music certainly is distinctive, and the pop songs match the overall mood of the rest of the underscore. That music in the film was constructed as a coherent object is testified to by the closing credit of Ian Hierons as musical supervisor 'for Still Moving Music'.

The songs establish a self-referential level in the film, yet their signification for the film is ambiguous. They certainly do not signify 'the future', as the music is (nearly) contemporaneous pop/rock music. Can pop/rock be 'futuristic'?[7] Or is it always of the moment, signifying 'the now'?[8] In recent years, pop music history has been converted into a continuum, for the benefit of record companies selling back-catalogues. The late 1980s, the time of *Hardware*'s birth, was the inauguration of an unprecedented period of back-catalogue re-selling, through the advent of CDs as well as recordings tied-in with films.

In terms of *Hardware*'s sense of 'the future', it is pulling the past into the present as much as it is representing the future. The reinvigoration of the record industry though CD sales led to the previous category of 'golden oldies' being integrated with the 'current' mainstream, both as re-releases and cover versions of 'classics'. This intrusion of nostalgia culture into the contemporary has created a perpetual present that includes both the past and the future (at least as an implication of the future as more of the same, a schizophrenic perpetual present). This simultaneously allows a 'nostalgia for the future', or for futurism – the phenomenon of 'retro-futurism' where we can desire the version of the future extrapolated from a very particular moment in the past. As Fredric Jameson notes, we are unable to imagine the future, because dominant representations of 'the future' now appear to us merely as projections from the past (1984: 238). Thus, in films, representations of the future can be relegated to mere design aspects.

In addition to its songs, *Hardware* includes a number of important cameo appearances, further establishing a significant esoteric level in the film. It showcases a couple of brief song excerpts, and as a counterpart to these contains brief appearances by three musical performers: Carl McCoy, Lemmy and Iggy Pop. McCoy, the singer from The Fields of the Nephilim, is the first person to be seen in the film, a mysterious figure (a 'zonetripper') who finds the fragments of Mark 13 half-buried in the desert sand. Stanley had made promo videos for The Fields of the Nephilim's 'Preacher Man' and 'Blue Water' in the late 1980s and the zonetripper figure was remarkably close to McCoy's stage and video persona. Lemmy, the singer from Motörhead, appears briefly as the taxi driver concurrent with his radiocassette playing Motörhead's 'The Ace of Spades', a short yet very self-consciously intertextual sequence where, referring to his group's song, he asks, 'Do you guys like music? Check out these boys!' The excerpt is largely the song's kinetic introduction, a full four bars, after which dialogue forces the verse into a lower volume. The third cameo is in voice only, where a disc jockey is featured on the soundtrack although no radio source is seen on the image track. The voice belongs to Iggy Pop and the first of his two voice-over appearances concludes with one of his own songs, 'Cold Metal', which he introduces as 'a golden oldie.' The song's lyrics begin with 'I play tag in the auto graveyard/I look up at the radio towers'. Although vague, the song's sense of negativity fits the dystopian character of the film. The song is based on a minimalist clipped staccato guitar riff on three chords, and its appearance confirms the radio as lacking any clear source in the film's diegetic world. This underlines the lack of importance of the music for the film as illusion, and emphasises music as a discourse in itself, through having both Iggy Pop and Lemmy introduce their own songs. The first effect of this is on an esoteric level as a kind of 'wink' at the audience; and secondly, it establishes a familiar type of music (if not the song itself) in a less familiar setting, manifesting a reassurance for the audience. Cameos, like the songs in the film, provide crucial cultural co-ordinate points. These are not mainstream pop stars, like Cliff Richard or Phil Collins, but artists with more extreme reputations who lend a strong sense of the esoteric to the film. Indeed, McCoy, Lemmy and Iggy Pop are not fully recuperable to (dominant) mainstream pop culture.[9] Instead, they indicate a specific area of pop music culture, like a minority channel on television.

The Time Machine: The film's two pop video-like sequences

While the pop music discourse in *Hardware* remains fairly consistent throughout the film, in order to engage it from time to time, the film is forced to make some radical shifts in its regime of enunciation. It moves between musical spectacles to narrative development in a manner reminiscent of traditional film musicals. It changes precisely like switching channels on a television set: from science fiction narrative to music and spectacle.

Hardware contains two pop video-like sequences, for 'The Order of Death' and 'Stigmata'. The former is a voyeuristic display of sex, with the Public Image Limited song cueing the limits of the sequence and the act of sex itself. It functions as a discrete unit within the film, an autonomous micro-narrative with its bounds set by the music and by the sex, the latter being a developmental narrative in opposition to the static repetition of the music's narrative. Thus, it bears striking resemblance to a pop video.[10]

Public Image Limited (known as 'PIL') released the song 'The Order of Death' on the album 'This is What You Want, This is What You Get' in 1984.[11] Shortly before the album's release, the group's singer, John Lydon (Johnny Rotten when with the Sex Pistols), had acted in an Italian-made film with Harvey Keitel: *Order of Death* (Roberto Faenza, 1983), alternatively titled *Cop Killer*. Lydon has a history of involvement with film (Donnelly 1998b: 101–14) from his appearances with the Sex Pistols in *The Punk Rock Film* (Don Letts, 1977) and *The Great Rock'n'roll Swindle* (Julien Temple, 1980) to his own representation (played by Drew Schofield) in *Sid and Nancy* (Alex Cox, 1986). He was originally to have provided the voice of the disc jockey Angry Bob in *Hardware* but withdrew to be replaced by Iggy Pop, another revered cult figure in the pop world (Stanley 1993).

It is possible that Public Image Limited produced the song as a part of the soundtrack for the film of the same name in which it then failed to be included, although the piece's availability under another name suggests otherwise. Lydon had commented earlier, 'I think a lot of soundtracks are really vile and I think films are being done a disservice. I think we could do a service to a film. Like with this Michael Wadleigh thing we wanted to go right down to a bottle banging on the table – *the whole lot*, not just music but sounds' (Martin 1981: 31). The proposed but ultimately unfulfilled collaboration with Wadleigh was probably *Wolfen* (Michael Wadleigh, 1981), and although the production and their involvement were beset by problems that halted activity for a time, Public Image Limited and Lydon were likely to have retained an interest in film music. Indeed, the song in *Hardware*, 'The Order of Death', not only lends itself to use within a film but also in many ways resembles film music more than it does the traditional pop song.

The piece has a totally rhythmic function and neglects to carry the melody, which is the defining aspect of popular music's capacity to provide a verbal developmental narrative. It is therefore easy to suggest that 'The Order of Death' is not a song at all but is better described as a musical piece, particularly as it does not work through the micro-narrative of the sung word. The temporal structure of the piece is based on a simple alternation of blocks of music over a repeated backing, rather than the more conventional song form. Each bar consists of a backbeat rhythm with bass drum semiquavers on the first and third beats. This drum beat is doubled by the repeated line of the song's title, making the whole seem mechanical and relentless. This suggests that the piece may not be as disruptive to the filmic narrative by its insertion into the cinematic context but may function in a way more like traditional film music.

This sequence is marked as discrete by the song fading in at its own beginning and then fading out at its conclusion, encompassing sixteen shots. The sequence as a whole is integrated with the narrative of the film by the elision of action at the start (cut to the couple in the shower) and at the conclusion (fifteen cuts later) where another point-of-view is established (a man watching through a telescope – reminding the audience of its voyeuristic position) to drive the narrative forward.

The opening shot is an establishing shot of Jill and Mo kissing in the shower as the non-diegetic music fades in. It immediately cuts to a slow zoom in on Mark 13's eye, then inside the eye and then to what appears to be a point-of-view shot of the couple from the machine's eye. This underlines the self-consciously voyeuristic nature of the sequence, which is further confirmed by the sequence closing with yet another point-of-view shot, that of the peeping-tom neighbour with a telescope. However, the sequence is not simply a collection of point-of-view shots, but contains the sort of shots one might expect from pop videos, with the camera encircling the couple and a succession of intercut shots of faces towards the end of the sequence that confirms Mark 13's point-of-view.

The discretion of the sequence is principally achieved by the music, which destroys almost all diegetic sound to become the foregrounded motor of the action. The edits take place around important moments in the music's development, such as the entry and exit of the guitar tune,[12] giving the firm impression that the images were cut to fit the music. It is rare in film and pop videos to cut the action on the first beat of a bar, but this takes place on one occasion during the sequence. The effect is to dramatise the action at that point, where the sequence replaces the micro-narrative of Mark 13's vision with the spectacle of sex. The cut coincides with the main variation in the music, where the guitar tune enters, so achieving maximum effect for the conduit into the spectacle. The piece is based on the alternation of four bar blocks. The regularity and easily recognisable (even subconsciously) format sets up certain expectations in the audience. The principal effect of utilising the music to drive the action of the sequence is that film time (editing rhythm, narrative time) is replaced by musical time (metronomic rhythm, musical beat). The temporal organisation of the sequence is thus built around a repetitive beat, a forward movement that is perceived as inevitable, and the image track is subordinated to musical organisation as the central carrier of filmic development.

In an interview following the release of Public Image Limited's 'The Flowers of Romance' in 1981, Lydon declared that the music on the album was better understood as 'minimalist film themes' (Martin 1981: 31) than conventional pop music. The group's interest in film soundtracks suggests that the song 'The Order of Death' might have returned to the medium that was a prime influence on it if not a direct inspiration for it. This is a testament to the degree of interaction and influence that has taken place mutually between pop music and film music, while pop music in its variety of forms has insinuated itself firmly in films in its own right as a replacement for more traditional film music.

The second pop video-like sequence in *Hardware* involves another discrete action set-piece in the image track, that of creating a sculpture, with the head of Mark 13 as the crown of the finished item. In this sequence, the music is diegetically motivated, through Jill turning the television to an MTV-like channel that is broadcasting what appears to be a pop video. She leaves the music channel on as a soundtrack to her sculpting and while the earlier parts of the sequence intercut television images (of the group and other things), as the sequence progresses there are increasingly only shots of her sculpting.

In terms of images the sequence is certainly kinetic; the act of sculpting involves welding, drilling and spraying and is intercut with dramatic television images that appear to be part of the pop video. On the television is the group who appear to be the source (the diegetic motivation) of the song that encapsulates the sequence, and yet it is not images of Ministry that materialize on screen but those of Gwar, a notoriously theatrical heavy metal band with outrageous costumes. This sleight of hand certainly adds to the esoteric level of the film and the observation of this will have given pleasure to members of the audience. This in-joke is a clear example of how the film made an effort to establish 'cult' appeal, as well as illustrating the film's intermittent music discourse that becomes almost fully uncoupled from the film's story. The television appears to show a montage of images as effects, including computer screens and infra-red images. The flow of footage includes a banned video from the group Psychic TV, as well as images from Psychic TV collaborator Monte Cazzaza and experimentalists Survival Research. Some of the images look like a snuff torture movie, although it also includes what appears to be some footage from a slaughterhouse.[13] The kinetic and aggressive television images added to the song denote an extremity of word, sound and image.[14] Fairly quickly, all the images are of Jill sculpting, displacing the emotional turmoil of the previous images for Jill's act of creation, the birth of what the film suggests is a surrogate child. The sequence as a whole is a collage of shots including many of short duration and from dramatic angles, containing only a few shots of above five seconds length while many of the television images are virtual flash frames. The visual style not only is related to pop video style but part of it actually appears to be a pop video.

Ministry's 'Stigmata' is built upon a relentless snare drum beat. The singing is consistently harsh and closer to shouting, part of the legacy of the punk style, while the electric guitars (both organic and synthetic) provide a heavy-metal style backing riff with a (synthetic) *portamento* rise in the chord pitch. At one point there is a thunderous roll on the bass drum. The structure of the song conforms to the four and eight bar patterns common to pop and popular music, while also conforming to the verse-chorus structure (known as 'song form'), but as a verse and variation (Kernfeld 1988: 396). The verse is sung and involves the guitars receding with a foregrounding of the beat and singing, while the variation sections lack vocals and bring the dense-textured but simple guitar riff to the fore. The dynamic effect of this is to make the variation more dramatic and kinetic than the verse, where the words hold the audience's attention. The song is based upon two bars of verse, with the second in each case allowing the vocals to the fore, while the 'chorus' (a loop of one bar) lacks any singing. However, the pitch bend upwards on the fourth beat of each of the chorus' bars is crucial, creating a fever pitch of excitement, particularly when added to by the distorted and aggressive vocals. While these contrasting sections do not directly structure the visuals, the comprehensive musical structure establishes a time scheme onto which the audience locks during the succession of images. Musical structure, in the case of both songs, has a high degree of significance, setting up particular time schemes for the film to access momentarily before its successive passage to another attraction, be it another piece of music, visual spectacle, or violent set-piece (Gunning 1990: 61).

Incidental music and musical regime

Although the two pop video-like sequences are discrete, almost autonomous in the film, and the songs appear almost is if they were inserted into the film like a foreign object, there are connections between the songs and the film's musical underscore. Kalinak noted the growing practice of having a couple of songs in films, often gracing the main or end titles (1992: 187). These songs in the vast majority of cases sit alongside some form of underscore. At the same time, pop music has increasingly inflected the underscores for films (Donnelly 2001a: 102–3), and the composer of the incidental music for *Hardware*, Simon Boswell, came to film scoring from a background in pop music, producing pop records by artists as diverse as chart star Amii Stewart and experimental pop group 23 Skidoo. Boswell (1990) described his score for *Hardware* 'as if a Celtic Ry Cooder on acid had discovered God and decided to write an opera ... [climaxing in] a scene in heaven – with Jimi Hendrix, Stravinski and the Moscow State Choir all jamming in a very small room'.

Boswell's score consists of the synthetic sounds that have become commonplace since the widespread availability of easily programmed and pre-set keyboard synthesizers and MIDI equipment in the middle of the 1980s. The music provides continuity for the film in that it has a recurrent theme and uses recurring devices and timbres. Perhaps the most commonplace device, the deep synthetic drone which adds tension to the image, has become one of the staples of electronic film scoring, as embodied by John Carpenter's music for his own films. Electronic drones are endemic in *Hardware*, providing a kind of aural wallpaper or ambience for the action and for the regular appearance of the film's main theme, which subtly intrudes. This is composed of a five note melody that contains two dramatic semitone falls in pitch, all accompanied by a droning bass note. The musical tension supplies a sense of unease across the whole film. The motif is established in the opening sequence of the film preceding the titles, where the theme is interpolated with minimal ancillary melodies including a short slide guitar figure that directly connotes Ry Cooder's music for *Paris, Texas* (Wim Wenders, 1984), especially as the image track shows a desert. The immediate connotation is of the music in spaghetti westerns,[15] referencing the frantic Spanish guitar in the scores of Ennio Morricone and others.[16] The music at this point is communicating with the audience through the use of overcoded musical instrument sound and musical genre. This playful use of music – having a mentally-processed effect rather than a purely subconscious effect – reflects the self-conscious use of music in the film as a whole. The music is not wholly unfamiliar. The film's main theme is often played on a string synthesizer, thus sounding like the banks of strings that provide more traditional orchestral underscores.

A moment of particular interest occurs when orchestral music rises from the midst of the synthetic underscore. It is Rossini's 'Stabat Mater' and comprises a substantial section in itself. Like the music, the film at this point is elegiac and slow (although there is a brief intercut section where Jill is revived downstairs). The 'Stabat Mater' plays as Mark 13 watches over the dying Mo, with the sequence including an extraordinary vision of Mark 13 as part of a crucifix formation with three television sets. The film is fairly explicit in its staging of the crucifixion to accompany music about the Virgin Mary's anguish at her child's fate.

In fact, the film opens with an epigraph card containing a Biblical quotation: 'No flesh shall be spared' from the Book of Mark, Chapter 13. This Biblical quotation adds a playful yet portentous edge to the film's unfolding, as well as helping to fulfil the traditional science fiction function of warning about potential developments already under way in the present. Indeed, the film has been retitled in some quarters as *M.A.R.K.13* to fully exploit the film's Biblical references, which also include a central character being called 'Moses' who, as he dies, informs Mark 13 that he is 'divinely protected'. Mo reads the Bible aloud, from the Book of Mark, Chapter 13: 'No flesh shall be spared … the earth will shake, rattle and roll.' The film has included so many pop music references that an immediate reaction might be to read this as a reference to the Big Joe Turner/Bill Haley & the Comets song. This quotation appears to marry the film's Biblical references with its esoteric pop/rock discourse, underlined by the conversion of Rossini's religious piece into a sequence that arguably resembles a pop video.

Conclusion

The two main strategies for music in science fiction films have been to contain futuristic music as a counterpart to a futuristic world on screen, or to provide a frame for these representations through wielding contemporary-styled music, in order to make traditional emotional and formal effects. While the score to *Hardware* does both to some degree, the film contains an insistent and fairly coherent musical strand that is wholly indifferent to the concept of the future or the film's representations.

Gunning has noted the similarity between some contemporary cinema and the 'attractionism' of early cinema (1990: 61). His approach sees film as a grab bag of effects and fragments of (often discrete) interest, rather than a fully-integrated work. Overarching narrative is therefore of less importance, and micro-narratives and incident tend to be of more interest. Thinking along these lines, perhaps 'the future' is less important in *Hardware*'s equation, as it is merely one of a selection of attractions. 'The future' is merely a pretext for 'readymades' of disaster which dystopian representations allow (war, radiation, technology, violence). Other elements of the film can take on more significance, and in the case of *Hardware*, music seems to have a degree of importance in the film that has almost no direct bearing upon the film's narrative or diegetic world. Within the body of *Hardware* the pop/rock songs presented like pop videos and the esoteric references function as discrete attractions and micro-narratives which break up the narrative elision. It remains another (almost independent) dimension in the film, setting up its own time schemes (of regulated musical time) and not bowing to those of cinematic convention. The dual context of the pop/rock music (within and without the film) means that it signifies intertextually, relating to the specifics of the music itself and the pop music discourse outside of the film's bounds.

Hardware was partially shot at the Roundhouse in Camden Town, London. This was a famed venue for rock music in the late 1960s, particularly 'psychedelic' groups like Pink Floyd and the Pretty Things. This shadow seems to have hung over *Hardware*, feeding its interest in pop/rock music, which has translated into a solid strand throughout the film. Pop/rock music is essential to the film, less as a part of the action and more as a self-referential object in its own right. *Hardware* thus demonstrates that pop music can function as an esoteric discourse within films, relying on extra-filmic knowledge for its effect, something which underlines the contemporary nature of the music and undermines the functioning of the music within the diegetic 'future' constructed by the film.

Notes

1 *Hardware* was a co-production of British film producers Palace Pictures, television company subsidiary Film on Four International, and the American production company Miramax (which later became a major Hollywood player).
2 In addition to its traditionally-styled film score, *Star Wars* also contained some 'futuristic' diegetic music played by the Cavatina Band in the film.
3 Some orchestrally-based scores aimed to mix the familiar and the unfamiliar, embracing the more dissonant sounds associated with twentieth-century art music. The best example was the *Alien* series, in particular Jerry Goldsmith's score for the first movie, *Alien* (Ridley Scott, 1979), which combined unfamiliar instruments (including electronics) and discordant orchestral harmonies to aid depiction of the exotic antagonist of the film's title.
4 Stanley went on to make *Dust Devil* (1992), a documentary about voodoo; and later was removed from directing the Hollywood production of *The Island of Dr Moreau* (John Frankenheimer, 1996).
5 This may be seen in the light of the disintegration of narrative in postmodern textuality, where it is no longer the omnipotent ruler of the text, but has had to cede prominence to other elements.
6 Although the soundtrack album also includes a piece of music that is credited to Lemmy and Kaduta Massi, and which appears consonant with the character of some of the film's incidental music.
7 The 'futurist' movement of early 1980s British pop music was at least partially inspired by the technological possibilities of cheap synthesizers. One of the principal groups of the time, Heaven 17, took their name from a fictitious group of the future in *A Clockwork Orange* (Stanley Kubrick, 1971).
8 Indeed, there is a paucity of pop songs about the future. Songs like Zager & Evans' 'In The Year 2525' and Sarah Brightman's 'I Lost My Heart to a Starship Trooper' lack any solid sense of 'futuristic' style, the idea of which is manifested almost wholly in the lyrics.
9 As I write this, twelve years after *Hardware*'s release, both Iggy Pop and Lemmy are as much alternative pop icons as they were twelve years before its release.
10 This song also appears at the end of the film, as radio DJ Angry Bob tells his listeners that Mark 13 is going to be mass-produced. The audience is then shown Carl McCoy walking in the Zone, after which the song continues across the film's end-titles.
11 It was released in a significantly different version as 'The Slab' on the unofficial Public Image Limited album 'Commercial Zone', also in 1984. This was a consequence of the group splitting and John Lydon re-recording the album to erase the work of the departed Keith Levene who, in turn, released the originally recorded tapes as an unofficial LP.
12 Upon the first guitar entry Mark 13's eye lights up, and upon the inauguration of the guitar tune's second block of four bars the film cuts to a *Psycho*-referencing shower shot (from underneath the shower head). The cut to images of sex arrives at the point of a dramatic chord change (from I minor to IV Major).
13 When I interviewed Richard Stanley, I asked him about this section. He was proud to have included footage that had been seen as problematic by censors, but was sceptical about the alleged 'snuff' status of the images.

14 The activities on television parallel those in Jill's flat. As Mark 13 slashes Jill's bed, the film cuts to images of butchery on television.
15 Boswell's score for Stanley's next film, *Dust Devil*, featured an Ennio Morricone spaghetti western-style melody as the main theme.
16 The film has few distinct musical cues, with only a few bursts of action music interrupting the deep droning synthesizer continuity. Slide guitar only occasionally appears after it has adorned the film's opening title sequence, such as during some of Jill's sculpting as well as accompanying images of the city at night.

Chapter Ten

'Music Inspired By...': The Curious Case of the Missing Soundtrack

Lee Barron

Introduction: I Don't Remember Hearing That Song...

Discussions of the relationship between film and music are not new; nor are discussions of the relationship between film and popular music. It is, as Mark Kermode has suggested, an association which is 'long-standing and multifarious. At its best, pop music can inspire and enliven directors; it can accompany, counterpoint, boost or ironically comment upon their visual work in a unique and sometimes spine-tingling manner' (1995: 11). Indeed, the precise moment at which this relationship came into being has been identified:

> When Richard Brooks decided to use Bill Haley and his Comets' 'Rock Around The Clock' as the theme tune to *The Blackboard Jungle* in 1955, he lent the film a sparkling air of 'now-ness' which no amount of scriptwriting or directing could have achieved. Despite the fact that the film featured no pop music other than in its opening and closing credits, *The Blackboard Jungle* has gone down in history as 'the first rock film' acknowledging the

awesome power of Haley's music to capture a critical moment in American social history. (ibid.)

The use of rock and pop music within film was to continue throughout the following decades, resulting in the routine appearance of the soundtrack album, which deftly allowed audiences to enjoy again the selection of songs utilised by directors; some, like 'Saturday Night Fever' became multi-million sellers. However, these albums would also become an increasingly intrinsic part of the overall merchandising package surrounding film releases. *Star Wars* (George Lucas, 1977), *Batman* (Tim Burton, 1989), *Shrek* (Andrew Adamson & Vicky Jenson, 2001), *Harry Potter and the Philosopher's Stone* (Chris Columbus, 2001) and *Lord of the Rings: The Fellowship of the Ring* (Peter Jackson, 2001) clearly possess enormous merchandising potential, of which soundtracks constitute only a small part. However, as Carla Freccero has noted, 'in recent years, the soundtrack album has become a genre unto itself, regardless of the quality, popularity or genre of the film, and sometimes with little or no relation to the narrative of the film' (1999: 91). What the near-obligatory release of soundtrack albums achieves is the provision of merchandising opportunities to films without obvious marketing potential, such as *An Officer and a Gentleman* (Taylor Hackford, 1982) and *Robin Hood: Prince of Thieves* (Kevin Reynolds, 1991) – successful films, but films not readily amenable to the conventional paraphernalia of linked commodities which includes toys, action figures, lunch boxes, comic strips, computer games, books, T-shirts and fast-food deals.

As a result, the use of popular music has become increasingly mandatory as a means of investing movies with a broader commercial presence. However, this might be seen to present an apparent problem for those which contain no, or very little, music *per se*. In response to this potential dilemma, a convenient solution has been simply to draw in popular songs under the mantle of 'songs inspired by the motion picture'.

The starting-point for this chapter can be traced back to my own first acknowledgement of the implications of the words 'music from and inspired by the motion picture'. Seeking to obtain a techno-dance track that accompanied a key scene from *Blade* (Stephen Norrington, 1998) in which vampires attend an illicit rave, I promptly purchased the soundtrack album. Not knowing the artist or name of the track, I eagerly put on the CD and waited. Eventually, by track 12, my patience was rewarded with New Order's 'Confusion', duly followed by other tracks I recognised from the film, by Expansion Union, DJ Krush and Junkie XL. But the majority of the songs on tracks 1-11 were absent from the original movie.

Although the CD is an attractive and enjoyable collection, and features songs by leading hip-hop performers whose lyrics do reflect some of the themes of the film, their inclusion on the soundtrack conflicts with their absence in the film.

In order to explain and illuminate these increasingly common contemporary practices, my intention is to revisit the concept of synergy in a manner which complements earlier discussions by Kermode (1995), K. J. Donnelly (1998a) and John Mundy (1999). However, I also want to examine some of the developments that have occurred since those discussions, in order to demonstrate the ways in which the soundtrack is increasingly acquiring an independent status as a cultural product *in its own right*. Where once, in their (often) orchestral form, they were the objects of desire for the dedicated film fan, they are now increasingly targeted at mainstream audiences. Furthermore, the use of soundtrack albums shows no signs of diminishing; rather, it is subtly changing to accommodate market needs and to take advantage of developments in CD technology to represent the patterns of synergy yet more effectively. And while my analysis will refer to various contemporary examples, I will specifically use the example of 'Josh's Blair Witch Mix' from the *The Blair Witch Project* (Daniel Myrick and Eduardo Sanchez, 1999) as a soundtrack album that clarifies and illustrates the concept of 'music inspired by'.

The soundtrack album, flexible accumulation, and the return of synergy

The most obvious conceptual tool with which to discuss the developments of the soundtrack album is that of synergy. In this context, synergy is that practice by which media products can be utilised to advertise or support other media products. Edward Herman and Robert McChesney have suggested that the activities of the Disney corporation provide a compelling demonstration of the nature and process of synergy:

> When Disney ... produces a film, it can also guarantee the film's showing on pay cable television and commercial network television, and it can produce and sell soundtracks based on the film, it can create spin-off television series, it can produce related amusement park rides, CD-Roms, books, comics and merchandise to be sold in Disney retail stores. (1997: 54)

Synergy is most closely associated with the nature of ownership and control of the media industries, and the drive towards their global expansion (Tunstall & Palmer 1991; Morley & Robins 1995). The creators of this potentially universal cultural space are the international entertainment and media corporations, whose strategies and practices demonstrate three levels of ownership: the studio, producing film, television and music; the distributor of media products, typified by MTV; the manufacturers of hardware. Of course, the primary objective for 'the real global players is to operate across two or even all three of these options' (Morley & Robins 1995: 13). The key to this lies in diversification and flexibility, policies which are grounded in social and structural consequences:

> The postwar boom from 1945 to 1973 was based on a Fordist-Keynesian system, but there has been a shift from Fordism to what might be called a 'flexible' regime of accumulation ... masses of capital and workers shift from one line of production to another, leaving whole sectors devastated, while the perpetual flux in consumer wants, tastes and needs becomes a permanent locus of uncertainty and struggle. (Sarup 1996: 99)

The cultural ramifications of this shift are far reaching:

> Flexible accumulation has been accompanied on the consumption side by a much greater attention to quick-changing fashions ... the relatively stable aesthetic of Fordist modernism has given way to all the ferment, instability, and fleeting qualities of a postmodernist aesthetic that celebrates difference, ephemerality, spectacle, fashion, and the commodification of cultural forms. (Harvey 1989: 156)

Furthermore, these processes have had significant effects upon the structure and form of media corporations:

> We are seeing the emergence of decentred corporations in which diverse media products (film and television, press and publishing, music and video) are being combined into overarching communications empires ... various forms of horizontal alignment are apparent, at both national and international levels, with new alliances between broadcasters, film and television producers, publishers, record producers and so on. (Morley & Robins 1995: 32)

The flexible accumulation economic systems envisioned by David Harvey are increasingly witnessing the fusion of information technologies with forms of entertainment. Media industry mergers of recent years, such as the $7.5 billion incorporation of Time-Life and Warner Communications, and the $37 billion merger of Viacom and CBS, reflected this tendency, while the $163.4 billion amalgamation in 2001 of Time-Warner and America On-Line (AOL) has resulted in an industrial-cultural conglomerate that combines a formidable range of media forms, including television, film, magazine, newspapers, books, information databases and personal computers; its union of media and computer culture has been seen as a key moment in the evolution of the 'infotainment society' (Best & Kellner 2001).

Within this economic/entertainment 'technocapitalist' culture therefore, the role of cultural products is especially significant; and this is particularly true of cinema, since 'the 'big screen' film is now just the beginning of a profit stream involving television, home video, CDs, computer games, clothing and so forth' (Smith 1998: 13). Thus, whereas the music to be found on the soundtrack album would originally function to set the mood, or convey character emotion, or heighten the dramatic impact of a film, its 'musical wallpaper' has now leapt from the screen to become a product in its own right:

> In recent years there has been a notable trend towards the youth promotion of often unremarkable films via rock and pop music tie-ins. Although this is nothing new, the 1980s saw a previously unparalleled explosion of the 'pop promotion' gimmick with often artistically bankrupt results, thanks largely to the rise of music video as a primary marketing tool. Ever since Joe Cocker and Jennifer Warnes hit the Top Twenty in 1982 with 'Up Where We Belong' ... for which the much played video was essentially an advertisement for *An Officer and a Gentleman*, producers and distributors have been loathe to overlook such potential free publicity. By the time Tony Scott's *Top Gun* (1986) passed into movie lore as the quintessential pop-promo 'feature', the 1980s had already become the decade of the 'pop soundtrack'. (Kermode 1995: 17)

Alongside *Top Gun*, films of the 1980s such as *Flashdance* (Adrian Lyne, 1983), *Ghostbusters* (Ivan Reitman, 1984), *Footloose* (Herbert Ross, 1984), *Beverly Hills Cop* (Martin Brest, 1984) and *St Elmo's Fire* (Joel Schumacher, 1985) produced related hit singles. This list has continued to grow through the 1990s and beyond: Wet Wet Wet's 'Love Is All Around' from *Four Weddings and a Funeral* (Mike Newell, 1994), Bryan Adams' 'Everything I Do' from *Robin Hood: Prince of Thieves*, Celine Dion's 'My Heart Will Go On' from *Titanic* (James Cameron, 1997) and Faith Hill's 'There You'll Be' from *Pearl Harbor* (Michael Bay, 2001). Crucially, and in all cases, the accompanying music videos contain not merely the performers, but a substantial montage of images from the films. In the case of Bryan Adams, his single 'Everything I Do' remained at Number One in the British charts for 17 weeks, thus affording a massive and consistent positive exposure for the film it promoted. And although soundtrack albums were, at this time, increasingly splitting into two genres – the composer's score and the pop album – it is notable that even in the late 1990s, 'traditional' soundtracks could still become huge hits. James Horner's soundtrack for *Titanic* and Hans Zimmer's orchestral albums for *The Thin Red Line* (Terrence Malick, 1999) and *Gladiator* (Ridley Scott, 2000) were commercial successes.

At the same time, however, 'the soundtrack album' underwent a strange conceptual mutation:

> Recent years have also seen the rise of a bizarre phenomenon in which two, or even three, music albums from the same film are released simultaneously, one featuring the score, another the songs, and yet another languishing under the weirdly conceptual banner of 'songs inspired by the movie' ... the 1994 British blockbuster *Four Weddings and a Funeral* spawned a soundtrack album in which the entire incidental score is reduced to a five-minute medley, while a wide-ranging collection of classic pop love songs packs out the rest of the album. Almost none of these songs appear in the movie but, cleverly intercut with snippets of dialogue from the film, they have served as an extraordinarily successful promotional item. (Kermode 1995: 19)

The significance of this development has also been noted by Donnelly:

> Soundtrack LPs provide a space for the plenitude of music; what may have been a few seconds and hardly noticed in the film can be enjoyed as an aesthetic object in its own right, its own logic undiluted by the exigencies of the film. *Batman* was the first film to institute the release of two soundtrack LPs, a strategy that has become more common since, examples being *Dick Tracy* (three LPs), *Addams Family Values*, *The Crow* and *Forrest Gump* (two LPs, one of them double). In each case, these soundtracks reveal a division of the films' music into orchestral and song compilations. (1998a: 145)

Donnelly focuses his attention on case studies of the scores for *Batman* (Tim Burton, 1989) and *Batman Returns* (Tim Burton, 1992), in which he investigates the relationship between Danny Elfman's scores and Prince's song-based album. Although his observations emphasise the continuing relevance of 'traditional' incidental scores, he notes that the secondary 'pop' album plays a new and central role in the promotion of popular motion pictures:

> *Batman* involves a cohabitation of Elfman's score with Prince's songs. Although the songs are marginalized, and indeed much of Prince's LP does not grace the film, it manifests an extension of the text beyond its traditional boundaries to include intersecting aesthetic products ... The album and the film are two separate works ... in two different media, complementing and supporting each other. (ibid.: 144–5)

As the 1990s progressed, these characteristics intensified and evolved. *The Matrix* (Wachowski Brothers, 1999) spawned two albums. One contained the original score by composer Don Davis; the second, and far more popular, album comprised dance/rock tracks by performers such as Prodigy, Propellerheads, Rob D, Rob Zombie, Marilyn Manson, Deftones, Monster Magnet, Meat Beat Manifesto, Rammstein and Rage Against The Machine. The motivation for an album which includes these tracks is twofold. First, such performers lend a controversial 'edge' and cultural credibility to the film. Secondly, if, as has been argued (Jenkins 1992), fandom constitutes an alternative social (and subcultural) community characterised by informed cultural consumption, the opportunity to tap into this fan community is potentially very profitable. Indeed, many fans may well purchase a soundtrack album which features a new track by their favourite performer, irrespective of their enjoyment or knowledge of the movie itself. Thus, *The Saint* (Philip Noyce, 1998) received generally mediocre reviews and disappointing box-office returns, whereas the soundtrack album attracted considerable interest because of its contributions from leading dance acts like Orbital, Moby, the Chemical Brothers, Daft Punk and Underworld.

Furthermore, there is an opportunity for 'playfulness' and novelty afforded to musicians who contribute to such soundtracks which has considerable appeal to the dedicated music fan. By playfulness, I mean the degree to which soundtracks can allow artists to experiment or record tracks that might otherwise fall outside their usual style. The rhythm section of U2, Adam Clayton and Larry Mullen, contributed their re-working of Lalo Schifrin's original television series theme to the soundtrack of *Mission Impossible* (Brian De Palma, 1996); Limp Bizkit repeated the exercise for *Mission Impossible II* (John Woo, 2000). Apollo Four Forty similarly re-interpreted the original television series theme for *Lost in Space* (Stephen Hopkins, 1998) and, like Orbital's theme music from *The Saint*, all became Top Twenty hits.

The logic which demands promotional videos that stress the attractions of the movie in order to reach the widest possible audience leads to differing outcomes. While marketing requirements may be satisfied, this development can threaten the integrity and mood of the albums, and may stray from the composer's own musical vision. And of course, the inclusion of such tracks may not always be made by those closely connected with the film's production. Kermode has reported that 'director Ridley Scott was forced by Universal executive Sidney Jay Sheinberg to scrap Jerry Goldsmith's orchestral score for the Tom Cruise fantasy *Legend* (1985) in favour of a soundtrack by Tangerine Dream … Sheinberg insisted that a more 'accessible' sound was needed to attract the youth audience' (1995: 19). That Tangerine Dream were perceived as the sound of 'youth' might be seen to reveal much about executive conceptions of popular music and its audiences; but nonetheless, the drive towards market accessibility is still the prerogative, no matter what violence may be done to the composer's initial ideas.

It should be stressed that there is nothing intrinsically cynical or deceitful in utilising popular music. Martin Scorsese has skilfully and convincingly demonstrated its effectiveness from *Mean Streets* (1972) to *Bringing Out the Dead* (1999). David Lynch's soundtrack for *Lost Highway* (1997) impressively combined Angelo Badalamenti's jazz-based score with songs by David Bowie, Smashing Pumpkins and Rammstein. And Dario Argento's consistent use of Goblin's music in *Profondo Rosso* (1975), *Suspiria* (1977), *Tenebrae* (1982), *Phenomena* (1984) and *Sleepless* (2001) has contributed much to the atmospheric quality of his films.

But while these are examples of music that is broadly and consciously part of the film narrative, there does remain a certain cynicism over the use of some particular songs. Many albums have been employed as vehicles through which record companies can dispose of previously unreleased tracks, which often have little connection – in form or content – to the movie. Moby's 'Flower', which is included on the soundtrack album of *Gone in Sixty Seconds* (Dominic Sena, 2000) is remarkably similar to the fusion of 1930s blues and contemporary dance beats that characterised his multi-million-selling 'Play' album, and appears to be an unreleased song from those sessions rather than a specially recorded piece reflecting the themes of the film. The desire to have a hit single remains paramount.

In recent years, an additional strategy has been the release of soundtracks which combine the conventional instrumental score with (often incongruously) a popular song. An early example was *Titanic*, in which the Celtic strains of James Horner's theme provided the backdrop to Celine Dion's 'My Heart Goes On', which became a huge hit and whose video featured extensive footage from the film. But, if you will excuse the pun, this would prove to be merely the tip of the iceberg. Post-*Titanic*, many soundtrack albums adopted the same strategy: Tan Dun's theme for *Crouching Tiger, Hidden Dragon* (Ang Lee, 2000) was supplemented by Coco Lee's 'A Love Before Time', Hans Zimmer's score for *Pearl Harbor* by Faith Hill's 'There You'll Be', and Howard Shore's incidental music for *Lord of the Rings: The Fellowship of the Ring* by Enya's 'May It Be'. Extensions of this idea can be seen on soundtrack albums such as Gabriel Yared's music for *City of Angels* (Brad Silberling, 1998), Billy Corgan's score for *Stigmata* (Rupert Wainwright, 1999) and Thomas Newman's theme for *American Beauty* (Sam Mendes, 1999), all of which combined incidental scores with collections of rock and pop songs from performers such as U2, Alanis Morissette, Jimi Hendrix, John Lee Hooker, Peter Gabriel, Eric Clapton, Goo Goo Dolls, Massive Attack, Natalie Imbruglia, Eels and The Who.

The curious case of the missing soundtrack: The Blair Witch Project

As first noted in Mark Kermode's observations about *Four Weddings and a Funeral*, within these overall strategies, a novel and audacious development has been a tendency to include tracks that may not appear at all in the films themselves, but creep in under the ambiguous justification of 'music inspired by the film'. A notable example of this is 'The X Files' associated album, 'Songs in the Key of X', which appears to consist of nothing more than the personal choices of the television programme's creator, Chris Carter. Although some of the tracks have filtered into the show (Nick Cave & the Bad Seeds' 'Red Right Hand') most have not, since the episodes are largely scored by Mark Snow's eerie keyboard-laden incidental music. 'Songs in the Key of X' was followed by 'The X Files: The Album', released to tie in with the movie *The X Files: Fight the Future* (Rob Bowman, 1998), and a second album, containing Snow's incidental score for the film, was also released at the same time. 'The X Files: The Album' contains some tracks which are present in the movie (Noel Gallagher's 'Teotihuacan', X's 'Crystal Ship') and others which are not (Mike Oldfield's 'Tubular X'). It also includes a 'hidden track' – a spoken narrative that reveals in detail the nature of the 'conspiracy' that has shaped the television series and the film. The track's inclusion is illustrative of a tactic that has characterised the science-fiction/fantasy market in recent years, whereby tie-in novels, DVDs, comics, videos, computer games, board games and trading cards are among additional texts promoted as part of general film- or programme-lore.

This synergistic function can proceed in other ways too. The soundtrack album to *Blade* identifies the film's star, Wesley Snipes, as the 'Soundtrack Album Executive Producer' allowing him – through his choice of tracks – to engage in a form of horizontal diversification and participate in the production of texts in a manner additional to that of his status as actor.

However, the most acute and revealing example of the incorporation of the soundtrack into a film's merchandising package can be seen in the design and promotion of *The Blair Witch Project*. 'The Blair Witch Project: Josh's Blair Witch Mix' is perhaps unique, in that it is the musical soundtrack to a film that has no musical soundtrack. *The Blair Witch Project* was a film that confounded all expectations to become a huge box-office success and which defied 'any easy categorization ... the story of three student film-makers who go missing in the Maryland woods while making a documentary about the myth of the Blair Witch [provided] a new twist on the horror genre' (Roscoe 2000: 3).

But despite the contradiction of a soundtrack to a film from which music is missing, the context, narrative and invented world of *The Blair Witch Project* informed and determined in very precise ways the subsequent release of that album. The film used

> documentary codes and conventions to construct a 'plausible reality' ... Myrick and Sanchez employed extra-textual material such as websites, advertising and a separate short documentary, *The Curse of the Blair Witch*, to further enhance this reality, a reality that plunged some of its audience into ontological doubt as to whether *The Blair Witch Project* was actually the missing Heather Donahue's documentary and the footage really discovered in the Black Hills was telling her true story. (ibid.)

A key component of the movie was its technology: 'made on an extremely low budget, it exploited new video technologies and the Internet, which fostered tremendous subcultural interest in the phenomenon' (Best & Kellner 2001: 241). Although it quickly became quite evident that its three protagonists (Heather Donahue, Joshua Leonard and Michael Williams) were actors who were very much alive, the powers and processes of an unusually potent synergy were soon at work. A variety of extra-textual spin-offs soon emerged, including a television documentary (*The Burkittsville 7*), an interactive computer game, and a teenage novel series. Perhaps the most notable, if only for its meticulous (re)construction, was a book, 'The Blair Witch Project: A Dossier' (Stern 1999), which documented the entire 'history' of the Blair Witch, was peppered with extracts of old manuscripts and police interviews from the investigation into the students' disappearance, and which repeated much of the material propagated by the film's official website that had contributed greatly to the word-of-mouth rumouring surrounding the film's success. This 'history' bears repeating here, since it was to serve as the platform upon which the film was erected, and helped to justify and explain the existence of the soundtrack album.

The tale of the Blair Witch begins in 1785 when, in a village in the Black Hills, Maryland, the reclusive Elly Kedward, accused of luring children into her home in order to draw blood from them, is found guilty of witchcraft and banished during a severe winter. By the midwinter of 1786, all the children who had accused Kedward, and many of the village's other children have mysteriously disappeared, and the settlement is abandoned. In 1824, Burkittsville is founded on a site near the original village. In 1886, eight-year-old Robin Weaver disappears, and search parties are sent out to find her. The girl returns but one of the search parties does not; their bodies are found some weeks later at Coffin Rock, tied down and disembowelled. The story re-emerges in November 1940, when seven children from Burkittsville disappear within six months. In 1941, a hermit, Rustin Parr confesses that he is responsible for their murders. The police find the children's bodies in the cellar of his house deep in the woods; all have been disembowelled. During police interrogation, Parr claims that a voice in his head, 'an old woman', had ordered him to kill the children. He is found guilty of the crimes and hanged. In 1994, Heather, Michael and Josh go into the woods and are not seen alive again, except on their video footage which is later discovered, edited and released as *The Blair Witch Project* in 1999.

It is the attempt to 'continue' this story that provides the underlying principle of 'Josh's Blair Witch Mix'. The only music in the film is the unattributed and indistinct grunge-like rock song played by Josh on the radio/cassette equipment in his car; this tape becomes the hook upon which the soundtrack album is hung. In passing, it is the lack of a score that immediately distinguishes the movie from most other horror films where, typically, a jarring musical soundtrack is perceived as one of the crucial ways in which the film attains its psychological impact (Urbano 1998).

The absence of any music stems from the conditions under which filming took place, which demanded that the actors were physically alone for the eight days of the shoot. Donahue, Williams and Leonard were sent into the woods to improvise elements of the film, assisted only by directorial notes left at checkpoint positions. Since they filmed much of the material themselves, there was no out-of-frame activity from a film crew. The sounds made at night, such as children crying, were the work of the film's directors and producer; they actually occur within the narrative and are not the products of added post-production sound effect technology (Collis, 1999). Sanchez and Myrick have explained: 'We wanted to shoot this thing in such a way that when you see it on the screen, it looks totally genuine, like a real documentary, like a real home movie' (Roscoe 2000: 5). Therefore, the characters hear the sounds in exactly the same way that the audience does.

But this novel approach to diegetic sound created an obvious problem for the release of an accompanying soundtrack album. Ingeniously, the solution was to build the album into the mythos of the film and the legend of the Blair Witch, by announcing that the soundtrack was a reproduction of the tape found in Josh's car. Its 'official' status was enhanced by the dedication to be found on the inlay packaging: 'Dedicated to the memory of Heather, Mike and especially Josh, whose great taste in music inspired this album. R.I.P.' The logic of the story was completed by two additional pieces of information printed on the inlay:

October 16 1997 – All existing material is turned over to the Families of Heather Donahue, Joshua Leonard and Michael Williams. Included in the evidence is a cassette tape taken From Joshua Leonard's car stereo labelled 'Josh's Blair Witch Mix'. October 12 1999 – Joshua Leonard's family releases 'Josh's Blair Witch Mix' to Chapter III Records for examination.

To purchase 'Josh's Blair Witch Mix' is therefore to buy into the mythology of the Blair Witch. However, the existence of the soundtrack manifests not so much the curse of the Blair Witch, as the curse of synergy-seeking media economics:

Synergy between the music and screen industries has become part of our everyday experience. The number of chart-topping singles and albums based on, featuring in, or relating to films is growing, and is clear evidence of this contemporary symbiosis between the screen media, popular music, and other forms of contemporary entertainment. (Mundy 1999: 27)

The Blair Witch Project is a stark demonstration of this symbiosis; although lacking the chart-topping single, it has significantly expanded the boundaries of entertainment-based marketing. The musical content of its album goes beyond the smattering of irrelevant tracks on 'The X Files' and 'Blade' albums discussed above. Just as Heather, Michael and Josh mysteriously disappear into the ether, so too do the songs that make up the soundtrack. Of the 12 tracks, only one is identifiable from the film (the minimalist instrumental 'The Cellar' by Antonio Cora, that plays over the film's closing credits). The remaining 11 tracks – purportedly indicative of Josh's musical tastes – belong in a broad category of gothic, punk, industrial, underground or 'cult' musicians, and are uniformly characterised, as their titles illustrate, by a prevailing and (now that we know of Josh's fate) entirely prophetic sense of morbidity and doom: Lydia Lunch, 'Gloomy Sunday'; Public Image Limited, 'The Order of Death'; Skinny Puppy, 'Draining Faces'; Bauhaus, 'Kingdom's Coming'; The Creatures, 'Don't Go To Sleep Without Me'; Laibach, 'God is God'; Afghan Whigs, 'Beware'; Front Line Assembly, 'Laughing Pain'; Type O Negative: 'Haunted'; Meat Beat Manifesto, 'She's Unreal'; Tones on Tail, 'Movement of Fear'.

In addition, the songs are combined with extracts of dialogue from key moments of narrative – the beginning of the journey, the first hints that something is stalking them, and the film's most noted point-of-view sequence in which the anguished Heather rues her decision ever to pursue the Blair Witch legend. By allowing these snatches of dialogue to segue into the music, the validity of the form and the relevance of the content are emphasised. The interaction also creates a 'virtual' soundtrack, independent of the original film; and this status is complemented by its Enhanced CD format which contains 'rare and exclusive film footage' that can be accessed by personal computer. That the imagery of the film can be brought to the soundtrack via the consumer's personal computer again challenges the conventional musical-narrative relationship.

At every level, therefore, 'Josh's Blair Witch Mix' is a triumph of synergy, ably aided and abetted by contemporary technology. Indeed, the Enhanced CD illustrates the nature of synergy *within* a single product, through its seamless marriage of sound and image. The developments illustrated by 'Josh's Blair Witch Mix' and other Enhanced CDs, such as Eric Serra's score for *The Fifth Element* (Luc Besson, 1999) which offers the possibility to simultaneously connect to the film's official website, provide the listener/viewer with a direct conduit into what has been variously termed the 'network society' (Castells 1996) or the synergy-driven realm of the new 'infotainment society' (Best & Kellner 2001).

Conclusion

Soundtrack albums are not simply items of commodity fetishism; nor are they products without artistic merit. Many of the albums discussed above – including 'Josh's Blair Witch Mix' – are interesting and enjoyable collections. But their claim to be 'official' film soundtracks is brazen and misleading. Both film and musician can benefit equally from the combinations of popular music and film;

synergistic practices bring benefits that are not merely uni-directional. In another context, this was made evident through the 'discovery' of the Versace-clad actress/ model Elizabeth Hurley at the premiere of *Four Weddings and a Funeral* which featured Wet Wet Wet's 'Love Is All Around' single. Thus, while…

> *that* dress did wonders for her own profile … it also enhanced the image of Versace. Front-page colour pictures in newspapers such as the Sun, the Mirror and the Evening Standard, as well as the broadsheets, turned Versace into a household name that functioned as a byword for show-stopping, sexy clothes. (Buckley & Gundle 2000: 341)

In this instance the process of synergism manifested itself on four distinct levels; it boosted Elizabeth Hurley's film and modelling career; it raised Versace's profile; advertised *Four Weddings and a Funeral*; which in turn helped Wet Wet Wet remain at Number One in the British charts for several weeks. Therefore, synergy's ability to assist all parties makes it the spur to creative marketing; and as technological advances continue, the opportunities can only increase. Significant developments may be already occurring. The DVD version of *The Ninth Gate* (Roman Polanski, 1999) allows the user to isolate Wojciech Kilar's incidental score (which is also available as a soundtrack album) and may herald the start of a process in which, if the DVD continues to displace video, purchase of the official soundtrack might similarly become redundant.

But until this becomes the case, the crucial element driving the desire to associate rock and pop songs with film releases is the search for mutual profit. Soundtrack albums are 'big business … the $1 million advance paid by Giant Records for the soundtrack for *New Jack City* was rewarded with sales of over two million album units. The soundtrack album from *Saturday Night Fever* has, to date, sold in excess of twenty million units' (Mundy 1999: 27).

It is hardly surprising therefore that producers remain keen to persuade popular musicians to contribute to film soundtrack albums, either as stand-alone products or as counterpoints to more traditional incidental themes. At the time of writing, a second album of music from *Moulin Rouge* (Baz Lurhman, 2001) has been released. It contains re-workings of those songs originally contained in the official soundtrack, performed here on versions which do not appear in the film, by musicians such as George Michael, Robbie Williams, David Bowie and T. Rex. Hence, in the true spirit of the synergy of the soundtrack album (and its economic rewards), it would appear that performers, producers and consumers alike seem set to continue to be 'inspired by the motion picture'.

Chapter Eleven

CASE STUDY 2: *THE BIG CHILL*

Melissa Carey and Michael Hannan

Jeff Smith's (1998) comprehensive historical guide to the practice of cross-marketing films and their soundtracks clearly demonstrates that the introduction of popular music forms into film was an important commercial device. The various stages in this development included the composition of title songs from which thematic material for underscoring could be derived, the composition of themes specifically designed for success on the popular music charts, and the composition of popular songs to assist the cues that form part of a film's narrative. However, since the 1960s, an increasing number of soundtracks have been constructed through the simple compilation of pre-existing popular songs, so that the practice of using freshly composed popular music has now been largely abandoned in favour of an exclusive reliance on existing recorded music.

The introduction of popular songs and themes to the movie soundtrack can be seen as a challenge to the traditional function of music in film. While it is widely understood that music has the psychological power to influence the viewer's feelings about a particular scene, without the viewer being aware of such manipulations (Gorbman 1987: 11–30), the use of existing and familiar songs, rather than a composed score, would seem to contest this. Popular songs, particularly in their lyrics and hooks, draw attention to themselves; in addition, they appear to be particularly unsuitable for underscore (as distinct from their diegetic use) because their naturalistic use is constrained by listener expectations of structure, duration, metre and mood consistency. By concentrating our examination on the placement and use of popular songs in *The Big Chill* (Lawrence Kasdan, 1983) we hope to provide a particular and substantive case study of the manner in which they effectively fulfil the general and theoretical functions of music in film.

The theory of film scoring

David Huckvale employs the term 'soundworld' to describe the various interrelated elements of music, sound effects and dialogue in film (1990: 10). The soundworld itself, however, cannot be analysed in isolation:

> Image, sound effects, dialogue, and music track are virtually inseparable
> during the viewing experience; they form a *combinatoire* of expression …
> it is the narrative context, the interrelations between music and the rest of
> the film's system, that determines the effectiveness of film music. (Gorbman
> 1987: 12–16)

In this respect, the consumer's experience of film is qualitatively and immediately distinct from other media forms: 'in novels, the author tells you what the characters are feeling, but in film it is often the score that does this' (Karlin & Wright 1990: 131).

Many writers have identified the crucial function of the film score to be its role in the process of interpretation and the attribution of meaning. Thus, Claudia Gorbman has argued that 'music "anchors" the image in meaning … it expresses moods and connotations which, in conjunction with the images and other sounds, aid in interpreting narrative events and indicating moral/class/ethnic values of characters' (1987: 84). This insight has been expanded by Nicholas Cook, who agrees that music interprets words and pictures, but points out that while words and pictures have a denotative function, and music a connotative function, music itself does not possess a meaning, but 'a potential for the construction or negotiation of meaning in specific contexts … it is a bundle of generic attributes in search of an object' (1994: 39).

But how does music impart meaning? Gorbman has referred to the existence of various shared codes which help us extract meaning from music on several levels

(1987: 13). The most powerful of these are cultural codes: as suggested above, we associate particular styles of music, instrumentation and production sound with particular socio-economic communities, ethnic groups, historical events or geographical locations. In addition, over many years of film production, cinematic codes have also been established. Audiences have learned to recognise and expect conventions of music in film, such as title music and beginning/end themes.

More precisely, the placement of music in film falls into two broad categories: diegetic and non-diegetic. Diegetic music springs directly from the narrative, in which its 'source' can be observed on screen – music on record-players, radios or television, and music in live performance, both public and domestic. Popular music has been traditionally and extensively used in film to perform a diegetic function. Non-diegetic music is music which lacks any naturalistic connection to the narrative; often it is heard as background music which accompanies action on screen – a low ominous tone might, for example, be used to alert the viewer to imminent danger.

Of course, the distinction between diegetic and non-diegetic music is often less than straightforward. An intimate scene in a restaurant may be accompanied by appropriately romantic music which is non-diegetic (merely intended to reinforce the romantic mood, and thus heard only by the cinema audience), or diegetic (performed by musicians who are present in the restaurant, and thus heard by all of its customers). Indeed, in many cases, what is initially interpreted as non-diegetic is revealed on screen as diegetic.

Overall, the identified functions of music in film (Karlin & Wright 1990: 127–75; Gorbman 1987: 11–30) can be summarised in the following ways:

- to create a broad level of structural and stylistic unity, or musical 'concept'
- to create a sense of period, location, or cultural background: 'setting the scene'
- to provoke a sense of epic grandeur: 'monumentalising'
- to accompany and support action, such as providing a musical emphasis to sound effects
- to provide pacing, both in individual scenes and on a broader structural level
- to underscore dialogue
- to link scenes
- to emphasise or highlight movement, mood or humour
- to de-emphasise or contrast visual movement, mood or humour: to go 'against the grain'
- to show changes in moods and feelings, and accumulating emotional states
- to pre-empt the mood of an upcoming scene

- to play the thoughts of characters, rather than the actions
- to play an additional character, such as a ghost, or something imagined
- to provide a subtext: to inform the audience of events or circumstances of which the movie characters are unaware
- to flesh out the aural environment, contributing to a sense of spatial reality (diegetic music only)
- to provide another level of rhythm to the rhythm of the editor's 'cut'
- to follow the movement of the camera

Our analysis of *The Big Chill* seeks to demonstrate that many of these functions can be achieved just as effectively through the use of a compiled soundtrack of existing popular music songs as through the employment of a composed soundtrack.

The Big Chill

What happens when a close-knit group of typically idealistic college friends from the 1960s grow up and go their separate ways in the real world? Can their commitment to change, their hope for a better world, and their friendship survive? Or must they inevitably conform and surrender to the impersonal capitalistic mainstream ethic of middle-class America?

When, a decade on from their graduation, they are brought together by the suicide and funeral of Alex, the most idealistic and non-conformist of the group, the friends are forced to take stock of their lives and priorities. The reunion takes place at the South Carolina mansion of the wealthy Harold and Sarah Cooper; it is here that Alex slashed his wrists, in the bathroom of their summerhouse. They meet Chloe, Alex's rather quirky young girlfriend. The next few days and nights are spent renewing acquaintances, revisiting their shared past, and trying to come to terms with Alex's death. There is much soul searching as all of the group recall their earlier values and aspirations, and reflect on the trajectories along which their lives have travelled.

Chloe, who superficially seems to be remarkably self-contained and unaffected by Alex's death, soon makes a connection with Nick. Physically emasculated in Vietnam, Nick has drifted aimlessly through his life, consuming and dealing drugs, and routinely joking, like Alex did. Nick clearly reminds Chloe of Alex. The handsome and charming Sam has become a successful television star, playing the part of *J. T. Lancer*, but estranged from his wife and young daughter, he feels there is a shallowness and lack of purpose in his life. Homemaker and mother Karen, bored with her marriage, had always been attracted to Sam in college and comes to the funeral hoping for a romantic resurrection. She is not disappointed. Sam is happy to oblige, but ironically his presence influences Karen's eventual decision to stay within the security of her marriage.

Meg, who altruistically entered law to help the socially disadvantaged, only to find herself working in corporate real estate, has also arrived with a personal agenda. Watching her biological clock ticking away while searching unsuccessfully for the right man, she has determined to have a baby on her own, and is hoping to persuade one of the male friends to help her out. After she fails to make progress with the impotent Nick, the unwilling Sam and the unsuitable Michael, it is left to Sarah and Harold to resolve her dilemma. Sarah, a respected doctor, persuades Harold to help Meg. Harold has no more difficulty in accommodating this demand than he does in living with the daily contradiction between his former college values and his prosperous lifestyle as the owner of a chain of shoe stores.

As the weekend progresses, it becomes apparent to all that sharing and maintaining their friendship is more important than sharing and maintaining values and ideals. Despite the shifts and disruptions in their personal and professional lives, it is that friendship which serves to hold them together and give them hope for the future.

Musical concept

Fred Karlin and Rayburn Wright have stressed the importance of a defining 'concept' to give a score unity and 'a consistent attitude and style' (1990: 81). Whether musical or instrumental, its stylistic unity or coherence needs to reflect the location and temporal setting of the movie, the nature and attitudes of the central character(s), and the relevant dramatic themes.

In *The Big Chill*, score concept is clearly defined by a unifying musical period: hit songs (predominantly American) from 1963 to 1971. Five of the songs derive from Motown, one of the most successful and distinctive sources of popular music of the mid-1960s (Fitzgerald 1996: 346) and on whose label the film's soundtrack album (which includes around half of the songs featured in the movie) was released. The musical styles reflect both the characters and the theme of nostalgia for the idealism of youth. Although the movie's dramatic narrative is located in the 1980s, the soundtrack reveals that the story really begins in the 1960s. In addition, some specific songs, such as Marvin Gaye's 'I Heard it Through the Grapevine', are suggestive of the film's geographical location: the 'deep south'.

Although a successful film score provides 'a clear and focused tone' (Karlin & Wright 1990: 96), the nature of that tone or attitude or mood may change, often radically, as the story unfolds. Shifts within movies from comedy to drama to action require commensurate musical shifts in tone, while maintaining relevance to concept. *The Big Chill* establishes its score concept (familiar hits from the 1960s), but then utilises various musical styles within this broader category (Motown, pop, soul, surf music, rock, country rock) to provide a variety of moods appropriate to the drama. Although it is constructed around the aftermath of a suicide, *The Big Chill* was promoted as a 'compassionate comedy' rather than a tragic drama, and the choice of music – many of the songs are cheerful and upbeat – reflects this attitude.

Tied to this underlying concept is the theme of nostalgia. *The Big Chill* presents an idealised memory of a time when things were better, before the friends all 'grew up' to go their separate ways. Among the eight types of soundtrack which may be used in contemporary movies, as discussed by Rebecca Coyle, is the 'old hits soundtrack, featuring songs known and loved from bygone eras' (1998a: 6). This is the category to which *The Big Chill* belongs, and which at the same time exemplifies her observation that 'music within films is becoming more linked to memorable moments than to a wash of accompanying and complementary sound' (1996b: 160). This is illustrated by the use within the film of Procol Harum's 'A Whiter Shade of Pale', in a way which very clearly draws attention to the centrality of nostalgia. As the friends relax in the lounge after returning from the funeral, they engage in a discussion which confirms the significance of the popular music of their youth compared to contemporary popular music. During the conversation, 'A Whiter Shade of Pale' is heard diegetically (presumably from the record-player). Its volume is low, allowing dialogue to be clearly heard, and its presence creates a pattern of expectations for diegetic cues throughout the movie, in that whenever the group is gathered in the lounge, music (diegetic or diegetically ambiguous) is heard.

Setting the scene

The movie opens with a scene of cosy domesticity – a father gently bathing his son. Prompted by the mention of 'Jeremiah', the little boy breaks into a rendition of 'Joy to the World', to which the father (Harold) clicks along, coaching the impromptu performance. The relevance of the 1960s influence is immediately established, and Harold's behaviour suggests the transfer of his musical influences to his young son. The performance of the song in this setting suggests a spontaneous, child-like and innocent world – an important starting point to introduce the theme of lost youth. And as the song is repeated at the end of the movie (in the hit single version by Three Dog Night), it might perhaps be considered to be a/the 'theme'.

Marvin Gaye's 'I Heard it Through the Grapevine' fades in as the opening credits roll, thus performing the function of title music. The long-established cinematic convention through which opening title music defines the genre of film, sets a general mood, and announces the narrative themes to be explored in the story also signals the audience to 'pay attention ... the story is about to start' (Gorbman 1987: 82). Relying on the audience's familiarity with the conventions of cultural codes, it also provides geographical and historical settings, and performs a 'reveille function' (Tagg 1979: 62), preparing us for what follows as each character in turn hears the news of Alex's death on the telephone, and travels to the funeral. Like most cues in the film, the song performs several roles, or functions, simultaneously. Bridging different scenes in different locations at different times, 'I Heard it Through the Grapevine' works to enclose those scenes and to provide spatial and temporal continuity.

Monumentalising function

Gorbman's account of film music's capacity to provoke 'epic feelings ... to elevate the story of a man into the story of Man' (1987: 81) has been described as its 'monumentalising function' (Huckvale 1990: 4). In their explanation of this ability, both authors draw on the earlier insights of Theodor Adorno into the ways in which music and drama together intoxicate the audience into a state of 'oceanic regression' (1981: 90–1). The employment of appropriate music makes the audience more susceptible to suggestion, reducing barriers of belief and acting as 'a catalyst to the suspension of judgement' (Gorbman 1987: 5). Furthermore, it associates narrative events with their intended meaning(s), it connects the audience member to the world of the story, and it links the audience member with other audience members. As a result, individual audience members are able to relate the relevance of the story and characters not only to their own lives, but to the human condition in general.

This effect is most apparent in the use of 'You Can't Always Get What You Want' within the funeral sequences. After the minister has spoken in his eulogy of the themes of lost hope and the inevitability of having to settle for less in life than one might have hoped, he then announces Karen will play 'one of Alex's favourite songs' on the church organ. As Karen's version of the opening of the song merges seamlessly into the original Rolling Stones' version, the boundaries are contested and broken between diegetic and non-diegetic music, and between reality and cinematic fantasy. The music's rupturing of sonic/spatial reality is emphasised by the increased volume (and thus, increased emotion) as Alex's coffin is brought outside the church. As the tone of the organ also intensifies at this point to additionally blur the diegetic/non-diegetic distinction, the drama is given its 'epic' qualities. The entry of the choir towards the end of the song, as the camera zooms out from the group standing around the graveside, supports the sense of drama and religious overtones, through its implied symbolic references to angels and an afterlife. Thus the 'monumentalising' function is complete as we move towards an awareness of Alex's idealistic dreams and his struggle to integrate them into an imperfect and uncaring world.

Against the grain

The extended accompaniment of 'You Can't Always Get What You Want' to the post-funeral scenes outside the church also provides an example of the irony which typifies 'against the grain' musical usage. In stark contrast to the previous scene in the church where most were on the brink of tears, here the characters are indifferent, engaging in humorous asides and flippant remarks. In the same way that the Rolling Stones themselves were considered by some to be the epitome of rebellious and anti-establishment forces in the 1960s, so their song recalls the 'wild' or carefree or nonconformist youth of this group of characters. The specific attention drawn to the revving engines in the music video-like funeral procession echoes the aggressive nature of the rock style, and the general disjunctions between the cultures of rock'n'roll and the behavioural codes of a funeral present a telling illustration of film music which 'blissfully lacks awareness or empathy' (Gorbman 1987: 24).

Music and action: editing to music

The songs in *The Big Chill* provide an editing framework for many scenes through techniques which resemble those found in the music video genre. Although the use of previously recorded popular songs does not allow for precise synchronisation with already-edited film, the reverse process of shooting and cutting the film to the music can be just as effective. During 'I Heard it Through the Grapevine', the characters move in time with rhythmic elements of the music; and at the lines 'when I found my' and 'just about to lose my mind', Michael is seen searching for something, and revealing his mental anguish. Chloe's stretching exercises appear to be choreographed to the music. The movements of dressing the corpse take place in time with the music, so that the sounds of dressing are exaggerated by volume and rhythmic placement on prominent beats which punctuate the song and integrate it with other components of the sound design, and the movements of the hands in knotting and sliding the corpse's tie are accompanied by the string glissandi in the song.

Of course, there are differing ways in which the fusion of action and music can proceed. On some movies, such as *Butch Cassidy and the Sundance Kid* (George Roy Hill, 1969) and *Shaft* (Gordon Parks, 1971), the action is edited directly to the structural dictates of the music; other editors prefer to work to a 'temp track' which consists of recorded music attached to a film by the director in order to give the composer some broad ideas of the type of music required; others work to a piece of randomly chosen background music which may help to give sequences a natural rhythm and flow, even though the music will not appear in the finished movie; and a screenwriter like John Hughes actually writes while listening to music, and specifies song titles in his screenplays (Karlin & Wright 1990: 29).

Throughout *The Big Chill* there are numerous examples of the similarities the film shares with that property of music video which defines the track as the starting point for visual accompaniment rather than, as in traditional film treatments, adding music only after the film has been finally edited. Much of 'You Can't Always Get What You Want' is choreographed around a sequence of synchronised actions: car doors close, engines start, headlights flash to the beat of the song. Even the cars themselves seem to be moving in time with the music.

Similarly, the increased energy of the scene in which the main characters play football in the backyard matches the increased volume of the Spencer Davis Group's 'Gimme Some Lovin'' which accompanies it. The rhythm and pace of the game repeat the rhythm and pace of the song. The players' shouts for the ball and responses to other's actions and movements duplicate the Gospel call-and-response vocals. Dialogue is placed within gaps in the lyrics. This is goodtime music, reminding the characters (and the audience) that giving some loving is something they (and we) need from each other.

A similar function is performed by the Temptations' 'Ain't Too Proud To Beg'. After the evening meal, Harold plays the song on the record-player, singing and dancing to the first few lines. As all the group join in the clearing away and tidying in the kitchen, they too begin to dance and sing with the music. Their movements around the room are shaped by the structure of the record. That the music is loud emphasises again the party spirit in which they all share.

Mood and pacing
The examples discussed in the previous section refer to pacing and mood, but the use of music also provides pacing on another level, as the frequency of musical cues increases in parallel with the overall dynamic profile of the movie. In the movie's early scenes, there are longer periods of musical silence between songs. Later, however, as the narrative drama begins to build to a climax, there is an

almost continuous string of songs with very little time between the end of one and the start of the next. In this way, as in movies with a composed underscore, music provides pacing on both micro and macro levels.

Shifts in emphasis

Within the narrative structure of *The Big Chill*, characters alternately switch from happy to sad to happy again in successive scenes. Given the circumstances of the plot, such frequent, often sudden, changes in emotional tone, as the characters shift between grief over Alex's death and joy over renewed friendships, are not unexpected.

The songs plainly echo these mood swings – bright, optimistic songs accompany light-hearted interludes, sombre songs accompany serious moments. So, for example, the serious mood of 'You Can't Always Get What You Want' and its 'epic' commentary on life is quickly followed by the playful 'Tell Him' by the Exciters. The cue starts in sync with Chloe closing the door on Michael. Starting a cue on a moment of shifting emphasis such as this is a technique frequently used to 'amplify' a change in focus indicated through dialogue, camera moves or actions (Karlin & Wright, 1990: 49). As the increased volume additionally alerts us to the change, the shift in mood, reflecting relief that the funeral is over, is immediate. We also move from the general commentary in the previous song to a much more personal level, which is supported by close camera shots of each character unpacking his or her personal effects. The liveliness of 'Tell Him' suggests that despite the circumstances of the reunion, the weekend will not be gloomy.

Spatialisation

Songs playing on the hi-fi system in the house provide an ideal opportunity for the viewer to understand the spatial interconnections of the rooms. As 'A Whiter Shade of Pale' is playing, the song bridges scenes in different parts of the house. Changes of volume (as a door to an upstairs room opens) give sonic reality and help create a sense of spatial orientation. When the cue ends in mid-phrase on a cut back to the lounge, a new song, 'Tracks of My Tears' by Smokey Robinson & the Miracles, is playing quietly, indicating that time has passed; the music provides spatial and temporal continuity. The sequence, reinforced by the mood and volume of these two songs, marks a quiet period in the profile of the movie and, as the last cue fades unremarkably, there is some very quiet background music from the television. The gradual volume decrease over the last few minutes has helped to shape the overall structural dynamic.

Highlighting

The Rascals' 'Good Lovin'' is another song that starts on a moment of shifting emphasis – in this case a cut to an open-road scene. Harold, Michael, Nick and Chloe are driving out to the cottage Alex and Chloe were renovating. Although a car scene typically represents an opportunity to present music diegetically (music playing on the car radio), in this instance it is used non-diegetically. The initial high volume level is faded down for a close-up of those in the car. In the front seats Harold is talking to Michael about the marriage problems of his business partner, when Chloe suddenly interrupts with the surprise announcement that 'Alex and I made love the night before he died. It was fantastic!' The end of her remark is timed to synchronise with a break in the music – a rather unusual (for a pop song) two second gap – in which the shock of the three men is apparent. This technique, referred to by Karlin and Wright as 'highlighting' (1990: 143), is a familiar device in conventional film scoring to emphasise a particular moment. In addition, the lyrics of the song are relevant to the conversation. One of Chloe's last memories of Alex is of 'good lovin'' and, as Nick observes after the music resumes, 'he went out with a bang, not a whimper'.

Playing the thoughts of characters

The specific use of music to illustrate the moods and values of characters is exemplified in *The Big Chill* by the use of Percy Sledge's 'When a Man Loves a Woman'. The song fades in as the camera, concentrated on Sarah's face, indicates that she is about to reach a decision. Sarah exchanges fond looks with Harold and Meg; Harold also looks fondly at Meg. We already know of Meg's desire for a child and her difficulty in finding a suitable male. The subtext supplied by the music suggests that Harold's love for Sarah is so great that he would do anything for her; and that he also loves Meg enough (though in a different way) to want to help her. The song lyrics also help to justify the unconventional arrangement about to be suggested.

Pre-empting the mood or narrative

Lyrics pre-empt developments in the next scene as the anticipated solution to Meg's problem is confirmed. Aretha Franklin's 'You Make Me Feel Like a Natural Woman' plays in, as Sarah says to Harold, 'It's about Meg'. The song underscores several romantic/sexual encounters which are happening simultaneously in different parts of the house, defining the mood and linking the scenes of different couples: Chloe asks Nick if she can sleep with him; Karen and Sam are also romantically engaged; Sarah declares her love for Harold; while, for Meg, the idea of conceiving a child 'makes her feel like a natural woman'. The multiple harmonies, lush brass and string orchestration, and complex chord movements make the song a richly textured and sensuous accompaniment to the scenes of lovemaking.

Intertextuality: song lyrics and film narrative

The use of lyricised songs departs from the conventional approach to film scoring by overtly foregrounding the soundtrack in the listeners' consciousness; lyrics draw attention to music. In past practice, this was considered undesirable, especially when lyrics competed with dialogue for attention: 'Dialogue, or any narratively significant sounds for that matter, must receive first priority in the soundtrack mix' (Gorbman 1987: 77).

In *The Big Chill*, dialogue is frequently interwoven with music by the employment of subtle but sophisticated techniques in the adjustment of volume levels. Often dialogue is timed to weave around lyrical or musical phrases, creating a shifting emphasis between various elements and directing our attention to what the film maker wants us to hear. At the same time, lyrics 'speak' for the characters, fulfilling a role that can be compared with the narrative commentary of a Greek chorus or 'as an anthem setting the narrative stage' (Gorbman 1987: 20). By using song lyrics in this manner, the commentary can be multi-dimensional, allowing for multiple readings on numerous levels: the same lyric can say different things on behalf of different characters, and communicate varying statements and ideas to varying audiences.

In *The Big Chill*, the lyrics of the majority of included songs comment on the scene in which they appear. For example, The Band's 'The Weight' is used as background to a montage scene, in which characters enter and exit the kitchen during the morning after a late night of partying. As well as the song providing continuity to these temporally disparate shots, its opening line, 'pulled into Nazareth, I was feelin' 'bout half past dead', describes the way most of the friends look – a little hungover and in need of coffee. But in addition to this general commentary, the lyrics also work on a more personal level. Meg's expression of her weariness caused by the burden of her unfulfilled desire for a child is picked up by the song's reference to sharing the burdens of life. The friends are, at this point, beginning to acknowledge that 'sharing' is one way to make the burdens of life more bearable, and the conversations that follow the song illustrate the idea of 'taking a load off' by talking a problem over with a friend.

The lyrics of the Beach Boys' 'Wouldn't It Be Nice' have literal and ironic connotations. While relating specifically to the hopes and ambitions of individual characters, they also provide a general observation about the aspirations for a better life that the group held in previous years: 'Wouldn't it be nice if we were older, then we wouldn't have to wait so long/And wouldn't it be nice to live together, in the kind of world where we belong?'

On another level, they relate specifically to the hopes and ambitions of individual group members. Meg's request to Sam to act as a sperm donor because he has good genes carries the message 'Wouldn't it be nice, Sam, to help me conceive a baby?' And in the same scene, where Michael and Nick are apparently trying to seduce Chloe, the lyrics of the next verse emphasise the romantic intentions that seem to be spreading to all corners of the house: 'Wouldn't it be nice if we could wake up, in the morning when the day is new/And after that to spend the day together, hold each other close the whole night through?' And the irony of juxtaposing the line 'wouldn't it be nice if we were older' with the scene of Nick and Michael doing drugs like teenagers reminds us that in this respect, at least, very little seems to have changed for them.

Many popular songs are so well-known that the lyrics do not need to be heard in order to convey meaning and intertextual commentary. The instrumental piped-music of Frank Sinatra's 'Strangers in the Night' which accompanies Sam and Karen's shopping expedition, during which Sam talks of his marital and familial problems, provides an appropriate diegetic cue for the supermarket scene, and is familiar enough for the relevance of the lyrics to be plain without our hearing them.

Just as the sequence of events in many music videos may enact a story derived from (often quite general) lyrics, the songs in *The Big Chill* frequently marry editing practices to lyrical content in a very direct way. During the funeral service, the lyrical/narrative associations of 'You Can't Always Get What You Want' are especially evident. The minister's announcement that Alex's death was suicide, his mourning of the young man's 'loss of hope', and his plea that 'ordinary pleasures' should be enough confirm the theme of the song; in this case, Alex wanted more from life than it was able to deliver, and his death was not what his friends would have wanted. The song's reference to 'the reception', which follows the announcement by the minister of the details of the post-funeral reception, is a preparation for that event and acts as a bridge to the scene, as we follow the procession of cars to the cemetery. Chloe's disappointment at not being allowed to ride up front in a limo shows us that, again, she too didn't quite get 'what she wanted'.

The complex levels of lyrical/narrative commentary are also demonstrated by the movie's use of 'Tell Him'. When Chloe rejects Michael's offer of company, she 'tells him' that she's not interested. At the same time a more general recommendation is implied in the repeated advice to 'tell him right now'. In the light of Alex's death, the conclusion seems to be that if you do love someone, don't leave it too long to tell him/her of your love. Sarah, in particular, is 'always gonna love him'. The frivolous mood ends abruptly. The shot of Sarah crying in the shower, profoundly affected by her loss, is intimate and emotional, and the music too ends. In this case, it is the sudden absence, rather than the addition, of music which is significant:

> Curiously, a powerful dramatic scene, especially one with a strong sense of realism or emotion, can be weakened by the addition of music – it can turn earnest drama into maudlin melodrama; it can take the searing edge off gritty, threatening realism and make the scene safely 'theatrical' so we no longer see it as reality. (Karlin & Wright 1990: 48)

Its effective combination of screenplay and soundtrack here ensures that the scene possesses a considerable impact. Later dialogue, referring to Sarah's past affair with Alex, invites us to revisit it and recall the strong emotions it encouraged.

At breakfast on the final morning, conversation centres around a shared commitment to keep in touch. As friends prepare to leave, addresses are exchanged and promises are made. The mood is one of agreement and harmony. Even Harold and Nick are happy to shake hands, having resolved a previous argument. Smokey Robinson & the Miracles' 'I Second That Emotion' sums up the mutual and genial mood.

This is followed promptly by Michael's statement, 'See, Harold, we took a secret vote. We're not leaving. We're never leaving'. This is the last line of dialogue in the movie and gives way immediately to the credits, which are themselves accompanied by Three Dog Night's version of 'Joy to the World'. The repetition of this song gives closure and in its reconnection with the movie's opening scene, suggests its function might be that of the theme song. The movie thus ends on an optimistic note, through the song's provision of a popular equivalent of the 'rising crescendo [and] loud and definite' (Gorbman 1987: 82) qualities ascribed to end-credit music. Although the movie is concerned with the tragedy of a suicide, its 'message' is finally projected as one of hope for the future.

Conclusion

Aside from commercial considerations, there are valid reasons to support the suitability of popular music within film. Its place in movies of the 1980s has been compared with the traditional Hollywood musical, where 'it is a matter of convention for the flow and space of the narrative to be disrupted by a musical number' (Gorbman 1987: 162). In the same way that romantic orchestral music became the earlier choice for film scoring – because of its 'quick and efficient signification to a mass audience' (Gorbman 1987: 4) – it has been argued that popular music too does not require the level of 'codal competence' that other styles do. In fact, one of its definitive characteristics is that it is capable of 'encoding the musical message in a such a way as to be decodable by a more heterogeneous audience' (Tagg 1979: 27) for whom such music is a familiar, often predominant, force in their lives.

The employment of popular music songs thus stands as an appropriate and plausible device which fulfils standard film scoring functions. But this does not mean that the practice is entirely without its shortcomings. For example, while film can be edited to existing songs, the songs themselves are not easily edited. That they do not lend themselves to fragmentation or musical manipulation can result in a loss of flexibility, as the rhythm of the song frequently becomes the rhythm of the cut. The opportunity to manipulate rhythm within the course of a cue (a technique commonly used in composed underscore) is also lost. Apart from comic or surreal effects, or a diegetic 'accident' involving the source of the music, the rhythm and tempo of the song cannot be altered.

Within a single cue, film composers often integrate subtle changes in other parameters, manipulating texture, mood or volume. And while composers of popular music may use many of the same techniques, the recorded song is an already complete artefact with most of its parameters set before it becomes part of the movie soundtrack.

Another technique used extensively by film composers is the repetition of a musical motif or theme, with variations reflecting a progression in a situation, or in a character's mental state, during the course of the narrative. Although repetition is common within the popular song, it is unlikely that audiences would appreciate the repetition of the same song many times in a movie, even if different recorded versions were employed. This is especially true of hit songs with which the audience is already familiar. By contrast, in a traditional score, thematic variations may be used in an unobtrusive way – typically, the viewer is unaware of the musical repetitions and variations – to influence audience attitudes and emotions through a specific narrative progression.

Many composed music cues, while simple in concept and construction, draw from a vast repertoire of effective film scoring devices – a low held note, a high tense string chord, a few notes tinkled high on the piano, a harp glissando. By limiting the score to songs, movie-makers are denying themselves some of the most powerful signifying devices in film.

Against the loss of some of the functions embedded in the traditionally composed instrumental soundtrack, a film such as *The Big Chill* nevertheless demonstrates how a 'concept' and a variety of moods within that concept can be supplied by the song-based film soundtrack. Through their generic associations, popular songs are able to set the scene, create a sense of epic grandeur, pre-empt the mood or the narrative direction, play the thoughts of a character, and provide shifts of emphasis in narrative meaning. By cutting the film to the song track, the traditional relationship between movement (action) and musical rhythm and texture can also be achieved.

The potential problem of conflict between lyrics and dialogue can be (and in this case, is) overcome by judicious changes in the dynamic level of the music and/or situating dialogue in instrumental sections of the music. Lyrics also bring to the soundtrack an enhanced level of intertextuality not present in the traditional instrumental soundtrack, supply a self-sufficient narrative allowing for a more abstract visual treatment, and, in so doing, demonstrate how the content and techniques of music video have penetrated narrative film making practices.

Rather than dismissing the use of popular music in film as a purely commercial exercise, it is useful to consider 'how listening habits and responses might have changed in response to these commercial interests and the changing relations between them' (Gorbman 1987: 163). Although aesthetic comparisons, both favourable and unfavourable, can be made between the use of composed music and recorded songs as underscore, it may well be that the latter practice is becoming the norm, and is functioning in a very different way than is recognised by film score theory. Thus, 'a semiotic phenomenology of the evolving relations between music and image, and, overall, of changes in the "diegetic effect" or disposition of representation, needs to emerge' (Gorbman 1987: 163). In relation to the practice of using recorded songs as underscore, a review of the creative techniques and aesthetic principles employed by the members of film-making teams (including directors, editors, music supervisors, music editors, composers, music producers and sound editors) is overdue.

Chapter Twelve

TRIUMPHANT BLACK POP DIVAS ON THE WIDE SCREEN: *LADY SINGS THE BLUES* AND *TINA: WHAT'S LOVE GOT TO DO WITH IT*

Jaap Kooijman

Lady Sings the Blues fails to do justice to the musical life of which Billie Holiday was a part, and it never shows what made her a star, much less what made her an artist. The sad truth is that there is no indication that those who made the picture understand that jazz is any different from pop corruptions of jazz. And yet when the movie was over, I wrote 'I love it' on my pad of paper and closed it and stuffed it back in my pockets. (Kael 1972: 152)

We don't see the kind of contrast Tina Turner actually sets up in her autobiography between 'I looked like a wreck one minute, and then, I went on that stage and projected all this energy.' [*Tina: What's Love Got To Do With It*] should have given us the pathos of that, but it did not at all, because farce can't give you pathos like that. (hooks 1996: 113)

> Hollywood biographies are real not because they are believable. Rather, one must treat them as real because despite the obvious distortions ranging from the minor to the outright camp, Hollywood films are believed to be real by many viewers. (Custen 1992: 7)

Taken together, the above observations sum up the limitations and the appeal of the Hollywood musical biopic. Both *Lady Sings the Blues* (Sidney J. Furie, 1972), which starred Diana Ross as jazz legend Billie Holiday, and *Tina: What's Love Got To Do With It* (Brian Gibson, 1993) in which Angela Bassett played Tina Turner have been criticised for presenting a historically distorted and melodramatic portrayal of the lives of the two legendary African-American female singers. Nevertheless, the commercial success of both films seems to suggest that the general public were indifferent to such shortcomings. Rather like Pauline Kael, viewers loved these films, in spite of any critical reservations they may have had. Although two decades apart, *Lady Sings the Blues* and *Tina: What's Love Got To Do With It* are remarkably alike in the way they present a compelling and attractive pop version of the tragedy and triumph that the fictionalised life stories of Holiday and Turner have come to represent. That both Diana Ross and Angela Bassett were nominated for a best actress Academy Award (neither won – in 2002, Halle Berry was the first African-American woman to win an Oscar in that category) reinforces the triumphant character of the two films.

In reference to *Tina: What's Love Got To Do With It*, bell hooks has questioned the emphasis on 'black female tragedy' rather than 'black female triumph' in American popular film. It is not Tina Turner's success in the music industry, but her relationship with the abusive Ike Turner that provides the main focus of the film: 'It's so interesting how the film stops with Ike's brutality, as though it is Tina Turner's life ending. Why is it that her success is less interesting than the period of her life when she's a victim?' (hooks 1996: 112). A similar insight can be applied to *Lady Sings the Blues*. Rather than focusing on Billie Holiday's musical career, the film's narrative is predominantly based on Holiday's struggle with her drug addiction and her almost pathological dependence on her strong male lover, Louis McKay. Yet, even though hooks presents a convincing argument, one can also perceive these films as showcasing struggle and survival, eventually leading to black female triumph. As Gerald Early has suggested, *Lady Sings the Blues* is 'not so much about the downfall of a brilliant artist as it is about the struggle of a black woman to become a respectable lady in this society with the help of a decent, proud [black] man' (1995: 120). In *Tina: What's Love*

Got To Do With It, a black woman's struggle is also central although, as the film emphasises, here the support comes from Tina Turner's faith in Buddhism which gives her the strength, courage and confidence to escape from an abusive and controlling relationship. In the end, both films, quite literally, present an image of black female triumph. The final scene of *Lady Sings the Blues* shows a triumphant Diana Ross performing 'God Bless The Child' at New York's Carnegie Hall, while Billie Holiday's sad decline and early death are merely mentioned in newspaper headlines appearing behind Ross on the screen. In a remarkably similar scene, *Tina: What's Love Got To Do With It* ends with Angela Bassett lip-synching 'What's Love Got To Do With It' at the New York Ritz, followed by footage of the 'real' Tina Turner giving an electrifying performance of the same song.

Even though both films eventually present an image of black female triumph, they are quite different in the way in which this triumphant image is constructed. *Lady Sings the Blues* strengthens the image of its star, Diana Ross, rather than its subject Billie Holiday, whereas *Tina: What's Love Got To Do With It* reaffirms the star image of its subject Tina Turner, rather than its leading actress, Angela Bassett. The distinction becomes especially obvious through the way pop music is used in the films – while Ross sings all the Holiday songs, Bassett lip-synchs to Tina Turner's voice. In this chapter, I will argue that the use of pop music (both in the film and on the soundtrack) and melodrama enables the construction of the images of Diana Ross and Tina Turner as triumphant black pop divas by simplifying and eventually eliminating the characters of the fictional Billie Holiday and (the very real) Angela Bassett.

Black pop divas in film

With the notable exception of the work of black film historian Donald Bogle, *Lady Sings the Blues* and *Tina: What's Love Got To Do With It* tend to go unmentioned in academic studies of popular African-American film (Bogle 1992; Diawara 1993; Guerrero 1993; Rhines 1996). Perhaps this exclusion stems from the fact that both films tell the stories of African-American women yet are directed by white men, and/or that the films are melodramatic biopics – a genre typically associated with classic (white) Hollywood rather than black cinema. More surprising, however, is the absence of both films from academic studies of popular music in film. Although these studies include a wide variety of films in which pop music plays an essential role – ranging from Elvis Presley's rock musicals and rockumentaries such as Talking Heads' *Stop Making Sense*

(Jonathan Demme, 1984) to such popular dance films as *Saturday Night Fever* (John Badham, 1977) and *Dirty Dancing* (Emile Ardolino, 1987) – musical films starring African-American women tend to be overlooked (Smith 1998; Mundy 1999; Shuker 2001: 175–80). The exclusion of *Lady Sings the Blues* and *Tina: What's Love Got To Do With It* is particularly surprising, as these two films are not only relevant examples of how pop music can merge with film (in both films the off-screen artist's existing songbook has been interwoven with a melodramatic narrative), but they are also clearly demonstrate how the image of African-American female stars in Hollywood is constructed through a connection to pop music.

Several authors (Dyer 1986; Alexander 1991; Tasker 1998: 184) have commented that films which feature black women in the female leading role are often based on the 'packaging of black women musical icons' (hooks 1996: 111). In addition to the two films considered here, they include *Mahogany* (Berry Gordy, 1975) and *The Wiz* (Sidney Lumet, 1978), both of which star Diana Ross; *Thank God it's Friday* (Robert Klane, 1978), starring Donna Summer; *The Bodyguard* (Mick Jackson, 1992) and *Waiting to Exhale* (Forest Whitaker, 1995), both starring Whitney Houston; *Poetic Justice* (John Singleton, 1993) starring Janet Jackson; and *Set It Off* (F. Gary Gray, 1996) starring Queen Latifah. Supporting black female roles are also often played by musical icons: Aretha Franklin as the singing waitress in *The Blues Brothers* (John Landis, 1980); Grace Jones as the evil James Bond girl, May Day, in *A View to a Kill* (John Glen, 1985), and Tina Turner as the exotic Aunty Entity in *Mad Max: Beyond Thunderdome* (George Miller/George Ogilvie, 1985).

Rather than going to the cinema to see 'serious' actresses portray a dramatic role, it would appear that audiences go to see these popular musical icons perform, regardless of whether they actually sing in the film – prompting bell hooks to pose the rhetorical question: 'Is this Hollywood saying we still can't take black women seriously as actresses?' (1996: 111). Of course, this packaging of musical icons is not limited to African-American female singers. The performances of Bette Midler in *The Rose* (Mark Rydell, 1979), Madonna in *Desperately Seeking Susan* (Susan Seidelman, 1985), Mariah Carey in *Glitter* (Vondie Curtis-Hall, 2001) and Britney Spears in *Crossroads* (Tamra Davis, 2002) have also been based on their appeal as pop musical icons rather than their ability as serious actresses. Nevertheless, the relatively large proportion of musical icons in films featuring African-American women continues to suggest that in Hollywood the connection between African-American women and pop music is considered to be an essential advantage or even a necessity.

The Hollywood biopic and realism

'Diana Ross *IS* Billie Holiday' reads the tagline of *Lady Sings the Blues*, while *Tina: What's Love Got To Do With It* promises the viewer 'The True Life Story of Tina Turner'. However, like most Hollywood biopics, both films have taken great liberty in adapting historical events to position the lives of Holiday and Turner within the conventions of the genre. As Custen has asserted, the Hollywood biopic presents an ironic paradox: 'While proclaiming the greatness of individuals by honouring them with a showcase about the uniqueness of their lives, Hollywood film really reduces individuals to part of a set of almost Proppian moves, a mass-tailored contour for fame in which greatness is generic and difference has controllable boundaries' (Custen 1992: 25–6). As a result, historical events are rearranged and often simplified to present an understandable and compelling narrative based on cause and effect, leading to a cathartic finale.

In *Lady Sings the Blues*, for example, the several men in Billie Holiday's real life are combined into one romantic figure, Louis McKay, who is presented as Holiday's main and only love interest. Moreover, a fictional character, Piano Man, is introduced, not only to stand as Holiday's faithful friend, but also to provide comic relief throughout the film. It is his dramatic death at the end of the film which triggers the catharsis of the film's narrative, showing the tragic and devastating effects of drug abuse, and prompting Holiday's return to New York where she gives her triumphant final performance. The film's producer Berry Gordy (founder and president of Motown records) explained these changes by pointing out that *Lady Sings the Blues* was supposed to be 'an entertaining thing … this picture is honest, but it's not necessarily true' (Thomas 1973: 28). In other words, the boundaries set by the conventions of the Hollywood biopic justify historical inaccuracies and misrepresentations.

Custen has identified the 1950s as the most productive and popular period of the Hollywood biographical picture; since the 1960s the genre has largely shifted to television, although *Lady Sings the Blues* and *Tina: What's Love Got To Do With It* are part of cinema's continuing interest in musical biopics. The films do fit within Custen's general definition of the biopic as 'a biographical film … that depicts the life of a historical figure, past or present' (1992: 5). Moreover, like many biopics, both films are (loosely) based on the published and commercially successful autobiographies of their subjects: *Lady Sings the Blues* takes its title from Billie Holiday's autobiography co-written with William Dufty, while *Tina: What's Love Got To Do With It* (its title coming from a Tina Turner hit single) is based on Turner's autobiography *I, Tina: My Life Story*, co-written with Kurt Loder (Holiday 1992; Turner 1987). In both cases, the biopic derives its authority and authenticity from its connection to the original autobiography and reinforces this connection by employing the title of one of its subject's songs as the film's title. Once such authority and authenticity has been established, the film can then break free from its autobiographical source, as was frankly recognised by Diana Ross in 1973: 'I believe that if we had stuck straight to what we had in the book, we would've had a documentary about a lady that was just one tragedy after another. I read between the lines and I tried to find that other side of Billie Holiday that wasn't in the book, that's not on the back of album covers' (Thomas 1973: 28).

Even within the contours maintained by the conventions of the Hollywood biopic, many critics have found that *Lady Sings the Blues* and *Tina: What's Love Got To Do With It* reduce the lives of Billie Holiday and Tina Turner to melodrama, thereby ignoring the complexity of historical circumstances and objectifying these black women as victims (Canby 1972; Cocks 1972; Kael 1972; Pearson 1993; Gillett 1994; hooks 1996: 111–13). James Baldwin believed that the off-screen Billie Holiday was far more complex and definitely less weak and passive than the character portrayed by Diana Ross: 'The film cannot accept – because it cannot use – this simplicity. That victim who is able to articulate the situation of the victim has ceased to be a victim: he, or she, has become a threat' (1976: 110). Similar problems in the portrayal of Tina Turner have been noted by hooks and Pearson, the latter primarily objecting to the 'inherently inflammatory' violence of the scenes depicting Ike's attacks on Tina. Instead of exposing the complexity of domestic violence (in the film, Ike's behaviour is 'explained' by his cocaine abuse), the situation is presented as 'helplessness in the face of evil' in an attempt to evoke the 'primitive fears' of the audience. Pearson concludes: 'Just remember that the worse the abuse depicted, the lower a representation of it will aim – viscerally … you think you've seen something important because you have been so deeply "moved" (that is, so well manipulated)' (1993: 335). Thus, it may not be historical distortions but oversimplified portrayals of black female characters and their social circumstances which are the most contentious issues within these movies.

The use of music

The appeal of musical biopics is in large part based on the inclusion of musical performances, giving the viewers a glimpse of the magic and the circumstances that made the film's subject famous. *Lady Sings the Blues* presents reconstructions of Billie Holiday's first performances in the New York of the 1930s, her performances with a big band while touring the South, and her final performance at Carnegie Hall. These historical reconstructions do not represent the actual Billie Holiday, of course, but present Diana Ross (dressed in gowns designed by Bob Mackie) singing Holiday songs like 'The Man I Love', 'I Cried For You' and 'God Bless the Child'. The musical sequences in *Tina: What's Love Got To Do With It* are more problematic, as Angela Bassett lip-synchs to Tina Turner's voice (conversely, the actor Laurence Fishburne does sing Ike's parts), making her performances more like imitations than interpretations. Nevertheless, the effect is similar, as Bassett's recreation seeks to evoke the atmosphere and energy of the original performances by taking the audience back in time through its depiction of Tina Turner's evolving style (including her typical costumes and moves) from the late 1950s up to the early 1980s around songs like 'Shake a Tail Feather', 'Proud Mary', 'Disco Inferno' and 'What's Love Got To Do With It'. The musical performances – not only the actual songs but also the fashions and styles of the times they reconstruct – make *Lady Sings the Blues* and *Tina: What's Love Got To Do With It* enjoyable showcases of (African)-American pop music.

In addition to their reconstruction of the original performances, the songs provide continuity through changes of time and space. In *Lady Sings the Blues* the performances of 'Gimme a Pigfoot' and 'I Cried For You' are used in montage sequences showing the progress in Billie Holiday's singing career and personal (love) life. In *Tina: What's Love Got To Do With It*, 'Proud Mary' is used in a similar way; while the soundtrack plays the song in its entirety, three different performances are shown whose location and time are indicated by a text line appearing in the corner of the screen: 'London 1968'; 'Chicago 1971'; 'Los Angeles 1974'. The montage sequence not only shows the evolving performance/ fashion style of Tina Turner (becoming more provocatively sexy), but also the increasing popularity of the band and – as suggested by the shouts of the audience – Tina Turner herself.

Moreover, songs are used to add a layer of meaning to the narrative. When Billie Holiday's drug addiction makes her insensitive to the advice of those around her, Holiday/Ross performs 'Ain't Nobody's Business If I Do,' reinforcing the message to 'leave her alone'. And Ike and Tina's wedding is accompanied by 'It's Gonna Work Out Fine', only to be followed by a montage sequence in which Tina is shown as submissive to Ike, accompanied by 'A Fool in Love'.

In *Lady Sings the Blues*, music has an important role in emphasising the film's romantic character. As Donald Bogle has noted, the film was the 'first full-fledged black romantic melodrama … [containing] some of the most romantic scenes thus far in the history of blacks in films' (1992: 245–6). During the scene which shows her first professional performance, as a bar singer, Billie Holiday is placed in juxtaposition to her fellow singers. In stark contrast to her colleagues, who sing coarse, rough blues songs and go from table to table to pick up dollar bills between their legs, Holiday is presented as a 'classy' jazz singer who is too embarrassed to repeat this method of collecting money. Subsequently, she is booed and ridiculed until an 'anonymous' arm holds up a dollar bill. Once Holiday finally notices the gesture, the camera presents her point-of-view shot, focusing first on the arm holding the bill. As the male voice asks 'Do you want my arm to fall off?' the camera slowly moves upward, ending with a lingering close-up of the face of Louis McKay (Billy Dee Williams), specifically focusing on his sparkling eyes and smile. After she has accepted the dollar bill, Holiday sings 'I fell in love with you the first time I looked into … them there eyes'. The song unequivocally validates the Billie/Ross and Louis/Williams romance, not only through its expression of their encounter, but also through its seduction of the audience, like Holiday herself, by the images and sounds of love at first sight.

A similar musical translation is made later in a sequence addressing racism rather than romance. When Billie Holiday is on the road in the South, she asks the driver to stop the tour bus so she can go to the toilet. In the middle of the countryside, in search of an appropriate spot, Holiday 'suddenly' stumbles upon a group of mourning Southern black Americans, standing around a dead black man hanging from a tree. The impact of being confronted with lynching for the first time makes Holiday act in a hysterical fashion. As the soundtrack plays the first notes of 'Strange Fruit', she stumbles back into the bus and sits staring out of the window. An intercut of Holiday performing 'Strange Fruit' in concert follows, but before the song is over, the camera returns to her contemplative pose in the bus. By using 'Strange Fruit' in this way, the film reduces racism to an isolated occurrence of horror in Holiday's personal life and suggests that her discovery of the lynching inspired her to compose 'Strange Fruit' (which in fact she did not).

Unsurprisingly, the lynch scene was strongly criticised for its melodramatic character (Canby 1972; Kael 1972). James Baldwin bluntly observed:

The best that one can say for this moment is that it is mistaken, and the worst that it is callously false and self-serving – which may be a rude way of saying the same thing: luckily, it is brief. The scene operates to resolve, at one stroke, several problems, and without in the least involving or intimidating the spectator. The lynch scene is as remote as an Indian massacre, occurring in the same landscape, and eliciting the same response: a mixture of pious horror and gratified reassurance. (1976: 109)

In addition to presenting a melodramatisation of racism, the scene undermines the provocative content of 'Strange Fruit'. The relatively short song is made even shorter, as the entire second verse and the first two lines of the third verse have been eliminated. The lines in which the 'gallant South' is connected to the pictures of 'bulging eyes' and 'the smell of burning flesh' are deleted: 'It may have been that those responsible for the movie … felt that audiences were still not ready for the song' (Margolick 2000: 137–8).

Music in *Tina: What's Love Got To Do With It* is used to emphasise Tina Turner's growing independence and the subsequent increase in Ike's abusive behaviour. In the scene recreating a 1960s television performance of 'Shake a Tail Feather', Tina is introduced to producer Phil Spector who invites her to record 'River Deep, Mountain High' with him. In a follow-up scene, the recording session is shown, including the full orchestra that is perceived as typical of Spector's productions. A similar recording session later in the film shows Tina singing 'Nutbush City Limits' at their home recording studio. That Tina has written the song herself is significant, and she explicitly mentions this fact. Both scenes seek to reconstruct the actual recording sessions (thus providing the audience with fictional 'behind the scenes' footage) but more importantly, they show Ike's growing jealousy of Tina's independence and solo success. Shots of Tina recording the songs are intercut with shots of Ike's frustration, boredom and use of cocaine, eventually culminating in his violent behaviour. What the two scenes tell us is that the success of 'River Deep, Mountain High' and 'Nutbush City Limits' leads directly to Ike's drug abuse and violence. His aggression is explicitly shown when he attacks Tina before she can complete the recording of the song she wrote herself.

The music also allows Tina to distance herself from Ike in that the two songs are characterised by a 'sound' which is markedly different to Ike's rhythm'n'blues repertoire. After Tina has left Ike (but before she makes her solo comeback), she informs her new (white) manager Rogier Davies that 'I ain't about blues anymore, you know' and that she wants to sing rock'n'roll like David Bowie and Mick Jagger. Through her self-transformation from blues singer to rock'n'roll singer, Tina Turner has left Ike not only physically, but spiritually too. Moreover, the film implies, but fails to problematise, her increasing movement away from her 'black roots' – at least musically.

Black triumphant pop divas

Like the image of the film star, the image of the pop star can be perceived as a star-text – a combination of different images and texts of the star, both on and off stage, including professional performances, interviews, promotional photographs and gossip. Taken together, these images and texts result in a collection of meanings that constructs the star persona. As a commodity of production and consumption, the star persona can contain a wide range of meanings, which often embody conflicting values and fantasies. The construction of the star persona is necessary not only to provide the audience with a point of identification, but also to secure the continuity of commercial success (Goodwin 1993; Dyer 1998; McDonald 2000). In the case of Diana Ross and (the real) Tina Turner, *Lady Sings the Blues* and *Tina: What's Love Got To Do With It* make significant contributions to the star-texts of these two black female pop personae. Both films present conflicting values by portraying the characters of Billie Holiday and the fictional Tina Turner as victims, and yet, simultaneously, by helping to construct the image of Diana Ross and the real Tina Turner as successful African-American pop stars. In other words, these films use the on-screen theme of black female tragedy to present an off-screen image of black female triumph.

As lead singer of the Supremes, Diana Ross had become an American pop cultural icon of the 1960s. To transcend this image of the ultimate pop singer, Ross had to leave the Supremes far behind and become a movie star (Bogle 1980: 175 81; Kooijman 2002). Motown's Berry Gordy utilised the legendary status of Billie Holiday to transform Diana Ross into a black Hollywood star by symbolically taking her 'back to the holy waters … [to be] rebaptized and born again. Diana, the princess of ghetto chic, a girl/woman known as plastic, goes through Billie's horrors and humiliations. By doing so, she acquires a certain depth and relevance' (Bogle 1980: 176–80). Gerald Early uses a similar metaphor in his description of *Lady Sings the Blues* as 'an ocean of pop-culture kitsch' used to complete the metamorphosis of Diana Ross: 'Holiday was the only sufficiently gigantic black bitch-goddess of popular culture whose art could legitimate Ross's own standing as the reigning black bitch-goddess of her own day' (1995: 119).

The 'rebirth' of Ross is completed in the film's final scene, in which she gives a dazzling performance of 'God Bless The Child' at New York's Carnegie Hall. Rather than presenting Ross as Lady Day performing her swansong, the grand finale presents a triumphant performance by D-I-A-N-A R-O-S-S, the newly established movie star. The irony of the film's paradoxical ending is not lost: 'The film fades out with a triumphant Billie who is already, however, unluckily, dead, singing on-stage before a delirious audience – or, rather two: one in the cinema Carnegie Hall, and one in the cinema where we are seated' (Baldwin 1976: 104). The fictional Billie Holiday has to 'die' to enable the rebirth of Ross; thus, unlike her screen persona, Ross can enjoy her new status as superstar: 'Diana Ross: Lady *Doesn't* Sing the Blues,' as the *New York Times* rightly noted (Harmetz 1972: D4). Significantly, while remaining critical of the film, Baldwin praised Ross's acting performance, thereby helping to shape the Diana Ross star image: 'Diana Ross, clearly, respected Billie too much to try to imitate her. She picks up on Billie's beat, and, for the rest, uses herself, with a moving humility and candor, to create a portrait of a woman overwhelmed by the circumstances of her life' (Baldwin 1976: 103). In her own 'real' life, the glamorous and triumphant star image of Diana Ross was reaffirmed by being nominated for a best actress Academy Award and by receiving a standing ovation after a special screening of *Lady Sings the Blues* at the Cannes International Film Festival.

The construction of the Tina Turner star persona in *Tina: What's Love Got To Do With It* is more complicated as she is the subject rather than the performing star of the film (at least visually; vocally, Turner is the film's performing star). In one of the film's pivotal scenes, Ike and Tina are in court to finalise their divorce, and Tina is willing to give up everything in exchange for the right to retain her stage name. Ironically, as the film makes perfectly clear, it was Ike who constructed Tina's original star persona, including the change of name from Anna Mae Bullock to Tina Turner. In an essay published before *Tina: What's Love Got To Do With It* was released, hooks pointed out this irony by arguing that Tina may have left Ike, but she did not leave behind the image he created of her:

> Without Ike, Turner's career has soared to new heights, particularly as she works harder to exploit the visual representation of woman (and particularly black woman) as sexual savage. No longer caught in her sadomasochistic sexual iconography of black female in erotic war with her mate that was the subtext of the Ike and Tina Turner show, she is now portrayed as the autonomous black woman whose sexuality is solely a way to exert power. (hooks 1992: 68)

The final scene of *Tina: What's Love Got To Do With It* presents a visualisation of the irony described by hooks. Like the triumphant final performance by Diana Ross in *Lady Sings the Blues*, the film ends with an equally triumphant performance of 'What's Love Got To Do With It' by the fictional Tina Turner at the New York Ritz. The performance symbolises Tina's final departure from Ike and the construction of her image as successful pop star. Just before her performance, Tina is visited by Ike in her dressing room where he threatens her with a gun. No longer afraid of him, Tina stands up and walks out onto the stage. As she sings, Ike wanders into the audience, stares at Tina, and lights a cigarette (here clearly signifying Ike's 'bad' character). Then he slowly turns and walks away, followed by the on-screen text: 'Ike Turner was later arrested on drug-related charges. He was convicted and served time in a California State Prison.' Once Ike is – literally – out of the picture, the camera returns to the stage, where Tina Turner/Angela Bassett has been replaced by the real Tina Turner, followed by the text: ' "What's Love…" hit Number One. Tina's first solo album won four Grammy Awards including Record of the Year. Tina has become one of the world's top recording artists. Her tours continue to break concert attendance records worldwide'. In stark contrast to the failure of Ike, Tina Turner is presented as the triumphant pop star whose victory is measured in commercial success. The film's final shot makes the construction of her star persona complete by presenting a freeze of the real Tina Turner smiling into the camera.

The implications of the replacement of the fictional Tina Turner by the real Tina Turner at the conclusion of the film was received with some disquiet. Henry Pearson comments that 'Suddenly, we breathe a sigh of relief and say: "This is how it's supposed to be; this is why she's a star." This intercut undercuts all the work Bassett has done up to this point' (1993: 335). And hooks notes that 'it's like saying that Angela Bassett isn't a good enough actress' (1996: 111). The explanation lies in the construction of the star persona. Just as the fictional Billie Holiday must 'die' to enable the construction of the Diana Ross star persona in *Lady Sings the Blues*, so too Angela Bassett needs to be 'eliminated' to make *Tina: What's Love Got To Do With It* a construction of the real Tina Turner as a successful star.

Star-text and soundtrack

The star personae of Diana Ross and Tina Turner are not only constructed through their performances in film, but also by their performances on the accompanying soundtrack albums. Since the 1970s, soundtracks have become an essential part of a larger synergy and cross-promotional strategy to market Hollywood films. Through the release of a possible hit single by a pop artist as the film's theme, the song and its accompanying music video can function as an advertisement for the film, and vice versa (Smith 1998: 186–229). In their own musical careers, both Ross and Turner have recorded film themes which have become hit singles:

Diana Ross's 'Theme From Mahogany' (1975), 'Endless Love' (1981), 'It's My Turn' (1981); Tina Turner's 'We Don't Need Another Hero' (1985), 'Goldeneye' (1995). However, with the soundtracks of *Lady Sings the Blues* and *Tina: What's Love Got To Do With It* the cross-promotional connection between film and soundtrack is even more explicit (and perhaps more effective) as a marketing tool, in that the film and the soundtrack both become part of the star-text that constructs the star persona.

The soundtrack of *Lady Sings the Blues* consisted of one disc containing excerpts from the film's dialogue and songs, and a second disc containing eleven Diana Ross studio recordings of Billie Holiday songs plus the film's instrumental 'Love Theme' and 'Closing Theme' (both composed by Michel LeGrand). Even though the album cover reads 'Original Motion Picture Soundtrack' the soundtrack is clearly presented as a Diana Ross solo album (a notion emphasised by the European edition, entitled 'Diana Ross Sings the Songs of Lady Sings the Blues' which only includes the second disc). The record was hugely successful in the United States, peaking at Number One in *Billboard*'s Album Chart, the only Diana Ross solo album ever to reach that position. The *New York Times* praised the soundtrack as 'a talented, very intelligent singer's homage to a jazz style of a sophistication never since matched by anyone', concluding that the Ross cover versions were 'about as good as you can get, barring the real things' (Canby 1972: 56). To tie in with the film, Motown released 'Good Morning Heartache' as a single and, although less successful than her chart-topping 'Ain't No Mountain High Enough' (1970) and 'Touch Me in the Morning' (1973), it shared the melodramatic quality of those songs: 'both a celebration of a relationship and the almost willing recognition of its passing and the exquisite pain of its passing' (Dyer 1979: 524).

By appropriating the Billie Holiday songbook, Ross was able to transform her image of a plastic pop singer into that of a serious jazz singer. Over the years, Ross would continue to sing a selection of Billie Holiday songs in her live concerts. Most notably, in December 1992, she performed the entire *Lady Sings the Blues* soundtrack live at the New York Ritz, broadcast on television as a 'once in a lifetime performance', and released on compact disc and DVD under the title *Stolen Moments: The Lady Sings ... Jazz and Blues*.

For the promotion of *Tina: What's Love Got To Do With It*, Tina Turner recorded a new song as the film's theme, entitled 'I Don't Wanna Fight,' co-written and originally recorded by British pop singer Lulu. Even though the song does not appear in the film until the end credits, 'I Don't Wanna Fight' clearly refers to the film's main theme, Turner's struggle to escape from an abusive relationship (in fact Turner sings that she does not 'wanna fight *anymore*', a relevant addition).

'I Don't Wanna Fight' became a huge international hit, reconfirming Turner's status as a global megastar, and was nominated for Grammy Awards in the Best Female Vocal Performance and Best Film Theme categories.

With its inclusion of the new hit single, the film's official soundtrack is, in effect, a Tina Turner 'Greatest Hits' compilation. The album predominantly consists of re-recordings of old hits, plus two original hit singles and three new songs. As a follow-up to 'I Don't Wanna Fight' Virgin released a new song, 'Why Must We Wait Until Tonight', a romantic love song which, unlike its predecessor, contradicts the film's main theme. The explicit connection to the film was restored with the third single, a cover version of 'Disco Inferno' (originally released by The Trammps), which is included in the film although, ironically, the fictional Tina Turner calls the song 'boring'. Like the *Lady Sings the Blues* soundtrack, the *Tina: What's Love Got To Do With It* soundtrack is presented as a Tina Turner solo album. In fact, only on the back cover is there any reference to the film itself. The front cover features a close-up photograph of Turner's face. The accompanying booklet consists primarily of Tina Turner pictures, including one of Turner sitting in a director's chair but with no mention of the film. As a result, the soundtrack and the film itself may be seen as marketing tools to promote the star Tina Turner, an insight emphasised by Turner's comments in the soundtrack's liner notes: 'With or without the film which brought these songs together, they are part of the soundtrack of my life.'

Conclusion

In her autobiography, Diana Ross reflected that by filming *Lady Sings the Blues*, she 'lived Billie Holiday's toughest moments of a very tough life', comparing her own experiences as a pop star to Holiday's experience of drug addiction:

> It's about being onstage when the highs are so high: the lights, the applause, the adoration. Then the performance is over and you go home or you're on the road and you're all alone in a strange hotel room somewhere. You want to escape that, you want the lights, the power, the energy. You want to keep the high, to stay in the exalted moment, to be excited all the time. But that can't be. (Ross 1993: 169–70).

Her observation suggests that *Lady Sings the Blues* is less about Billie Holiday than it is about the hardships she has come to symbolise, including those faced by a glamorous and successful pop star.

The paradox of the Hollywood biopic is its foregrounding of the universalism in an extraordinary life. Although *Lady Sings the Blues* and *Tina: What's Love Got To Do With It* fail to do justice to the complexity of Billie Holiday's and Tina Turner's 'real' lives, the power of both films is based on their ability to present a simplified yet compelling perspective on life's struggles. This is what both Pauline Kael and bell hooks recognised as the corruptions of pop: an appealing yet 'false' pathos, which presents a melodramatised version of black female tragedy, by turning such complex social and historical issues as racism and domestic violence into personal problems. Moreover, in spite of their eventual triumph, the films objectify Billie Holiday and the fictional Tina Turner as victims, who need either a strong man or a strong faith in Buddhism (and a white manager) to triumph over those problems. Ironically of course, in the end neither character succeeds, as both Holiday and the fictional Turner are eliminated to enable the triumphant finale of Ross and the real Turner.

In their construction of the star personae of Diana Ross and Tina Turner, *Lady Sings the Blues* and *Tina: What's Love Got To Do With It* are films about black female triumph rather than black female tragedy. By appropriating Billie Holiday's tragic life (and her songbook) Diana Ross was able to transcend her pop star image and become not only a Hollywood star but a serious singer. In a similar way, Tina Turner appropriated her tragic life with Ike (and their songbook), strengthening her own solo career and reconfirming her status as a 'soul survivor'. The films therefore are not historical representations, but vehicles whose use of music – in the cinema and on the soundtrack – constructed and reconfirmed the iconic status of Diana Ross and Tina Turner as triumphant black pop divas.

BIBLIOGRAPHY

Adler, Renata (1968) 'Screen: Upbeat Musical', *New York Times*, 27 December, 44.

Adorno, Theodor (1981) *In Search of Wagner*. New York: Schocken Books.

Agajanian, Rowana (2000) 'Nothing Like Any Previous Musical, British or American', in Anthony Aldgate, James Chapman & Arthur Marwick (eds) *Windows on the Sixties*. London: I. B. Tauris, 91–113.

Aldworth, Winston (1997) 'Topless Tracks Like Nun Other', *Sunday Star Times*, 17 August, F7.

Alexander, Karen (1991) 'Fatal Beauties: Black Women in Hollywood', in Christine Gledhill (ed.) *Stardom: Industry of Desire*. London: Routledge.

Altman, Rick (1999) 'Nickelodeons and Popular Song', in Philip Brophy (ed.) *Cinesonic: The World of Sound in Film*. Sydney: AFTRS, 244–56.

Andrews, Nigel (1998) *Travolta: The Life*. London: Bloomsbury.

Anon. (1983) 'The Stinger', *Daily Mirror*, 24 November, 16–17.

Atkins, Irene Kahn (1983) *Source Music in Motion Pictures*. London: Associated University Press.

Atkinson, Michael (1995) 'Long Black Limousine: Pop Biopics', in Jonathan Romney & Adrian Wootton (eds) *Celluloid Jukebox*. London: BFI, 20–31.

Attali, Jacques (1985) *Noise: The Political Economy of Music*. Minneapolis: University of Minnesota Press.

Auslander, Philip (1999*) Liveness: Performance in a Mediatized Culture*. New York: Routledge.

Baillie, Russell (1999) 'Radio Celluloid', *Weekend Herald*, 7–8 August, D5.

Baldwin, James (1976) *The Devil Finds Work: An Essay*. New York: The Dial Press.

Beatles, The (2000) *The Beatles Anthology*. London: Cassell.

Bennett, Andy (2000) *Popular Music and Youth Culture: Music, Identity and Place*. London: Macmillan.

Bernstein, Charles (2000) *Film Music and Everything Else: Music, Creativity and Culture as Seen By a Hollywood Film Composer*. Beverly Hills, California: Turnstyle Music.

Best, Pete (1995) Personal interview, Newcastle-upon-Tyne, 22 September.

Best, Steven & Douglas Kellner (2001) *The Postmodern Adventure: Science, Technology and Cultural Studies at the Third Millennium*. London: Routledge.

Billman, Larry (1997) *Film Choreographers and Dance Directors*. Jefferson, North Carolina: McFarland.

Black, Andrew (1991) 'Hardware', *Samhain*, 26, April/May, 31.

Bogle, Donald (1980) *Brown Sugar: Eighty Years of America's Black Female Superstars*. New York: Da Capo.

_____ (1992) *Toms, Coons, Mulattoes, Mammies, & Bucks: An Interpretive History of Blacks in American Films*. New York: Continuum.

Booker, Christopher (1969) *The Neophiliacs*. London: Collins.

Bordwell, David & Noel Carroll (eds) *Post-Theory: Reconstructing Film Studies*. Madison: University of Wisconsin Press.

Boswell, Simon (1990) Liner notes, *Hardware* soundtrack CD (Milan Records CDCH627).

Bowen, José A. (1999) 'Finding the Music in Musicology: Performance History and Musical Works', in Nicholas Cook & Mark Everist (eds) *Rethinking Music*. Oxford: Oxford University Press, 424–51.

Bowman, Wayne D. (1998) *Philosophical Perspectives on Music*. Oxford: Oxford University Press.

Brackett, David (1999) 'Music', in Thomas Swiss & Bruce Horner (eds) *Key Terms in Popular Music and Culture*. New York: Blackwell.

Brown, Gerry & Rick Sky (1983) 'Sting the Space Gangster', *Daily Star*, 21 September, 14–15.

Brown, Robert (1982) 'Brimstone and Treacle', *Monthly Film Bulletin*, 49, 584, 195–6.

Brown, Royal S. (1994) *Overtones and Undertones: Reading Film Music*. Berkeley: University of California Press.

Bruch, Michel Gert (1996) *Sting: Enquête de Police*. Paris: Editions Hors Collection.

Bruun, Seppo, Jukka Lindfors, Santtu Luoto & Markku Salo (1998) *Jee Jee Jee: Suomalaisen Rockin Historia*. Porvoo: WSOY.

Buckley, Reka C.V. & Stephen Gundle (2000) 'Flash Trash: Gianni Versace and the Theory and Practice of Glamour', in Stella Bruzzi & Pamela Church Gibson (eds) *Fashion Cultures: Theories, Explorations and Analysis*. London: Routledge, 331–48.

Budd, Malcolm (1985) *Music and the Emotions: The Philosophical Theories*. London: Routledge.

Buhler, James, Caryl Flinn & David Neumeyer (eds) (2000) *Music and Cinema*. Hanover, New Hampshire: Wesleyan University Press.

Burt, George (1994) *The Art of Film Music*. Boston: Northeastern University Press.

Canby, Vincent (1972) 'Screen: Billie Holiday', *New York Times*, 19 October 1972, 56.

Carr, E. H. (1961) *What is History?* London: Macmillan.

Carroll, Noel (1982) 'The Future of Allusion', *October*, 20, 51–81.

_____ (1988) *Mystifying Movies: Fads and Fallacies in Contemporary Film Theory*. New York: Columbia University Press.

Cassell, David (1982) 'Brimstone and Treacle', *Sunday Telegraph*, 12 September.

Castells, Manuel (1996) *The Rise of the Network Society*. Oxford: Blackwell.

Chase, Malcolm & Christopher Shaw (1989) 'The Dimensions of Nostalgia', in Christopher Shaw & Malcolm Chase (eds) *The Imagined Past: History and Nostalgia*. Manchester: Manchester University Press, 1–17.

Chion, Michel (1994) *Audio-Vision: Sound on Screen*. Trans. Claudia Gorbman. New York: Columbia University Press.

Clarkson, Wensley (1995) *Sting: The Secret Life of Gordon Sumner*. New York: Thunders Mouth Press.

Clayson, Alan (1991) *Ringo Starr*. London: Sidgwick & Jackson.

Cocks, Jay (1972) 'Holiday On Ice', *Time*, 6 November, 86–7.

Cohen, Annabel J. (2000) 'Film Music: Perspectives From Cognitive Psychology', in James Buhler, Caryl Flinn & David Neumeyer (eds) *Music and Cinema*. Hanover, New Hampshire: Wesleyan University Press, 360–77.

Cohen, Barney (1984) *Sting: Every Breath He Takes*. New York: Berkley Books.

Coleman, John (1982) 'Androids', *New Statesman*, 104, 2686, 27–8.

Collins, Jim (1992) 'Genericity in the Nineties: Eclectic Irony and the New Sincerity', in Jim Collins, Hilary Radner & Ava Preacher Collins (eds) *Film Theory Goes to the Movies*. New York: Routledge, 242–62.

Collis, Clark (1999) 'Hapless Campers', *Empire*, November, 92–100.

Cook, Nicholas (1994) 'Music and Meaning in the Commercials', *Popular Music*, 13, 1, 27–40.

_____ (1998) *Analysing Musical Multimedia*. Oxford: Clarendon.

_____ (1999) 'Analyzing Performance and Performing Analysis', in Nicholas Cook & Mark Everist (eds) *Rethinking Music*. Oxford: Oxford University Press, 239–61.

Cook, Nicholas & Mark Everist (eds) (1999) *Rethinking Music*. Oxford: Oxford University Press.

Cook, Richard (1983) 'Brimstone and Treacle', *New Musical Express*, 18 September, 27.

_____ (1985) 'Sting's 'Stein Stinks', *New Musical Express*, 2 November, 25.

Coyle, Rebecca (1998a) 'Introduction: Tuning Up', in Rebecca Coyle (ed.) *Screen Scores: Studies in Contemporary Australian Film Music*. Sydney: AFTRS, 1–14.

_____ (1998b) 'Sonic Semaphore: Music in the Films of Yahoo Serious', in Rebecca Coyle (ed.) *Screen Scores: Studies in Contemporary Australian Film Music*. Sydney: AFTRS, 141–63.

Custen, George F. (1992) *Bio/Pics: How Hollywood Constructed Public History*. New Brunswick: Rutgers University Press.

Darke, Chris (1996) 'The Grotesque', *Sight and Sound*, 6, 8, 50.

Davies, Hunter (1985) *The Beatles*. London: Jonathan Cape.

Davis, Fred (1979) *Yearning For Yesterday: A Sociology of Nostalgia*. New York: Free Press.

Denisoff, R. Serge & George Plasketes (1990) 'Synergy in 1980s Film and Music: Formula for Success or Industry Mythology?', *Film History*, 4.3, 257–76.

Diawara, Mathia (ed.) (1993) *Black American Cinema*. New York: Routledge.

Doane, Mary Ann (1985) 'Ideology and the Practice of Sound Editing and Mixing', in Elisabeth Weis & John Belton (eds) *Film Sound*. New York: Columbia University Press, 54–62.

Donnelly, K. J. (1998a) 'The Classical Film Score Forever? "Batman" and "Batman Returns" and Post-Classical Film Music', in Steve Neale & Murray Smith (eds) *Contemporary Hollywood Cinema*. London: Routledge, 142–155.

_____ (1998b) 'British Punk Films: Rebellion into Money, Revolt into Innovation', *Journal of Popular Culture*, 1.1, 101–14.

_____ (2001a) *Pop Music in British Cinema: A Chronicle*. London: BFI.

_____ (ed) (2001b) *Film Music: Critical Approaches*. Edinburgh: Edinburgh University Press.

Durant, Alan (1984) *The Conditions of Music*. London: Macmillan.

Dyer, Richard (1986) 'Mahogany' in Charlotte Brunsdon (ed.) *Films For Women* London: BFI, 131–37.

_____ (1995) 'In Defense of Disco', in Hanif Kureishi and Jon Savage (eds) *The Faber Book of Pop*. London: Faber, 518–26.

_____ (1998) *Stars* (Revised edition). London: BFI.

Early, Gerald (1995) *One Nation Under a Groove: Motown and American Culture*. Hopewell: Ecco Press.

Easthope, Anthony (1993) *Contemporary Film Theory*. London: Longman.

Eckstein, Jeremy (1993) *Cultural Trends 19*, 3.3. London: Policy Studies Institute.

Edelstein, David (1985) 'Material Girl', *Village Voice*, 3 September, 54.

Evans, Mike (1984) *The Art of The Beatles*. New York: Beech Tree.

Falck, Daniel (no date) 'Voyages on the Line' (author's manuscript).

Feuer, Jane (1992) *The Hollywood Musical*. London: Macmillan.

Finscher, Ludwig (ed.) (1996) *Die Musik In Geschichte Und Gegenwart, Zweite, Neubearbeitete Asugabe, Sachteil, Volume 5*. Kassel: Bärenreiter: Kassel/Metzler: Stuttgart.

Fitzgerald, Jon (1996) *Popular Songwriting 1963–1966: Stylistic Comparisons and Trends Within the U.S. Top Forty*. Unpublished PhD thesis. Southern Cross University, Australia.

Flinn, Caryl (1992) *Strains of Utopia: Gender, Nostalgia and Hollywood Film Music*. New Jersey: Princeton University Press.

Floyd, Nigel (1989) 'An American Without Tears', *New Musical Express*, 21 January, 20.

Forlenza, Jeff & Terri Stone (eds) (1993) *Sound For Picture: An Inside Look at Audio Production for Film and Television*. Emeryville, California: Hal Leonard.

Freccero, Carla (1999) *Popular Culture: An Introduction*. New York: New York University Press.

Friedlander, Paul (1996) *Rock and Roll: A Social History*. Boulder, Colorado: Westview Press.

Frith, Simon & Angela McRobbie (1978) 'Rock and Sexuality', *Screen Education*, 29, 3–19.

Frith, Simon (1988) *Music For Pleasure*. Cambridge: Polity Press.

_____ (1996) *Performing Rites: On the Value of Popular Music*. Cambridge, Massachusetts: Harvard University Press.

Getz, Steve (1985) *Sting*. Port Chester, NY: Cherry Lane Books.

Gillett, Charlie (1994) 'Truth and Tina', *Sight and Sound*, 4, 1, 64.

Goodwin, Andrew (1993) *Dancing in the Distraction Factory: Music Television and Popular Culture*. London: Routledge.

Gorbman, Claudia (1980) 'Narrative Film Music', *Yale French Studies*, 60, 183–203.

_____ (1987) *Unheard Melodies: Narrative Film Music*. Bloomington: Indiana University Press.

Gowers, Rebecca (1996) 'The Grotesque', *Daily Telegraph*, 14 June, 20.

Grossberg, Lawrence (1993) 'The Media Economy of Rock Culture: Cinema, Post-Modernity and Authenticity', in Simon Frith, Andrew Goodwin & Lawrence Grossberg (eds) *Sound and Vision: The Music Video Reader*. London: Routledge, 185–209.

Guerrero, Ed (1993) *Framing Blackness: The African American Image in Film*. Philadelphia: Temple University Press.

Gunning, Tom (1990) 'The Cinema of Attractions: Early Film, Its Spectator and The Avant Garde', in Thomas Elsaesser & Adam Barker (eds) *Early Cinema: Space, Frame, Narrative*. London: BFI.

Harmetz, Aljean (1972) 'Diana Ross: Lady *Doesn't* Sing the Blues', *New York Times*, 24 December, D4, D17.

Harrison, George (1982) *I Me Mine*. London: W. H. Allen.

Harron, Mary (1988) 'McRock: Pop as a Commodity', in Simon Frith (ed.) *Facing the Music*. New York: Pantheon, 173–220.

Harvey, David (1989) *The Condition of Postmodernity*. Cambridge: Blackwell.

Hawkins, Stan (2002) *Settling the Pop Score: Pop Texts and Identity Politics*. London: Ashgate.

Heal, Sue (1989) 'Stormy Monday', *Today*, 20 January, 28.

Heck, Thomas F. (1999) *Picturing Performance: The Iconography of the Performing Arts in Concept and Practice*. Rochester: Rochester University Press.

Heister, Hanns Werner (1996) 'Konzertwesen', in Ludwig Finscher (ed.) *Die Musik In Geschichte Und Gegenwart, Zweite, Neubearbeitete Asugabe, Sachteil, Volume 5*. Kassel: Bärenreiter: Kassel/Metzler: Stuttgart, 686–710.

Herman, Edward S. & Robert W. McChesney (1997) *The Global Media: The New Missionaries of Corporate Capitalism*. London: Cassell.

Hirn, Sven (1981) *Kuvat Kulkevat: Kuvallisten Esitysten Perinne Ja Elävien Kuvien 12 Ensimmäistä Vuotta Suomessa*. Helsinki: Suomen Elokuvasäätiö.

Hogue, Peter (1982–83) 'Radio On', *Film Quarterly*, 36, 2, 47–52.

Holiday, Billie and William Dufty (1992) *Lady Sings the Blues*. (Revised edition). New York: Penguin.

Honka-Hallila, Ari (1995) 'Elokuvakulttuuria Luomassa', in Ari Honka-Hallila, Kimmo Laine & Mervi Pantti (eds) *Markan Tähden: Yli Sata Vuotta Suomalaista Elokuvahistoriaa*. Turku: Turun Yliopiston Täydennyskoulutuskeskus, 11–68.

Hollows, Joanne, Peter Hutchings & Mark Jancovich (2000) *The Film Studies Reader*. London: Arnold.

Holman, Tomlinson (1997) *Sound for Film and Television*. Boston: Focal Press.

hooks, bell (1992) *Black Looks: Race and Representation*. Boston: South End Press.

_____ (1996) *Reel to Real: Race, Sex, and Class at the Movies*. New York: Routledge.

Huckvale, David (1990) 'Twins of Evil: An Investigation into the Aesthetics of Film Music', *Popular Music*, 9, 1, 1–35.

Jalkanen, Pekka (1992) *Pohjolan Yössä: Suomalaisia Kevyen Musiikin Säveltäjiä Georg Malmsténista Liisa Akimofiin*. Helsinki: Kirjastopalvelu Oy, 206–38.

_____ (1996) 'Popular Music', in Kalevi Aho, Pekka Jalkanen, Erkki Salmenhaara & Keijo Virtamo, *Finnish Music*. Helsinki: Otava.

Jameson, Fredric (1984) 'Progress Versus Utopia: or, Can We Imagine the Future?', in Brian Wallis (ed.) *Art After Modernism: Rethinking Representation*. Boston: The New Museum of Contemporary Art.

Jenkins, Henry (1992) 'Strangers No More, We Sing: Filking and the Social Construction of the Science Fiction Community', in Lisa A. Lewis (ed.) *The Adoring Audience: Fan Culture and Popular Media*. London: Routledge, 208–36.

Jenkins, Keith (1995) *On 'What Is History?'* London: Routledge.

Jones, Alan (1992) 'The Devil and Mr Stanley', *Shivers*, June, 24–5.

Juva, Anu (1995) *Valkokangas Soi! Kirja Elokuvamusiikista*. Helsinki: Kirjastopalvelu Oy.

Kael, Pauline (1972) 'Pop Versus Jazz', *The New Yorker*, 4 November, 152–8.

Kalinak, Kathryn (1992) *Settling The Score: Music and the Classical Hollywood Film*. Madison: University of Wisconsin Press.

Karlin, Fred & Rayburn Wright (1990) *On the Track: A Guide to Contemporary Film Scoring*. New York: Schirmer Books.

Kassabian, Anahid (2001) *Hearing Film: Tracking Identifications in Contemporary Hollywood Film Music*. New York: Routledge.

Keightley, Keir (2001) 'Reconsidering Rock', in Simon Frith, Will Straw & John Street (eds) *The Cambridge Companion to Pop and Rock*. Cambridge: Cambridge University Press, 109–42.

Kermode, Mark (1990) 'Hardware', *Monthly Film Bulletin*, October 1990, 297.

_____ (1995) 'Twisting the Knife', in Jonathan Romney & Adrian Wootton (eds) *Celluloid Jukebox*. London: BFI, 8–19.

Kerner, Marvin M. (1989) *The Art of the Sound Effects Editor*. Boston: Focal Press.

Kernfeld, Barry (1988) (ed.) *The New Grove Dictionary of Jazz*. London: Macmillan.

King, Barry (1985) 'Articulating Stardom', *Screen*, 26, 5, 27–50.

Kirby, Tim (1991) 'Pride and Prejudice', *Sight and Sound*, 1, 3, 20.

Kooijman, Jaap (2002) 'From Elegance to Extravaganza: The Supremes on "The Ed Sullivan Show" as a Presentation of Beauty', *The Velvet Light Trap*, 49, 4–17.

Lack, Russell (1997) *Twenty Four Frames Under: A Buried History of Film Music*. London: Quartet Books.

Laiho, Antero & Timo Toivonen (1997) 'Just Wanna Go To a Movie Show: Elvis Presleyn 50-Luvun Elokuvat Ja Niiden Vastaanotto Suomessa', in Anu Koivunen & Hannu Salmi (eds) *Varjojen Valtakunta: Elokuvahistorian Uusi Lukukirja*. Turku: Turun Yliopiston Täydennyskoulutuskeskus, 120–5.

Lapedis, Hilary (1999) 'Popping the Question: The Function and Effect of Popular Music in Cinema', *Popular Music*, 18, 3, 367–79.

de Lauretis, Teresa (1984) *Alice Doesn't: Feminism, Semiotics, Cinema*. Bloomington: Indiana University Press.

Lerner, Laurence (1972) *The Uses of Nostalgia*. London: Chatto & Windus.

Levinson, Jerrold (1996) 'Film Music and Narrative Agency', in David Bordwell & Noel Carroll (eds) *Post-Theory: Reconstructing Film Studies*. Madison: University of Wisconsin Press, 248–82.

Limbacher, James L. & Stephen H. Wright (1991) *Keeping Score: Film and Television Music 1980–1988*. Metuchen, New Jersey: Scarecrow Press.

Limbacher, James L. & Alvin H. Marill (1998) *Keeping Score: Film and Television Music 1988–1997*. Lanham, Maryland: Scarecrow Press.

Lowenthal, David (1989) 'Nostalgia Tells It Like It Wasn't', in Christopher Shaw & Malcolm Chase (eds) *The Imagined Past: History and Nostalgia*. Manchester: Manchester University Press, 18–32.

Maasø, Arnt (2000) 'This Goes To Eleven: "High" And "Low" Sound in Television' (author's manuscript).

Maltby, Richard (1995) *Hollywood Cinema*. Oxford: Blackwell.

Margolick, David (2000) *Strange Fruit: Billie Holiday, Café Society, and an Early Cry For Civil Rights*. Philadelphia: Running Press.

Martin, Gavin (1981) 'Company Lore and Public Disorder', *New Musical Express*, 14 March, 30–1.

Marwick, Arthur (1996) *British Society Since 1945*. Third Edition. Harmondsworth: Penguin.

McArthur, Colin (1981) 'Historical Drama', in Tony Bennett, Susan Boyd-Bowman, Colin Mercer & Janet Woollacott (eds) *Popular Television and Film*. London: BFI and The Open University, 288–301.

McClary, Susan (1991) *Feminine Endings: Music, Gender and Sexuality*. Minnesota: University of Minnesota Press.

McDonald, Paul (1998) 'Reconceptualising Stardom' in R. Dyer, *Stars*. London: BFI, 175–200.

_____ (2000) *The Star System: Hollywood's Production of Popular Identities*. London: Wallflower Press.

McKay, Peter (1981) 'Brimstone and Treacle', *Daily Mirror*, 17 September.

McClary, Susan (1991) *Feminine Endings: Music, Gender and Sexuality*. Minneapolis: University of Minnesota Press.

McLuhan, Marshall (1964) *Understanding Media*. Cambridge: MIT Press.

McRobbie, Angela (1984) 'Dance and Social Fantasy', in Angela McRobbie & Mica Nava (eds) *Gender and Generation*. London: Macmillan, 130–61.

Medhurst, Andy (1995) 'It Sort of Happened Here: The Strange Brief Life of the British Pop Film', in Jonathan Romney & Adrian Wootton (eds) *Celluloid Jukebox*. London: BFI, 60–71.

Middleton, Richard (1990) *Studying Popular Music*. Milton Keynes: Open University Press.

Miles, Barry (1997) *Paul McCartney: Many Years From Now*. London: Secker & Warburg.

Moore, Allan F. (2001) *Rock: The Primary Text*. Aldershot: Ashgate.

Morley, David & Kevin Robins (1995) *Spaces of Identity: Global Media, Electronic Landscapes and Cultural Boundaries*. London: Routledge.

Mundy, John (1999) *Popular Music on Screen: From Hollywood Musical to Music Video*. Manchester: Manchester University Press.

Munz, Rudolf (1998) 'Theatralität Und Theater: Konzeptionelle Erwägungen Zum Forsch-ungsprojekt Theatergeschichte', in Rudolf Münz (ed.) *Theatralität Und Theater: Zur Historiographie Von Theatralitätsgefügen*. Berlin: Schwarzkopf & Schwarzkopf, 66–81.

Murphy, Robert (1992) *Sixties British Cinema*. London: BFI.

Nasta, Dominique (1991) *Meaning in Film: Relevant Structures in Soundtrack and Narrative*. New York: Lang.

Neaverson, Bob (2000) 'Tell Me What You See: The Influence and Impact of The Beatles Movies', in Ian Inglis (ed.) *The Beatles, Popular Music and Society: A Thousand Voices*. London: Macmillan, 150–162.

Nelmes, Jill (1996) *An Introduction to Film Studies*. London: Routledge.

Newman, Kim (1986) 'Bring on the Night', *Monthly Film Bulletin*, 53, 628, 166–7.

_____ (1989) 'Stormy Monday', *Monthly Film Bulletin*, 56, 661, 58.

Norman, Philip (1981) *Shout! The True Story of The Beatles*. London: Hamish Hamilton.

Nowell-Smith, Geoffrey (1979–80) 'Radio On', *Screen*, 20, 3–4, 29–39.

O'Brien, Alan (1982) 'Brimstone and Treacle', *The Sunday Times*, 12 September, 34.

O'Sullivan, Charlotte (1997) 'Quadrophenia', *Time Out*, 29 January, 68.

Palmer, Gareth (1997) 'Bruce Springsteen and Masculinity', in Sheila Whiteley (ed.) *Sexing The Groove: Popular Music and Gender*. London: Routledge, 100–17.

Pantti, Mervi (1998) *Kaikki Muuttuu … Elokuvakulttuurin Jälleenrakentaminen Suomessa 1950-Luvulta 1970-Luvulle*. Turku: Suomen Elokuvatutkimuksen Seura Ry.

Pearson, Harry (1993) 'What's Love Got To Do With It?', *Films in Review*, 46, 334–6.

Peltonen, Matti (1996) *Rillumarei ja valistus: Kulttuurikahakoita 1950-luvun Suomessa*. Suomen Historiallinen Seura 1996.

Perry, George (1989) 'Taking the Tyne by Storm', *The Sunday Times*, 22 January, 3.

Piccarella, John (1986) 'Jimi Hendrix', in H. Wiley Hitchcock & Stanley Sadie (eds) *The New Grove Dictionary of American Music Volume 2*. London: Macmillan, 370–2.

Pym, John (1979) 'Radio On', *Monthly Film Bulletin*, 46, 500, 233–4.

Rautiainen, Tarja (2001) *Pop, Protesti, Laulu: Korkean Ja Matalan Murroksia 1960-Luvun Suomalaisessa Populaarimusiikissa*. Tampere: Tampere University Press.

Rhines, Jesse Algeron (1996) *Black Film/White Money*. New Brunswick: Rutgers University Press.

Romney, Jonathan (1989) 'Geordie Fame', *New Musical Express*, 21 January, 18.

_____ (1995) 'Access All Areas: The Real Space of Rock Documentary', in Jonathan Romney & Adrian Wootton (eds) *Celluloid Jukebox*. London: BFI, 82–93.

Romney, Jonathan & Adrian Wootton (eds) (1995) *Celluloid Jukebox*. London: BFI.

Roscoe, Jane (2000) 'The Blair Witch Project: Mock-Documentary Goes Mainstream', *Jump Cut*, 43, 3–9.

Rose, Cynthia (1993) 'The Riddle of the Rock Biopic', *Sight and Sound*, 3, 10, 14–16.

Rosenberg, Eric (2000) 'Bursting at the Seams: Architecture and the Films of The Beatles', in Mark Lamster (ed.) *Architecture and Film*. New York: Princeton Architectural Press, 241–50.

Rosenbluth, Jean (1988) 'Soundtrack Specialists: Maximising Cross-Market Connections', *Billboard*, 16 July, S-4.

Rosenstone, Robert A. (1995) *Visions of the Past: The Challenge of Film to Our Idea of History*. Cambridge, Massachusetts: Harvard University Press.

Ross, Diana (1993) *Secrets of a Sparrow: Memoirs*. New York: Villard Books.

Sandford, Christopher (1998) *Sting, Demolition Man: A Biography*. New York: Carroll & Graf.

Sarup, Madan (1996) *Identity, Culture and the Postmodern World.* Edinburgh: Edinburgh University Press.

Schafer, R. Murray (1993) *The Soundscape.* Rochester, VT: Inner Traditions International.

Sellers, Robert (1989) *Sting: A Biography.* London: Omnibus.

Selvin, Joel (1992) *Monterey Pop.* San Francisco: Chronicle Books.

Shore, Michael (1984) *The Rolling Stone Book of Rock Video.* New York: Quill.

Shuker, Roy (1998) *Key Concepts in Popular Music.* London: Routledge.

_____ (2001) *Understanding Popular Music* (Second edition). London: Routledge.

Smith, Jeff (1995) *The Sounds of Commerce: Popular Film Music 1960–1973.* Unpublished doctoral dissertation, University of Wisconsin, 230–47.

_____ (1996) 'Unheard Melodies? A Critique of Psychoanalytic Theories of Film Music', in David Bordwell & Noel Carroll (eds) *Post-Theory: Reconstructing Film Studies.* Madison: University of Wisconsin Press.

_____ (1998) *The Sounds of Commerce: Marketing Popular Film Music.* New York: Columbia University Press.

Smith, Murray (1998) 'Theses on the Philosophy of Hollywood History', in Steve Neale & Murray Smith (eds) *Contemporary Hollywood Cinema.* London: Routledge, 3–20.

Sonnenschein, David (2001) *Sound Design: The Expressive Power of Music, Voice and Sound Effects in Cinema.* Seattle: Michael Wiese.

Stanley, Richard (1993) Personal interview, Norwich.

Steiner, Fred & Martin Marks (1986) 'Film Music', in H. Wiley Hitchcock & Stanley Sadie (eds) *The New Grove Dictionary of American Music Volume 2.* London: Macmillan, 118–25.

Stern, D. A. (1999) *The Blair Witch Project: A Dossier.* Basingstoke: Boxtree.

Straw, Will (2001) 'Dance Music', in Simon Frith, Will Straw & John Street (eds) *The Cambridge Companion to Pop and Rock.* Cambridge: Cambridge University Press, 158–75.

Tagg, Philip (1979) *Kojak: 50 Seconds of Television Music. Towards the Analysis of Effect in Popular Music.* Unpublished PhD thesis. University of Göteborg, Sweden.

Tasker, Yvonne (1998) *Working Girls: Gender and Sexuality in Popular Cinema.* London: Routledge.

Taylor, John Russell (1971) 'The Musical', in George Perry (ed.) *Cinema: The First 75 Years.* London: Thomson, 69–77.

Thomas, Michael (1973) 'Diana Ross Goes From Riches To Rags', *Rolling Stone,* 1 February, 28–31.

Thompson, Kristin (1988) *Breaking the Glass Armour: Neoformalist Film Analysis.* New Jersey: Princeton University Press.

Trampert, Lothar (1994) *Elektrisch! Jimi Hendrix: Der Musiker Hinter Dem Mythos.* München: Piper/Mainz: Schott.

Tribe, Keith (1981) 'History and the Production of Memories', in Tony Bennett, Susan Boyd-Bowman, Colin Mercer & Janet Woollacott (eds) *Popular Television and Film.* London: BFI & The Open University, 319–26.

Tunstall, Jeremy & Michael Palmer (1991) *Media Moguls.* London: Routledge.

Turner, Tina & Kurt Loder (1987) *I, Tina: My Life Story.* New York: Avon Books.

Urbano, Cosimo (1998) 'Projections, Suspense and Anxiety: The Modern Horror Film and Its Effects', *Psychoanalytic Review,* 85, 6, 889–908.

Uusitalo, Kari (1981) *Suomen Hollywood On Kuollut: Kotimaisen Elokuvan Ahdinkovuodet 1956–1963.* Helsinki: Suomen Elokuvasäätiö.

Vernallis, Carol (1998) 'The Aesthetics of Music Video', *Popular Music,* 17, 2, 153–85.

Waksman, Steve (1999) *Instruments of Desire: The Electric Guitar and the Shaping of Musical Experience.* Cambridge, Massachusetts: Harvard University Press.

Wenner, Jann (1971) *Lennon Remembers.* London: Penguin.

INDEX

SOUNDSCAPE

THE SCHOOL OF SOUND LECTURES 1998–2001

You wish to see, listen. Hearing is a step toward vision.
– Saint Bernard of Clairvaux

The School of Sound is a unique annual event exploring the use of sound in film, which has attracted practitioners, academics and artists from around the world, raising the profile of sound production in film, television and multimedia. *Soundscape* is the first compendium of the event's presentations that investigate the modern soundtrack and the ways sound combines with image in both art and entertainment. Directors, sound designers, composers, editors, artists and theorists define and interpret their personal use of sound from both traditional approaches and radical new perspectives. Topics range from the practical to the aesthetic to the metaphysical, exploring sonic environments, non-naturalistic sound, sound as metaphor, human sound perception and sound for multimedia.

The contributors include directors David Lynch and Mike Figgis; sound designers Walter Murch, Owe Svensson and Randy Thom; composers Carter Burwell, David Burnand and Stephen Deutch; producer Bob Last; theorists Laura Mulvey, Michel Chion and Ian Christie; critics Peter Wollen, James Leahy and Shoma Chatterji; screenwriter Phil Parker; film-makers Mani Kaul and Amie Siegel; music producer Manfred Eicher; anthropologist Thanos Vovolis; and poet Tom Paulin

'Highly approachable and refreshingly jargon-free, this lucidly explained compendium sheds light on the aesthetics and perceptions of sound in a suprisingly entertaining manner. Sign up for a class now!' ****
– Howard Maxford, *Film Review*

April 2003   1-903364-59-0 (pbk)   £15.99   1-903364-68-X (hbk)   £45.00